"Muscle"
A Minor League Legend

By George Stone

Copyright © 2003 by George Stone

Cover photo courtesy of North Carolina Department of Cultiural Resources

Photo by Raleigh News and Observer

ISBN 0-7414-1507-0

Published by:

PUBLISHING.COM

519 West Lancaster Avenue
Haverford, PA 19041-1413
Info@buybooksontheweb.com
www.buybooksontheweb.com
Toll-free (877) BUY BOOK
Local Phone (610) 520-2500
Fax (610) 519-0261

Printed in the United States of America

Printed on Recycled Paper

Published July 2003

This book is dedicated to the memory of
Leo "Muscle" Shoals who passed away
at the age of 82 on February 23, 1999.

A tremendous baseball player,
a loving husband, a dedicated father,
a true patriot and a good friend.

Acknowledgements

When I first began the project of writing a manuscript on the life of Leo "Muscle" Shoals, I was so naïve as to think several hours of one-on-one interviews would be sufficient in gathering the needed information to turn that manuscript into a book. I would later discover that writing a book meant pouring through mountains of microfilm and playing detective in tracking down long-forgotten minor league baseball players who last played almost a half-century ago.

I also discovered that I would have to rely on the support of individuals who were total strangers. But where do you begin to thank those individuals who researched vital bits of information for a project in which they had no personal interest? And how do you not overlook someone when handing out your appreciation? But I shall try to thank those who played a prominent role in helping me put this book together.

First and foremost I would like to thank especially the family of Muscle Shoals for allowing me to continue this book, which I was hoping to finish in time for him to enjoy. However, at the age of 82, Muscle left us. I deeply appreciate Helen Sholes and her patience on my many visits to their home and to son Greg who I have reached out to for insight into his father. But I also would like to thank sons Ronnie, Tim and Gary and daughter Yvonne.

The forward was eloquently written by Furman Bisher of the Atlanta Journal-Constitution, whose writing style I have long admired and someone who knew Muscle in days gone by. It was an honor to have Furman Bisher add his touch of class to the book.

I would like to extend a special thanks to William Palmer (Curator Emeritus, Herpetology) of the North

Carolina State Museum of Natural Science in Raleigh for his tireless efforts in supplying me with articles and microfilm reprints from many papers which contained a rich supply of information. Palmer also shared his personal memories of Muscle growing up in Raleigh and paying visits to Devereux Meadow to watch Shoals lift one out.

I am indebted to Robert Anderson, a fellow sportswriter while at the Bristol Herald Courier and currently prep editor at the Roanoke Times, for his diligent reading and editing of my manuscript.

I also want to thank the staff of the Bristol Public Library who taught me what a valuable service interlibrary loan can be.

There were some great stories and columns written about Muscle over the years. I'm sure I missed a few as it was just not humanly possible to wade through every newspaper in every town in which Shoals visited as a player. However, there were a couple of columns which did not escape and excerpts were reprinted within these pages. A column written in 1950 by Eddie Allen of the Charlotte Observer was reprinted in its entirety with permission from the Charlotte Observer with the copyright to the article owned by The Charlotte Observer.

Also, excerpts used in this book were taken from the following newspapers: Monessen Daily Independent, Albuquerque Journal, Albany Herald, Johnson City Press, Tyler Morning Telegraph, El Dorado Daily News, Kingsport Times-News, Chattanooga Times, Charlotte Observer, Reidsville Review, Raleigh News and Observer, Durham Morning Herald, Greensboro News and Record, The State, Knoxville News-Sentinel and Asheville Citizen-Times.

I could not have written this book without the help of many former teammates and opposing players for their contributions in sharing memories of Muscle Shoals. I only wish that I could have contacted many more, especially key figures in the Shoals' story such as George Souter, Harry Hatch, Aldo Salvent, Louis Knight and Zip Payne. But tracking down many of these former players was a frustrating process. A few certainly had passed on and others could not be located with their most recent address being whatever town they last played in.

Many of the photos used in the book are from the Sholes' family private collection. A few photos were procured from libraries and others from former teammates. Very few photos of Muscle could be found from early in his career and that was a major disappointment. Photo credits were given as best as could be acknowledged to the original source.

I wish to thank Bill Lane, sports editor of the Kingsport Times-News, who called Shoals a friend and who, as a youngster, saw Muscle play at J. Fred Johnson Stadium in Kingsport.

A very special thanks goes to Gabriel Chavarria of Infinity Publishing who patiently came to my rescue time after time in formatting the manuscript prior to publication.

And this book would not have been possible without the encouragement from my loving wife of 23 years, Marcia, who would often lift me up when all seemed impossible.

I very much wanted this book published for the enjoyment of my mother Jeanette and my father Paul. However, my mother passed away on August 29, 2002. It was my parents who fueled my passion for baseball by taking me on those many trips to major league baseball parks, especially that first trip to Shea Stadium in 1965 and an unforgettable visit to the shrine of all ballparks – Yankee Stadium – in 1966 where my hero wore No. 7. I will forever be indebted to them. I also want to thank my brothers Paul Jr. and John for allowing me to use their gloves as a kid and for the times we had playing catch in the backyard.

I would hope my passion and love of the game of baseball, which had followed me through my 50 years, would be passed on to my son Michael and daughter Katrina, so that they may enjoy a truly great pastime.

To all who helped turn a manuscript into a book – thanks!

– George Stone

Prologue

Driving north on Interstate 81 to Glade Spring, Virginia from my home in Bristol, Tennessee, a distance of about 30 miles, I contemplated the questions I was going to pose to Leo "Muscle" Shoals for a newspaper story I was writing for the Bristol Herald Courier.

I naturally had to inquire about the 55 home runs he hit for the Reidsville Luckies, which set a Carolina League record back in 1949. It's a record which has stood the test of time for over a half a century as Tony Solaita has been Shoals' closest pursuer hitting 49 home runs in 1968 while playing for High Point-Thomasville. I also had to ask about his .427 batting average for Kingsport of the Mountain States League in 1953 and the near triple crown in his final minor league season in 1955 with Kingsport, then in the Appalachian League.

But more than what I was going to ask this minor league baseball legend, it was a question of what I was not going to ask. Do I dare approach the subject of how he was shot during a roadhouse scuffle in 1939 while a member of the Johnson City Cardinals? Do I get personal and ask about his reputation for being a hard drinker and womanizer?

I exit I-81 and wind around the backroads of Southwest Virginia, following the signs to Glade Spring. Shoals had given me directions and I fumbled with the slip of paper I had scribbled them on. Shoals' last words to me before I embarked were: "You can't miss it."

On the phone Shoals' voice was gruff and to the point and that remained with me as I pulled into the driveway of his two-story white-frame house on Oak Street. As a kid I had heard of Muscle Shoals, although I always thought it was Muscles Shoals. I had never met the man who is often referred to as the Babe Ruth of the minor leagues. Nor did I ever see him play, since I was three when he hung up his cleats for the final time.

As I reached for my tape recorder and note pad in the seat beside me, I was trying to visualize what a man named Muscle must look like. I once saw a picture of him during his playing days sitting in the dugout. The most noticeable feature was the huge arms plunging like mammoth tree trunks beneath the cutoff sleeves of his uniform

I pushed the button to ring the doorbell. There was no answer so I waited a few seconds and pushed it again. The front door was open and the only partition separating me from the inside of the house was a simple screen door. Then I heard the distinctive voice of Shoals, the same voice I had conversed with over the phone.

"I'll get it Helen. Must be that sportswriter from Bristol."

I was a little apprehensive. I don't know why. I wasn't as nervous conducting interviews with Ted Williams or Henry Aaron as I was now, waiting for Muscle Shoals to appear at the door. I was expecting this Goliath to demand what I wanted.

In the darkened house I could see the silhouette of the man who owned 362 career minor league home runs approaching. He reached out, swung open the screen door and greeted me with a wide smile and a welcoming handshake.

"Hi, I'm Muscle Shoals."

From that day in the spring of 1981 until his death in February of 1999, I came to know Muscle Shoals as a man who did not fit his renegade reputation. Muscle in the ensuing years would welcome me in his home with open arms many times, as would his wife Helen, during the period that I visited while putting together the manuscript for this book.

It was painful for Muscle Shoals to talk about his beer drinking and woman chasing days, but he did knowing that if a book was to be written, he had to open up and tell all. It was a past he admitted to living, but it was also a past he made up for when he married Helen and became a loving and devoted father to sons Greg, Ronnie, Tim and Gary and to daughter Yvonne.

A visit with Muscle would not be complete without the latest pictures of his eight grandchildren and three great-grandchildren, as well as his nieces and nephews. It was difficult linking this caring and loving man to the one I heard could just about outdrink any man alive.

We all change our ways at some point and so had Muscle when he found that he wanted to spend the rest of his life with Helen Perry of Kingsport, Tennessee.

As I began this book, through the urging of Jack Honaker of Abingdon, Virginia, – my former editor at the Herald Courier – I discovered that I was just not writing about a minor league player, but a baseball player who was feared when he brought his 5-foot-11, 220-pound frame to the batter's box. A left-handed power hitter from the late 1930s to the mid-1950s, Shoals was such a drawing card that fans would arrive early to the ballparks to see just how far a ball would travel off his 35-inch, 35-ounce bat during batting practice. Today, Shoals is 12th on the all-time minor league home run list.

The stories about Muscle Shoals are now legendary to those who remember the slugger. For those fans, former teammates and opposing players who knew Shoals and who saw Shoals play baseball, the name Muscle Shoals is revered.

The stories in this book are how Muscle remembered them. A great deal of research did take place while putting this book together, but not every story told by Muscle could be documented. Such as the one he tells about overhearing the sale of Dizzy Dean. Then there was the story he tells of getting a hit off Lon Warneke of the St. Louis Cardinals in spring training in Albany, Georgia in 1939. A boxscore of that game in the 1939 Albany Herald shows Muscle going 0-for-3. But, before we take the boxscore as fact and Muscle's version as fiction, let's assume that the boxscore was in error. Newspapers do make mistakes. Then there's the story on how he got the nickname Muscle. According to Shoals, it came during a longball-hitting contest during spring training of 1938 in Albany when a sportswriter coined the phrase adding Muscle in front of Shoals playing on the name of the dam in nearby Alabama. A check of the Albany Herald from 1938 shows that Shoals, indeed, came up with the nickname just that way. However, in the Asheville Citizen of June 8, 1948 an article states that Shoals got the Muscle nickname from Bill McDonald, a sports editor for the Johnson City Chronicle in 1939.

Every recollection by Muscle in this book was researched, but some of those recollections could neither be proven nor disproven. So, in those cases, I would just as soon take Muscle's word for it.

Muscle loved to talk baseball. Most of the time it was not about his career, but it was about the Atlanta Braves, who he watched religiously on television, or about the Patrick Henry High School team in Glade Spring, Virginia, to which he would offer his vast knowledge of hitting to those young players who would listen.

Muscle would be recognized for his accomplishments later in life. He was selected to the Carolina League's 50th Anniversary All-Star first-team along with the likes of Carl Yastrzemski, Ray Jablonski, Gregg Jefferies, Curt Flood, Leon Wagner, Brad Komminsk, Dwight Gooden, Harvey Haddix and Woody Fair. He was also selected to the Northeast Tennessee Sports Hall of Fame.

It was not uncommon, as a matter of fact it was almost routine, that my telephone at the newspaper office would ring around one a.m. two to three times a week, and it would be Muscle just wanting to chat. He always ended the conversation with "Come on up when you get a chance."

Unfortunately, when I became sports editor, my schedule would not allow me to make many visits. I knew his health was failing. Muscle was experiencing circulatory problems and I noticed that the phone calls had almost stopped. However, I never realized what serious health problems Muscle was suffering. My last visit was as a pallbearer at Muscle's funeral.

The major part of this book is based on fact through countless hours of research and much is from the memory of a man who last played over 45 years ago. To those readers of *Muscle: A Minor League Legend*, I hope you enjoy the story of a truly great baseball player.

Muscle never made the major leagues, but he's in a much higher league now and you can bet he's belting some tape measure home runs against some of the best there ever was. I just wish I would get that call telling me all about it.

– George Stone

Forward

These were heroes of the backwoods, the minor leagues of baseball before the pirates of television invaded their privacy. Muscular men who spoke volumes with the big sticks they carried. They conjured up names that matched their bulk and their feats – Moose, Ox, Dynamite, Rip, Ike, and Babe, of course. We zero in here on one called "Muscle," Leo Shoals, who borrowed the name from a dam in Alabama. Muscle Shoals was a man of might who left dents in many a minor league wall, left by the impact of those clouts that didn't leave the park. Three hundred and sixty two did.

Minor league baseball was a social event in many an American town, not to mention Canada and Mexico. Every city of any size, down to county seats and mill towns had a minor league team, and they were cherished. These heroes had a presence in the towns where they played, prominent in local conversation, recognizable as they walked the downtown streets and approachable. Charge for an autograph? Don't be ridiculous. The baseball team melted down social barriers. Lawyers, bootleggers, preachers, filling station operators, the high school principal, postmaster and judges sat side by side, and they spoke of baseball, and the team.

A personal aside here: One year in the '50s I sat with a Federal judge and an oldtime catcher, since retired, dressed in old denims and wearing soxless sandals, watching the Brunswick team play in Georgia. The judge and the catcher were on common ground. So was the Brunswick center fielder, a kid named Mario Cuomo, not long for the game, playing to pay his way through law school.

Towns like these were stops on Muscle Shoals' trail through the minor leagues, from 1937 in Pennsylvania to 1955, back home in Kingsport, Tennessee. He never got a whiff of the major leagues, but that never dimmed his enthusiasm. He so loved what he did that he wanted to share the story with people who would understand. Baseball people. Fans who knew the real meaning of hero worship. Smalltown people. The largest place he ever played was Chattanooga.

I came across him in Charlotte, much a bustling metropolis now, then a mild country town with ambitions. He was having a good season, but the team wasn't, and the town wasn't. It's a matter of consuming pride that your team, although beloved on occasion, is more beloved when winning.

Muscle Shoals played through it all, occasionally tempering the drudge with a libation. Oh, yes, Muscle would take a drink, and often kept a bottle on the table in his hotel room. But he never let it interfere with his time at bat, and if the pitcher made the mistake of trying to sneak a fastball by him, he never let him forget it.

Well, Leo found the right man for the book. George Stone never saw him play, but he knew well enough to let Leo tell the story, and he listened. I know so much of it so well. You'll find yourself sharing Johnson City, El Dorado, Rock Hill, Reidsville – especially Reidsville – Kingsport and all those other stops along with him. It's minor league baseball brought to life as so many of us remember it and loved it.

– Furman Bisher
Atlanta Journal-Constitution

Chapter One

Raindrops pelted the roof as I lay in that half-conscious state when one first awakens in the early morning. The panes in the partially opened window rattled as a clap of thunder seemed to jolt the two-story house from its foundation. As the rumble drifted into the distance, a cool June breeze lifted the curtains, causing them to flutter.

I pulled the sheet a little tighter under my chin and it seemed as if only seconds had passed before the blare of a car horn disrupted whatever peace remained in my Sunday morning. I peeked at the clock on the nightstand and it was almost eight. Helen, who was five months pregnant with our first child, had already dressed and gone downstairs to cook breakfast.

The tantalizing aroma of eggs and bacon sizzling in the frying pan caught my attention real quick and changed my attitude about being uprooted from my sanctuary at such an ungodly hour. I sat on the edge of the bed a moment or two, listening as the rain poured from the sky.

The rain was not unwelcomed. If anything, it was a godsend. I, along with the rest of my Reidsville Luckies baseball teammates, was scheduled to be in Greensboro for an afternoon game in the Carolina League. It now appeared as if the drenching rain might alter those plans. There was no question we could use a day of rest. The Luckies were 10 games under .500 at 21-31 and we hadn't had a break in our hectic schedule in over three weeks.

We squandered a double-header in Winston-Salem Friday night and then we returned home to Kiker Stadium for a Saturday night game against Greensboro. We coughed up four runs in the 10th inning and got thoroughly embarrassed 13-9 before 2,657 fans, our largest home crowd of the season to that point.

Helen called up from the kitchen that breakfast was ready, so I finished dressing. I walked over to the window

1

and the rain had slacked off to just a sprinkle. A car splashed through a puddle on the street below, sending a shower of water onto the sidewalk.

I meandered downstairs and to the kitchen where Helen had the table set and the radio on. In between ads for Wade's Gulf Station, which offered good Gulf gas and oil, and Hudson-Lester Hardware Company, where Devoe paint – the paint to transform worn and weary old houses – was sold, the weatherman was predicting the rain to let up around noon with a nice, clear day to follow. Helen was wondering whether we would play ball, even if the rain did stop. She and a couple of the other wives were planning to make the drive down to Greensboro.

As Helen poured a cup of coffee, I peeked out the window and the rain was nothing more than a mist with the sun breaking through the scattering clouds. I told Helen that if we got rained out we could take in the new Kirk Douglas movie, *The Champion*, at the Redi Theater.

After breakfast, I walked down the street to get a Sunday's paper. The newsstand wasn't far from our boarding house at 310 Lindsay Street, which was right next door to the City Funeral Home. Reidsville's only paper, *The Review*, didn't publish on Sunday so I bought a copy of the *Greensboro Daily News*. I walked back to the house and sat in the swing on the front porch, catching up on all the news, starting with L'il Abner.

I had just sat down and was reading where Cary Middlecoff won the U.S. Open by a stroke over Sam Snead and Clayton Heafner, when Sue Cranford, who owned the house we boarded in, came by and asked if I thought we would be playing ball. Sue was like a lot of the folks in Reidsville, North Carolina, a town of about 12,000, who came to Kiker Stadium to cheer on the Luckies. She was a diehard baseball fan and so were a lot of other people in Reidsville. I would walk down Scales Street and people I didn't even know would come up to me and say: "Good luck tonight Muscle, hit one out."

Sue and I chatted for a few minutes before she went in to visit with Helen. I went back to reading about the Major League pennant races. Brooklyn was leading St. Louis in the National League and the Dodgers had beaten Cincinnati 11-3 Saturday on home runs by Pee Wee Reese and Roy Campanella. In the American League, the New York Yankees were battling the Boston Red Sox for first place and the Bronx Bombers had won over Cleveland 12-7 the day before with a nine-run first inning as Bob Feller pitched to only eight Yankee batters before leaving the game.

I tried to keep up with what was going on around the majors, but I can't say I was all that interested. My main focus wasn't the Dodgers and Yankees or Cardinals and Red Sox, it was on the Danville Leafs, the Raleigh Capitals, the Greensboro Patriots and the Burlington Bees. While Major League attention was centered on Yankee Stadium, Ebbets Field, Sportsman Park and Fenway Park, my attention was directed toward Southside Park in Winston-Salem, Elon Park in Burlington and Devereux Meadow in Raleigh.

I turned the page and there was the headline of our loss the night before streaming across the top: **Ellis's Grand Slam Homer Paces Pats Over Luckies By 13-9**. Ed Ellis hit his grand slam in the 10th inning over the scoreboard in right field at Kiker. Meanwhile, my contribution was an uninspiring 0-for-2 in the game.

I read on down to some of the other games in the Carolina League played the night before. Durham beat Danville 7-4 at League Park on home runs by Earl Richmond, Carl Linhart and Ed Komisarck. Paul Stegman spun a six-hitter as Raleigh edged Winston-Salem 2-1 at Southside Park and visiting Burlington scored three runs in the 10th inning to beat Martinsville 12-9 at English Field.

I don't think there will ever be another year like there was in 1949 for baseball, and I'm not talking about the Major Leagues. I'm talking about minor league baseball and the popularity it had attained following World War II. In 1949, there were 59 minor leagues with 464 teams, 44 of those clubs were in North Carolina. There were close to 9,000 players in the minor leagues and attendance was over 42 million. Nowadays, you have about half that many teams in the minors. Minor league baseball in the late 1940s and early '50s was enjoying its most prosperous era, as you couldn't drive 50 miles across the country without running into a town which had a minor league team.

Those days are gone now, just like a thirty-cent loaf of bread down at Freeman's Grocery in Reidsville. Television had a lot to do with that. In 1950, when TV began broadcasting major league games, there were 58 minor leagues, but attendance dropped from 42 million in 1949 to 34 million in 1950.

I was 32 years old in 1949 and I had been playing professional baseball for eight years when I joined the Reidsville Luckies of the Carolina League, which had been upgraded from a Class C League in 1948 to a Class B League in '49. I was 38 years old when I finally retired in 1955 and I would have had a couple more years on my resume, but Uncle Sam wanted me on his team for almost four years from 1941 to 1945.

But 1949 was the highlight of all my years in baseball as I had career highs in at bats (501), runs scored (131), total hits (180) and home runs (55). Not bad for an old geezer of 32.

I enjoyed playing in the Carolina League, which had the greatest fans of anywhere I'd ever played. Even when we played on the road, the fans showed their appreciation to a ballplayer if you put forth the effort and had a good night. They might boo you when you came to bat, but they'd pat you on the back if they saw you walking around town during the day or have something nice to say as we would leave the ballpark after a game. Just great fans and, even today, you won't find better baseball fans, or any more knowledgeable fans, than what you have across the state of North Carolina.

I finished reading the paper and got another cup of coffee. I sat on the porch, still visualizing the game the night before. With each loss, it takes something out of you. I was still trying to figure out how we blew that game and I was blaming myself some. If only I had a hit here or there. The only thing I could do was to make up for it today, if we played. The sun was shining bright now and it was almost 11 o'clock, so I called a cab and went on down to Kiker Stadium. The team would meet there and ride the bus the 30 miles south on Route 29 to Greensboro and War Memorial Stadium.

The fellows started straggling in and they all were pretty much like me in that they would just as soon have had the day off. When I got to the clubhouse Glenn Rawlinson, our second baseman, was already in uniform and ready to play. I guess if there was anybody among us who didn't like having a day off it was Glenn. Glenn was a veteran of the minor leagues, like me, and he always came to play. We all did, don't get me wrong when I say I didn't want to play this day. It's just after such a long stretch without a day off, you need a break – mentally as well as physically.

Harry Hatch, our manager, came out of his little cubbyhole of an office and said he had spoken with Greensboro manager Wesley Ferrell and that the game was still on. The outfield was going to be a little soggy and the infield might be a little soft, but that they could get the field ready by 3 o'clock. So, we loaded our equipment on the bus and rumbled down the highway to Greensboro.

War Memorial Stadium was built in 1926 and today it's the only stadium still in use from when I played in the Carolina League. Durham Athletic Park hung on until 1994, before the Bulls moved into their new park in 1995.

I liked hitting at War Memorial. The dimensions were 327 feet to both left and right fields and it was 401 to dead center. The fence in right was a double-decker with advertising on both levels.

We had played the Patriots seven games so far and we'd lost five, so our luck against Greensboro wasn't so good with the most recent loss being that 10th inning debacle the night before. But, in baseball, each day's a new beginning.

On this Sunday afternoon, we had right-hander Harold McKinley pitching while Greensboro started left-hander Paul Wargo. Being a left-handed batter I preferred not having to bat against left-handed pitchers, but there were some left-handers who I didn't have a bit of trouble with. I wasn't sure about Wargo because he had just joined the Pats a couple of days before.

Greensboro jumped on us early with a run in the first inning then, in the top of the second, George Souter walked to get us started and I followed with a single. Bob Downing lined a pitch in the gap in right-center which rattled around long enough for Souter and me to score, as Downing legged out a triple. We took the 2-1 lead into the fourth then we went up 3-1 on my 20th home run of the season, which just cleared the fence in right-center.

But we couldn't hang on to the lead. In the fourth, McKinley walked a couple and gave up a couple of hits and, before we knew it, we were down 5-3. So, Harry brought in Lew Hester. We went back up 7-5 in the sixth as I hit another solo home run to right field, but it was Hester who did the damage with a three-run home run.

In the seventh, we broke the game open with four runs. Ferrell went to his bullpen and brought in Roger Powell to pitch and Souter greeted him with a line shot off the fence for a double to drive in two runs. I was up next. I remember one time that Ferrell had made the statement that, after I had hit a home run to beat him, he would walk me intentionally if I ever came up in a situation again where I could beat him, even with the bases loaded.

With two home runs and a single already, I was itching to take some more rips against Powell, who I felt comfortable in facing. Powell put a pitch right down the middle of the plate and I hit it solid for my third home run of the game, again to left-center, which tied a record set just three weeks earlier by Rip Repulski of Winston-Salem. Rip, by the way, would go on to play nine years in the big leagues.

We didn't have bat weights back in those days. I usually just grabbed me three
bats to loosen up.

(Photo courtesy Sholes family)

Despite our 11-5 lead, the Greensboro crowd seemed to be on my side and wondering, like I was, whether I would get a shot at a fourth home run. As it turned out, I would get the opportunity.

The ninth inning came around and I was due up second in the order. Souter led off with a walk and you could feel the anticipation in the crowd. I heard a few voices saying, "Come on Muscle, hit another one out."

I took the first pitch from Powell and it was a fastball high, but I held off and took it for a ball. It could have been a pitch I might have driven out, but I just didn't pull the trigger. I wasn't a first-pitch swinger anyway. Powell came right back with almost the exact same pitch and this time I swung, but foul-tipped it for strike one. I was mad at myself for missing that one.

Powell wasn't changing his pitching pattern. It was obvious he was going to make me chase a high fastball. He followed the 1-1 pitch with another fastball up over the letters, but I took it for ball two. With Souter getting his lead off first, Powell went into a full windup and threw a fourth straight fastball up around the letters. I took a big cut but missed, almost screwing myself into the ground.

Powell may have tried to get the 2-2 pitch up as well, but it was a fastball that backed me off the plate and filled the count. I stepped out of the box to get a breather and relax. I knew Powell would get something over the plate, he didn't want to back down and end up walking me. The home crowd would probably have booed him out of the park if he had given me a free pass. There was no reason to think that he wouldn't come back on the full count with another fastball.

I was thinking that he would be trying to guard against the base-on-balls and bring the next one down about an inch. I was right on the money. Powell's 3-2 pitch was a fastball just below the letters, maybe the best pitch I'd seen all day. I swung and the ball jumped off the bat and went soaring toward right field. The crowd let out a roar and rose to its feet. Powell turned on the mound and watched the flight of the ball. I was running hard to first and was set to go into my home run trot, then I realized the ball is bouncing around and right fielder Emo Showfety was picking it up. I put it into high gear heading around first as the relay throw came into second just as I slid in with a double.

> *"Muscle was a straightaway hitter. The outfielders always got right up next to the fence, as far back as you could and hope he didn't hit one over your head.*
>
> *"I don't see how he hit those home runs with the stomach he had which was something we used to tease Muscle about, and he always said that it was the stomach that gave him the power, joking of course. There was another guy who had a`pretty big stomach and he did all right – Babe Ruth.*
>
> *"But that night at the stadium, I thought he had his fourth home run. It looked to me as if it was heading out. But the ball missed leaving by about a foot or less. It hit the top of the double-decker fence in right field.*
>
> *"Muscle put on a hitting exhibition that day that I've never forgotten."*
>
> *– Emo Showfety,*
> *outfielder, Greensboro*

I remember being disappointed at not getting the home run, but I couldn't be too unhappy going 5-for-5 with three home runs and scoring five runs and driving in four more. I recall the Greensboro crowd standing up and applauding as I went back to first base in the bottom of the inning. That's what I mean by good fans, cheering an opposing player like that.

Oh yeah, we ended up winning the game 13-6.

"I was covering the game. Even if I hadn't been working, I would have been there to see Muscle. People didn't come out to see Reidsville play, they came out to see Muscle Shoals swing the bat. After he hit those three home runs, everyone was pulling for him to hit his fourth. I know he hit the ball and everyone thought it was gone out of the park. The only question seemed to be whether or not it was going to be fair or foul, because it was down the line. Then it hit off the top of the fence. I remember looking down at Muscle on second base and he was shaking his head like he couldn't believe the ball didn't go out of the park. Muscle was a pure joy to watch hit. There never was one like him before or since. He put electricity in the ballpark."

– Moses Crutchfield,
official scorer and writer
for Greensboro Daily News

After the game, down in the clubhouse, Willie Duke came by and congratulated me. Willie and I were great friends. Willie once played in the high minors with Ted Williams and he liked to tell about the time that he had a double, triple and home run off Whitlow Wyatt, who pitched for 16 years in the big leagues, while the Splendid Splinter struck out four times. Willie played quite a few years in the minors and had a .331 lifetime batting average.

Willie started the '49 season playing and managing at Winston-Salem, but got fired a few months into the season because they weren't winning.

Willie, a former North Carolina State star, was hitting .352 with 10 home runs when he was replaced by George Ferrell, who in turn was replaced by Roland Leblanc just two days later. As a matter of fact, Willie got the ax right after

Winston-Salem bounced us in a doubleheader in which Willie got five hits in seven at bats with five RBIs. A little while after that he joined Danville playing the outfield for Woody Fair's Leafs. In between jobs, Willie would attend games in Greensboro and he was there the night I almost had my fourth home run.

> *"I know when we used to play Reidsville, I hated to see Muscle come to the plate, especially with runners on base because he seemed to bear down even more. The thing about Muscle was you couldn't pitch around him. He had a great eye at the plate, but he could still go out after bad pitches and hit them out of the park.*
>
> *"I basically told our pitchers that if Muscle came to the plate in a win-lose situation, put him on.*
>
> *"When you did pitch to Muscle, you had to challenge him. He had major league potential, but he just never got the breaks. He was certainly a great hitter and a funny guy.*
>
> *"I know one time I got on first base and Muscle was playing the bag and I noticed that Muscle was sweating profusely. I figured he had a little too much to drink. I asked Muscle if he was OK because he was looking a little shaky. Muscle said, 'I'm OK Wee Willie, that's only yesterday's lemonade coming out.'"*
>
> *– Willie Duke*

A lot of writers and broadcasters began talking about me going after Gus Zernial's Carolina League record of 41 home runs, which he set in 1946 with Burlington. I didn't want to say anything brash to make me look cocky, but after people started talking, I thought to myself that the record was

11

a possibility. I had 22 home runs and it was only the second week of June. There was a lot of time left in the season as long as I stayed healthy.

> *"Shoals and his wife lived in a two-room apartment at my mother's house. My mother was Mrs. E.M. Cranford (Sue) who passed away in January of 1974.*
>
> *"I had just returned home from service and I remember when Shoals came home after a game, his wife would have him a whole fried chicken ready to eat.*
>
> *"I slept in a room next to the kitchen and I would wake up and listen to him telling his wife every detail about the game.*
>
> *"He really put his heart into the game. He had a real husky voice and I really got a kick out of lying there and listening to him describe those games.*
>
> *"He was well-liked by everyone in Reidsville. My mother was a baseball fan and really thought a lot of him and his wife. She was real sorry when they left Reidsville."*
>
> *– Ralph H. Brown*

I didn't know if Helen was at the game or not that day. Usually, if she goes on the road, I'll spot her in the stands. I didn't see her so I assumed she wasn't up to going.

When the bus rolled back into Reidsville and we pulled up to Kiker Stadium, Helen was there to meet me. We missed that Kirk Douglas matinee, but we still had time to get down to Short Sugar's Barbecue for a bite to eat. June 12, 1949 was a special day in a special season in the Carolina League.

Chapter Two

I guess it was appropriate that I was born in a lumber town. I never in my wildest dreams ever imagined how lumber would eventually take over my life, in a manner of speaking. But, more about that later.

I've lived and traveled all over the United States but, when it comes down to it, I guess you'd have to call me a native West Virginian. I was born Lloyd Cleveland Sholes Jr. on October 3, 1916 at a dot on the map called Camden on Gauley, a rather poetic sounding place in the southern half of West Virginia, about 100 miles east of Charleston, which sets right off route 19 on the western edge of the Monongahela National Forest. I actually lived my young years just outside of Camden on Gauley in Gauley Mills, which was nothing more than a sawmill town.

Camden on Gauley today probably isn't much bigger then when I was a young boy there. Camden was actually the town, which back then couldn't have been more than a thousand people. Gauley Mills was basically a company store and a post office and, of course, the mill which employed close to 500 people. But in Camden was where the school, church, drugstore, hardware store and moviehouse were all located.

Camden would be bustling on a Saturday with the men off from the sawmill bringing their families into town. As a kid we'd head to the moviehouse and it would be packed on a Saturday morning. Back then it showed mostly silent movies and I can still remember sitting there watching Tom Mix, who was my favorite cowboy hero, riding across the big screen. Lucille Caudy would be down front playing the piano and when the horses were riding across the screen she would play the piano real fast and then she would slow down when somebody got shot. We'd leave the moviehouse and all day we'd play cowboys. Naturally, all the kids wanted to be Tom Mix and nobody ever wanted to be the bad guys.

Not too far down the street from the moviehouse was where Doc Hill had his office. He seemed like an old codger to us kids, but at the time he probably wasn't that old, maybe in his 50s. It seemed like every time I sneezed, here would come ol' Doc riding that brown horse of his. He would be carrying that black bag in one hand and holding the reins in the other. I hated seeing him come.

One time, I don't know how old I was, maybe four or five, I swallowed a toothpaste tube cap. My mother panicked and called Doc up. It took Doc a little while to get there but he came into our house, his black boots all covered with mud, and I can still smell that odor of medicine, which he seemed to wear like some cheap cologne. I wasn't feeling bad, but mother had me in bed. I guess she was afraid I might die from swallowing a toothpaste tube cap and, after a couple of hours of wringing her hands, she had me worried too.

Doc comes into the bedroom, leans over me, pecked hard on my stomach a couple of times and laughed. "Oh, he'll pass it. It ain't going to kill Leo." He was still laughing when momma thanked him and he got back on his horse and rode down the dirt road.

Ol' Doc was all we had there in Camden on Gauley and, I guess if you looked past his rough exterior, he wasn't a bad doctor. At least I never heard of too many people dying on him after swallowing a toothpaste tube cap.

I was the second of Lloyd and Anna Sholes' children. I was Lloyd, Jr., but everybody called me Leo. I had three sisters, Mona was eight years older, Lucille was two years younger and Garnet, who we called Chloe, was a year older. Harold, who was five years older than me, was my only brother. Like most brothers and sisters we fought, but we were a close-knit family.

In Camden on Gauley most of the people who lived there did one thing for a living and that was work at the sawmill, owned by the Cherry River Boom and Lumber Company. Of course, our family was one of 'em.

Cherry River ran south of Camden. The north and south fork of the river ran together close to Richwood, a town about three times the size of Camden located 20 miles south.

The company, which was owned by a family out of Scranton, Pennsylvania, was really a pretty big operation. My father was a talleyman at the mill and he'd sit in this little building and look out a window at the lumber passing by and in a book he'd mark down whether it was chestnut or oak or whatever type of wood it might be. It was a pretty good job as far as jobs went in the sawmill industry. At least he didn't have to do a lot of hard labor.

The logs would be brought down out of the forest and off the mountain on flat rail cars pulled by an old cog engine, chugging at a snail's pace and billowing smoke that you could see for miles. The train, stacked with the fresh cut trees, would stop at the pond and those logs would be dumped into the water. The logs would eventually go through the mill where they would be sawed into lumber and the lumber would be stacked for what seemed as high as the mountains they came from.

I don't know how many years my father worked as a talleyman, but the boss liked the way my dad made his figures in the book and, because of that, offered him a job of running Gauley Mill's company store which serviced the mill town. Anything you wanted you could buy there. Everything from a cradle to a casket.

The workers at the mill were paid once a month. They'd cash their checks and come to the store for supplies and, after paying, they wouldn't have much money left. Just like the Tennessee Ernie Ford song "16 Tons". You know, "What do you get, another day older and deeper in debt. Owe my soul to the company store." There were people in Gauley like that.

But dad made a decent living. We never wanted for anything that I can recall. As a matter of fact, dad made

15

better working in the store than working at the mill. I know growing up I had a rifle, traps, ice skates and a bicycle. Dad was a hard worker, but he always had time for us kids and he

That's my mother and father, Anna and Leo, standing outside our Parkersburg, West Virginia home. They were two of the sweetest people you could ever meet.

(Photo courtesy of Sholes family)

always found time for his two greatest loves – squirrel hunting and baseball. We used to go camping in the mountains behind our house and we even built a little cabin out of scrap lumber. I worked a little as a nine-year-old. I had the only paper route in Camden delivering the

Clarksburg Telegram. I got two cents for each paper and I thought I was rich at the end of the week when I had a couple of dollars.

Dad never played any organized baseball, but he loved the game just the same. I know when I was about nine or 10, dad ordered me a subscription to *Baseball Magazine,* which was THE magazine for baseball fans. I used to cut out the pictures and tack them on my bedroom wall at home. Babe Ruth, Rogers Hornsby, Walter Johnson and Ty Cobb. They were all my heroes.

As I got older I was a pretty big kid. I wanted to be a catcher, so dad ordered me a catcher's mitt for the right hand, since I threw left-handed. We used to catch the Baltimore and Ohio train and ride to Richwood to play games on Saturday and Sunday. That was a big trip for us little boys. We didn't have organized leagues like they do now with Little League. A bunch of us boys in Camden and around the mill would get together and we'd play a game whenever and wherever we could find a team to play us. We didn't have uniforms. We never even thought about that. We'd just play in our old clothes and we had an old pair of shoes we'd wear so our mommas wouldn't fuss at us when we got back home.

Camden had an adult team, like most towns back then, made up of men who didn't play for money, just for the fun. Our team was made up mostly of men down at the mill. Camden's team played on top of this hill, not far from the mill, which had been flattened out and turned into a baseball diamond. The players wore steel cleats and you could hear them coming down the boardwalk that went past our house and linked Gauley Mills with Camden on Gauley. The click, click on those wooden planks and I'd come running and walk up the hill with them. They were big old bushers and they were heroes to us boys. You'd get up on the hill and there'd be a crowd of people. It was a big event on a Saturday afternoon.

I can still taste the lemonade they used to sell there on those hot days in the summer. There would be a big block of ice with sawdust on it to keep it from melting so fast and the person taking care of it would take an ice pick and chip off a piece of ice and put it in a glass. You would drink the lemonade, rinse the glass out in a bucket of water next to the stand and hand it to the next customer.

I used to dream about playing on that team, but I never got the chance. I was about 10 years old when my family had to move from Camden on Gauley after dad lost his job at the company store. I take after my dad in some respects. He was a little headstrong and I don't deny that I'm the same way at times. Nothing wrong being that way, but you have to exercise a little control, which was the downfall for my dad. He couldn't control his temper and it cost him his job.

This handsome lad is me at the age of six. I was a stout kid for my age.

(Photo courtesy of Sholes family)

My dad was a strong Democrat. I emphasize strong. The owners of the mill were Republicans. Dad was always arguing politics with them. At the company store, right behind the cash register, hung a picture of the Governor of West Virginia from 1917 to 1921 by the name of John J. Cornwell, who happened to be a Democrat. One day, dad came to work and the picture was gone. He didn't know what had happened to it and found out later that the head honcho at the mill, a supervisor by the name of Charles Badgett, didn't want that "SOB" Democrat's mug hanging in his store any longer. Dad exploded. He told the man to take his store and shove it. Dad quit before the man could say you're fired.

Dad wasn't worried about finding another job, but he knew that it would have to be somewhere other than the mill. His days there were done. Somehow he got wind that there were plenty of jobs to be had in Akron, Ohio. Akron was a booming town with plenty of factory jobs available. Dad made the trip of about 250 miles to Akron and, in a matter of days, was hired on as a foreman at a rubber plant.

Momma and the rest of us stayed in Camden on Gauley while dad went to Akron, but it wasn't too long before he sent word to momma to have an auction and get rid of everything and come on up. Momma did sell everything except our clothes. She even sold our black 1928 touring car to a family friend. I remember that old car with its running boards and side curtains.

We took the train to Akron, which was a whole lot different than what I had been used to back in West Virginia. It was the big city. On every block there would be a speakeasy. I sold many empty liquor bottles, getting a penny for a pint, two cents for a quart, and a nickel for jugs. This was during prohibition. Me and some other boys, we would go up to a door of a speakeasy, ring a bell and somebody would peep out a little hole and see who it was and then let you in. They would pay us for our bottles and then we'd scat out of there. There were some rough places we went to and some rough characters. They were certainly no places for little boys. But it was hard times back then and you made money where you could.

I know one time some of us kids were playing outside in the street next to a speakeasy, and the police raided the place. They knocked down the door to the house, but there wasn't anybody there. We snuck up and went in for a look and the bootleggers had cut a hole in the kitchen floor and had a copper still set up. In every room there were barrels of corn mash and down in the basement there must have been 100 cases of bottles – some full, some empty.

The cops went in and chopped up the still and we ran off with as much of the copper as we could. Copper was selling for about 10 cents a pound. Not bad money.

Akron wasn't a bad place to live, but we moved around three times trying to find something suitable to live in. Then dad decided it might be best if momma and us kids headed back to West Virginia until things got a little more stable in Akron. So, we went back to West Virginia, to Parkersburg, to live with my Aunt Belle Furr.

We had been in Parkersburg a few weeks and one day I came into the kitchen and found momma crying. Momma wasn't one to cry a lot because she was a strong woman, but she knelt down on her knees, grabbed me by my shoulders and said she had some bad news about dad. She explained that dad had been in an accident at the factory and got his hand caught in a machine. The injury was so bad that he was going to have to have four fingers on his left hand amputated.

As it turned out, his life wasn't in danger and he lost three fingers, but it was a situation where he had a family to support in The Depression and now he was unable to work. Dad sued the company and got $8,000 and joined us in Parkersburg where we raised a garden trading vegetables to stores for sugar and coffee and other staples. We also sold Christmas trees and when dad got better he got a job as the maintenance supervisor of the Wood County state roads.

Dad was my best friend during my childhood and my mother was the sweetest lady you'd ever meet. They were good to me and gave me all I could ask for. Mom died in 1952 and dad remarried after a couple of years. Then dad passed away a few years later after a stroke. But, to this day, they're with me every waking moment. I think of them all the time. I think about the fishing trips my dad and I used to make up the Cherry River every Thanksgiving. We also went duck hunting. Dad would go upstream and I would stay downstream. Dad would shoot the ducks and they'd be in the water and float down to where I had waded out in the shallow part.

Christmas was always a fun time as mom and dad tried to make Santa Claus as real as possible. The family next door to us had four boys about the same age as us and their dad had died. They used to tell me there wasn't a Santa Claus, but I didn't believe them. My folks would raise the window a little on Christmas morning and put a shoe print out there and the slice of cake my mom had left for Santa was always gone.

I tried to help out financially with a newspaper route for the *Parkersburg Morning News* during the week and on Sunday I delivered the *Pittsburgh Press* along the Kanahwa River. One customer I'd soon as not had was Miss Eddie. She was a tough old lady, a big woman with tattoos all over her arm. I'd knock on her door and say, "Miss Eddie, I need to collect for the paper." She'd stick out a finger and say, "Listen, you hit that plank and get out of here." I didn't have to be told twice, running as fast as I could down the plank from her houseboat across the water to the bank of the river.

She would always pay, but it was when she wanted to. She could well afford it because she was in the home brew business. She had buckets of it hanging around and pints of moonshine on shelves. I had several customers along the Kanahwa, most of them lived on houseboats like Miss Eddie. But, unlike Miss Eddie, most of the rest were pretty easy to get along with.

I usually got through with my run early and I'd go back home and momma would have me breakfast and she would fix me a couple of bologna sandwiches to take to

21

school. I wasn't much interested in school, but I didn't have any choice in the matter. If only I could have gotten as interested in my books as I was with baseball. We didn't have a school team, but we did have an American Legion team I was on.

Ever since back in 1925 when dad took me to Washington D.C. to see the Senators play the New York Yankees in a doubleheader, I wanted to play baseball. I can still remember Joe Judge hitting a home run for the Senators. But it was Babe Ruth who I wanted to see smack one, but he never got one out of the park that day. Babe was my biggest hero, just like he was the hero of about several million other boys. I wanted to be like the Babe. He was left-handed and so was I. To me, that was enough in common to think about following in his footsteps. I went down to the railing along the field between games and I was able to get the Babe's autograph. He was such a big man and he had this warm smile. I don't know what I ever did with that autograph. It got lost over the years.

But I thought to myself that one day that would be me. Just like the Babe, I was going to hit home runs and have kids come up to me wanting my autograph. Baseball was going to be my life and there was never any doubt in my mind.

Chapter Three

Hindsight, as they say, is 20-20, but if I had it to do all over again I would put a lot more effort into school than I did. It's tough making it in the world without a solid education, but try telling that to a young kid who had baseball on his mind every waking moment.

Since we didn't have a baseball team at Parkersburg High School, my freshman year I was on an American Legion team. When we first moved to Parkersburg after leaving Ohio, I was too young to play with the team, but I hung around and practiced with them. The team went to the state tournament that year and got beat. I got to go along and it was a thrill. The next season, I finally was old enough to join the team and we went back to the state tournament and this time we beat Clarksburg for the championship.

After the Legion season was over, I started hanging around the twilight league. It was a league comprised of men who worked at different jobs during the day and in the evening, at 6 o'clock, they would put on their uniforms and set out for the nearest diamond.

I was going to be a sophomore in high school and I was pretty big for my age. Toward the end of the season I was allowed to play some in the twilight league at first base and I got to pitch a little. The only reason I got to pitch was because I was left-handed and there weren't too many lefties around. But I could bring the ball up to the plate pretty good and I had a curve that bent a little.

We took a trip over to Wheeling to play one of the better teams in the league and the Wheeling team had a couple of guys who had played some minor league ball. Here I was, a boy practically, playing against grown men. The manager of our team decided he was going to pitch me against Wheeling because he felt Wheeling wasn't used to seeing a left-hander.

I thought, "Oh boy. They'll clean my clock." But I pitched five innings and didn't do that badly. I'd walk a guy, hit a guy and give up a hit. It was that kind of game. I was lucky enough to have a decent fielding team and my defense kept me out of trouble, turning five double plays. But one of the teams we played found out I was still in high school and raised a stink over the matter. So, that was it for me in the twilight league for the time being.

I was a pretty decent athlete. Not only did I play baseball, but I played halfback on the Parkersburg High School football team. I liked football. I was big and strong for a 15-year-old and when I got hit it was usually the other guy who got his bell rung. But, in 1931 at 15, I dropped out of school after my sophomore year. The Depression was hitting everyone hard and I felt like I could do better performing odd jobs and making some money to help my family.

Momma and Daddy said I was old enough to make my own decisions, but looking back I didn't know what I was doing. I know Ross McHenry, my football coach, tried to talk me into staying in school. He said I would regret it later on. I really feel Coach McHenry had my best interests at heart, but I also think he didn't want to lose me off the football team.

Our family was surviving the hard times. Dad was working again, as a carpenter. And we helped ourselves by raising a garden. We'd raise vegetables and trade at the store for sugar and coffee and other staples. I remember dad used to accuse me of cutting down the corn when I hoed. He was just kidding of course. Dad had a good sense of humor in those tough times. We were able to make ends meet, somehow.

People talk about being in the right place at the right time, well, I guess I was. At one of my Legion games, where I had a couple of hits and a home run, there was a man in the stands by the name of John Cochran. Cochran was a foreman at the Ames, Baldwin and Wyoming Company, located in Parkersburg, which was a manufacturer of tools such as shovels, picks, posthole diggers and things like that. The company also sponsored a team in the twilight league.

Cochran must have liked me because after the game he walked up to me outside the ballpark and asked if I'd like to come work for him and be on the company team. I told him I was just 16. He said I looked 18, and that he'd get me on at the company.

The country was still in the horrible grip of The Great Depression. Folks all over were having tough times and people out of work would take just about any job if it meant drawing a paycheck.

It was up in the winter before I went for my interview with Cochran and, as I approached the front gate of the company, people were standing four deep in freezing conditions just to get an application for a job. Here I was, just turned 17 and not in dire straits like most of those who were trying to keep warm huddled around big barrels with fires blazing up.

I walked up to the gate, whispered my name and told the man Mr. Cochran was expecting me. The man took me right in. I didn't dare look back because I knew those poor souls waiting to get in must have thought what is this young kid doing going in ahead of us. I felt guilty knowing there were people so desperate for jobs. Some of them with large families to support and here I was getting the VIP treatment just because I was going to play on the company baseball team.

I was led down a hall and to a door with Cochran's name on a gold plate. I went in and Cochran got up from behind his desk and asked me if I was ready to go to work. I said I was and he offered me a job of running a turning lathe at $18 a week making handles for axes and other tools. The job sounded pretty good to me. Making $18 was a lot of money and, on top of that, I was going to be playing baseball.

I played a few years in the twilight league while working at ABW. I had a great time. I couldn't wait until work was over during the day so I could put my uniform on and play ball. That's what I lived for. When winter came, it seemed like the cold months in West Virginia lasted forever. All I could think about was wondering when the snow would melt, the grass would turn green and we'd be back on the diamond hearing the crack of the bat.

In the twilight league I played first base when I didn't pitch. I liked pitching OK, but I enjoyed standing up at the plate and taking my hacks. But as long as I was playing every day it didn't matter a whole lot whether I was pitching or playing first, just as long as I was on the diamond.

Dick Hoblitzell was an umpire in the league and he called a lot of our games. Dick was from Waverly, West Virginia originally and he had played some major league ball. He was a former first baseman and had played for the Cincinnati Reds and Boston Red Sox. He played 11 years, got in a couple of World Series and even led the National League in at bats for two straight years.

Dick took me aside one day and we had a long talk. Dick seemed to think I might have some potential to play baseball professionally. I never really thought about having that much talent. I thought that maybe Dick was just trying to be nice to me. Shoot, I was content playing in the twilight league. For all I knew, this was as good as it got. Every time I would run into Dick he said he was going to see what he could do to get me a professional contract. I said sure and would go on about my business, never giving it a second thought, just thinking Dick was talking nonsense and trying to humor me.

One evening, we had just finished a game where I had three hits, including a home run. I was leaving the field when a guy comes running up behind me calling my name. I turned around and this fellow wearing a felt hat introduced himself as a scout for the Brooklyn Dodgers. I couldn't even tell you his name now. I'm not sure I even heard him tell me when he made the introduction. He went on to say that he had been following me around for a couple of games and liked the way I swung the bat. Then he floored me. He asked me right there on the field if I'd like to sign a professional contract with the Brooklyn Dodgers.

I'm sure I stood there with my mouth hanging open, muttering and stuttering. I didn't know what to say. Today, if you sign a contract, you have to be drafted or sign as a free agent, back then it wasn't quite that organized. This was during the days when you could sign with anybody who asked you first.

The scout said if I signed, I would report to Dayton, Ohio of the Middle Atlantic League. All this came right out of the blue and I really didn't know what to tell the guy. Then I thought I would get Dick's opinion. Dick had been around and he might offer me some advice.

I told the scout that I'd like a while to think about his offer and he said OK, that he would come by my house in a couple of days to talk about it. I saw Dick at our next game and told him about the Dodgers' offer and he shook his head and told me to stay away from the guy. Dick said the Brooklyn organization was a lousy franchise and that I could get something better.

I was at home one evening and there was a knock on the door and it was the scout. He asked me if I had considered the offer. I had mixed emotions, but I trusted Dick, so I told the scout that I had to decline his offer. It took the poor fellow by surprise. He was thinking that I would jump at the chance. He stayed there at the house a couple of hours trying to convince me to sign and I just kept telling him that I wasn't interested in playing for the Dodgers.

The scout finally left and when he did I started questioning myself as to whether I did the right thing. An offer to play pro ball, despite what Dick told me, might not come again. But Dick insisted that I not worry, that my chance would come. He said he would make sure of it. Dick kept saying the Dodgers weren't the only pro team out there, that baseball clubs were beating the bushes looking for prospects and that me being left-handed, that I would have no problem signing.

The twilight season came to an end in 1936 and during the entire winter I never saw or heard from Dick. Then one day I got a letter from a fellow by the name of Willis Countryman, a lumber dealer in Ohio. He explained in his letter that he sold lumber for a living but, as a hobby, he sniffed out baseball talent. He wasn't actually a scout but what's called a bird dog. A bird dog is someone who finds talent and then passes the information along to a pro scout. If the player signs, the bird dog may get a few bucks for his trouble.

Anyway, Countryman said he had heard about me from Dick Hoblitzell and wanted to know if I'd be interested in attending a tryout in the spring with the St. Louis Cardinals in Portsmouth, Ohio. He said if I didn't have a way up to Portsmouth, that he would drive to Parkersburg to pick me up and even pay all my expenses. This sounded almost too good to be true. I wrote Countryman back and told him I could use the ride up.

It seemed as if the next couple of months went so slow and I was afraid the tryout would never come about. I was afraid a letter would come telling me they'd changed their minds. One day I went to the mailbox and there was a letter from Countryman. I opened it up and he told me when he would be coming and to be ready.

It was sometime in mid-April and there I was sitting in the car next to Countryman, a man in his 50s, rolling across Highway 7 to Portsmouth. I had my suitcase packed with my cleats and glove and my uniform. We got to the park late in the afternoon and I put on my uniform, which had a shovel across the front of the jersey representing the ABW factory. I had bright red socks on. I must have been a real sight. I was a real busher.

I didn't know what to expect, because I'd never been to a tryout before. What I didn't expect to see was about 200 other ballplayers hoping to get their chance at pro ball, just like me. We all got in a line and had numbers pinned to our back. A couple of wooden desks were set up behind the home plate screen and that's where the scouts sat and did their evaluations.

It were these tryout camps which made the St. Louis organization such a great one. The tryout camp was the idea of Branch Rickey, who had these camps all over the country. He had scouts scurrying the backwoods for ballplayers. Of course, they had to have someplace to put these ballplayers and it was Rickey who began the farm system in 1920. The St. Louis farm system grew so large that, in 1940, the Cardinals had 32 minor league teams and a working agreement with eight other clubs with over 600 players.

Anyway, at these tryout camps every player got a chance to hit. After I lined a few shots down the right field line, Charlie "Pop" Kelchner, who was the chief scout for the Cardinals and who organized the tryout camp, got out of his seat and yelled out my number to come over. He said to follow him and we walked down to the left field area and he told me to sprint. Pop wanted to see what kind of speed I had. It's a wonder I wasn't told to go home right there because running wasn't one of my strong suits. I ran a few sprints and Pop asked me if I had ever broken my leg. I told him no and he said it looked like I was favoring my left leg. He asked me if I ever played the outfield. I told him no that all I ever done was play first base and pitched a little. Pop told me to stay put. He walked away and I could see him talking with the other scouts behind home plate and then I could see him heading back my way. He got to where I was standing, looked me in the eye and said, "Son, we'd like to sign you for $75 a month."

I did some quick adding and subtracting in my head and figured I'd be making less playing pro ball than what I was making at ABW. I thought I'd be making more. I told Pop that there was nothing more I'd like to do than to sign with the Cardinals, but that I had to make at least $100 a month.

Pop told me to wait again and he comes back and said, "OK, we'll give you $100 a month, but don't breathe this to anybody else. We just don't start our players off here with more than $75. But we want you in our organization."

In the matter of five minutes, Pop handed me a contract and, at the age of 20, I was a professional baseball player with the famous St. Louis Cardinals' organization.

At the tryout, I had met Mike Euroko. He was a pitcher hoping to sign and we had become friends. He had made several cuts and it looked like he was going to get a chance to sign too. I got him to one side and said, "Mike, they'll offer you $75 a month, but don't take it. Tell them you have to have $100." Countryman had me staying at some hotel that night and it just so happened Mike was there too and I ran into him later at dinner. He said, "Leo, you were right. They offered me $75 and I asked for $100 and got it."

This was a new beginning for me. I was young, excited and ready to begin my adventure into baseball as a professional. I was a member of the St. Louis Cardinals and I was floating on cloud nine.

Chapter Four

I kept repeating to myself over and over, "Leo, you're a professional baseball player." It was just hard for me to comprehend. This was something I had only dreamed about and now it was a reality. Heck, at this stage, it didn't matter whether I was going to be playing for the St. Louis Cardinals or some Class D team, which is exactly where I was sent – Class D, not St. Louis.

Pop told me that I would probably be reporting to Monessen, Pennsylvania of the Class D Pennsylvania State Association. I didn't a bit more know where Monessen was but Pop told me it was close to Pittsburgh. As it turned out, it was only about an hour or two from Parkersburg.

In all my excitement, I just remembered something. I still had my job at Ames-Baldwin. I would be making a little more playing Class D ball than I was making at the company, but there was the problem of September to March. I wouldn't be collecting a baseball check during those months and I couldn't afford not having a winter's job.

As it turned out, Mr. Cochran found out I made the Cardinals and he told my folks to tell me that when the season was over to come back to work. That was a load off my mind. Now I could go play baseball and not have to worry about a job when I put the spikes away for the winter.

This is not to put the city of Portsmouth down, because Portsmouth was a fine town, but it's not the ideal place to hold spring training. Florida sounds a lot better, but that's how clubs did it back then. Not everybody went to Florida. While April in Portsmouth ain't exactly shirt-sleeve weather, I wasn't complaining. I was in seventh Heaven.

I had just reported to Portsmouth and the big news was the arrival of the St. Louis Cardinals in town to play an exhibition at Riverside Park against the Portsmouth Red Birds, their farm club in the Mid-Atlantic League. The Cardinals, managed by Frankie Frisch, had completed spring training in Florida and were on their way to St. Louis for an exhibition series against the Browns. Branch Rickey, the Cardinals vice president and general manager who was born just a little ways from Portsmouth in Stockdale, decided to stop in for a game against the local minor league club.

The Cardinals arrived from Chattanooga, where they had played an exhibition, on the Norfolk & Western Railway. The team had dinner at the Hurth Hotel in Portsmouth and dressed for the game at the hotel before going to the ballpark.

The whole town of Portsmouth shut down for the Cardinals. Stores closed at 2 o'clock, schools were dismissed and even the government facilities were closed for a half a day. I was one of the 5,000 spectators there at the ballpark who saw Don Gutteridge and Don Padgett crank home runs in an 11-0 St. Louis win. Dizzy Dean didn't pitch, but he pinch-hit and flew out with the bases loaded.

Meanwhile, it was back to work after the Cardinals left town. You talk about a cluttered training camp. There were players all over the place trying out for the various minor league teams in the St. Louis organization. I know at one point they cut 90 rookies, fortunately I wasn't one of them.

We worked out and we played exhibition games against some of the other clubs and then it was time to break camp and leave Ohio bound for our summer home in Monessen. There were nine players on my team who broke camp in Portsmouth, including John Lynch, a former captain of the University of Pennsylvania squad, who was our catcher and manager and the elder statesman at the ripe old age of 22. Also along for the ride was our business manager Andy French. We didn't have a fancy, air-conditioned bus to make the trip. Instead, we piled into three cars heading for Monessen. We left on Friday and were supposed to be in Monessen later that night. Well, we left on Friday all right but instead of being in Monessen that night, we were somewhere between Portsmouth and Monessen on a lonely stretch of highway in Ohio with a broken down car. We were close to some little town so small it had no motel and there was none within 20 miles. It was late at night so we all bedded down right there in the cars. The next morning John was able to get a mechanic to fix the car for us and we headed out again to Monessen.

That would be the end of the story except somewhere near the West Virginia line another car had a flat tire and it took the better part of the day to find somebody who could repair it. We didn't have a spare in either of the cars. It was getting dark and it was pouring down the rain and John didn't much want to drive in those conditions. I remember him saying something about the brakes not working too good when they got wet on the car he was driving. So, we spent another night in those cars. Finally, on Sunday morning, we hit the road again for Monessen.

Meanwhile, unbeknownst to us, they were holding a contest in Monessen to guess when we would arrive. We were supposed to have been there three days ago. Anyway, this contest ran in the paper in Monessen and whoever guessed the correct time that we would arrive would win two free tickets for the season's opener. I don't know who ended up winning the tickets, but I do know we rolled into town at one in the morning.

Monessen was a steel town of about 10,000 located on the Allegheny and Monongahela rivers. Professional baseball was kind of new to Monessen. The town had a team in 1934, but it folded after the 1938 season. The Pennsylvania State Association, which began in 1934, didn't last too long either as it went under after the 1942 season.

As a matter of fact, just a month before we arrived in Monessen the league was on shaky ground. Three teams were certain, but three other teams were holding out because they wanted to operate in the league not as independents, but as major league farm clubs. Of course Monessen was a farm club of the St. Louis Cardinals while Butler hooked up with the Yankees and Beaver Falls was a franchise for the Boston Bees. Jeanette, McKeesport and Greensburg were the three waiting for a big league team to come along and adopt them.

The Brooklyn Dodgers agreed to take over Greensburg. PSA president Elmer Daily and officials from the major league clubs of the teams represented were able to convince the operators at Jeanette and McKeesport to open the season and they would attempt to get a working agreement before the season was over.

Our ballpark wasn't exactly the Taj Mahal, but it had a diamond and that was all we needed. Tin Plate Field it was called. I don't know where that name came from but it has to be one of the most unusual names for a ballpark I've ever heard. Southwest Pennsylvania had had some terrible flooding just a few months prior to our coming and they were in the process of trying to make some repairs at the field. Several of us pitched in one day and helped out. I was in charge of putting up some chicken wire around the wooden stands behind home plate.

After we got there, the Cardinals began moving some other players into town and we were up to our 16-player limit. I remember the day at the park when we were issued our uniforms. Our home uniform was white with a red R on the cap and our away uniform was gray and had a baseball with a pair of red wings, since we were called the Redwings, sprouting out from our jersey front.

Our season, which had a 110-game schedule, was due to open on May 13. Everyone was looking forward to it. I was standing on the diamond taking infield and I could see the fans coming through the gates. Adults got in for 35 cents and kids were admitted for 15 cents. But on this day the fans had to use their raincheck because we were postponed even before the game got under way. We didn't play the next day either, nor the next day after that. The first three games of the season were washed out.

Finally, though, the rains ended and my professional career had begun. Our games started at 5 o'clock because we didn't have lights, and we could have used lights in our opener as we were tied 6-6 at Tin Plate against the Greensburg Greensox when the game was called because of darkness. But, I was happy enough. I batted four times, had two hits, including a double, and I scored two runs.

A couple of days later I hit my first professional home run in a 21-9 loss to Jeanette at Tin Plate with two runners on. Beyond the right field fence, which was about 320 feet, there were some railroad tracks and I hit the ball over those tracks. It was a pretty good blow if I say so myself.

I was later introduced to night baseball in the Penn League. The Penn League and the Northern League were the only two leagues in organized minor league baseball going into the 1937 season that didn't have lights. But when Brooklyn went into Greensburg, the Dodgers put up lights at the high school field where the team played. It wasn't too many weeks later that Butler followed suit and installed 288,000 kilowatts of lighting. McKeesport jumped on the bandwagon and made plans for lights at Cycler Field.

As you might expect, a lot of people didn't want lights. Now we're not talking about the lights you see at minor league parks these days where it's like daytime at night. It took some getting used to. One writer in a local paper wrote: "I can't imagine anyone eating popcorn in the dark. Imagine a crowd which no longer can watch as a home run disappears over the fence." One of the arguments of putting in lights was that it would allow the steel workers, who made up a great deal of the workforce in that area, to get to the games after working an 8-to-4 shift. Our games started at 5 o'clock and if a guy at the factory wanted to come he would get there around the third inning. With lights, we could start later and allow the workers plenty of time to arrive at the park. At least that was the argument.

In the middle of July, Monessen was only averaging 100 people a game. Andy French began pushing to put in lights at Tin Plate in hopes that it would increase attendance and it was announced that indeed we would get lights before the season was over. Monessen mayor James Gold, who was also president of the Redwings, put in an order to the Frederick Lighting and Service Company in Akron, Ohio to come to Monessen and begin installation. The cost would be $2,500, which was a lot of money then.

But, there was one problem – money. As August rolled around, the club was about $1,500 short of the funds needed to put up lights. Gold was going to put up $1,000 through the club with the idea that the Chamber of Commerce would come up with the remaining $1,500. But the chamber denied ever having made that deal. So much for lights at Monessen. As for me, I'm glad we didn't put 'em up because I know I would have trouble adjusting. I didn't like playing at Butler because of the lights and the same with Greensburg. McKeesport, which was to get lights, never got them and it's probably a good thing they didn't. On June 11, McKeesport, along with Jeanette, dropped out of the league, which left us with only four clubs.

I don't know how Monessen managed to stay in the league, unless the Cardinals helped pay some of the bills, which they might have. I can't blame the fans for not coming out. Right after that 21-9 loss to Jeanette, we took a 17-5 lead into the ninth inning at Tin Plate against Beaver Falls, but ended up losing when the Bees came up with 16 runs to beat us 21-17.

Andy French tried everything to get people into the park. He would stage all kinds of contests. There was one contest in which the players participated by pushing a wheelbarrow blindfolded. I was a contestant one of those times. After putting on the blindfold, you'd grab hold of the wheelbarrow and someone would spin you around on the mound and then point you in the direction of second base. The objective was to push the wheelbarrow to second base. If you reached the bag, the prize was a sports shirt from Pokeys. I don't think I won that shirt. While it was fun for the players, the Monessen fans didn't exactly pack the ballpark for that event.

There was a lot of talent that year in the PSA. Butler, a farm club of the Yankees, had Bill Johnson, Frankie Slavanick and a big first baseman who later won a batting title in the big leagues by the name of Hank Sauer. Beaver

Falls had Whitey Weitleman, Chet Ross and Clyde McCullough and Greensburg had Eddie Lopat.

Lopat went up to the big leagues in 1944 with the White Sox, but he had his really big years with the Yankees. He pitched 12 years in the majors, winning 166 and losing 112 and was in five World Series. He later managed for a few years.

But in 1937 with Greensburg, Lopat pitched a little but they were trying to make a first baseman out of him. He hit just .229 and someone thought he might have better success throwing curves rather than trying to hit them.and that someone turned out to be right. I remember one of the rare times that Lopat got on first base he said, "Leo, the next time you see me I'll be pitching because I can't pull the ball and I can't hit the dang curve."

Class D ball was as low on the ladder as you could get and still be in pro ball. You had to do a lot of things yourself and each player was pretty much his own groundskeeper. They didn't have a crew come out and manicure the field before a game. Every infielder used a rake on his particular position to get the field in shape to play. Can you imagine players doing that today? If you were lucky, somebody would come along and mow the grass about once a week. Sometimes that grass would get pretty high. That is if you had grass on the field.

Clubs back then were working on a limited budget and they were always looking for ways to save a few bucks here and there. One way was to cut costs on baseballs. Baseballs were $22 a dozen and to cut costs on the balls they would use large rubber erasers to get the green grass stains off and then reuse the balls the next game. Today, you get a smudge on the ball and out it goes. Kids used to stand outside the park waiting for foul balls. They would get 25 cents per ball in return and the team would use them over.

I played first base all season, except one game where we were getting whipped pretty bad, and I was brought in to pitch. Hank Sauer was the first batter I faced and I wound up and gave him the best fastball I had. He swung and crushed the ball over the left field fence for a home run and I don't think he even got the meat part of the bat on the ball. I faced about six batters and I think they all got hits. I didn't stay in too long. Needless to say, I didn't do a lot of pitching for rather obvious reasons and no one was happier about that than me.

About the most excitement we had at Monessen that season was when the St. Louis Cardinals came into Pittsburgh for a series. The series was to start on a Tuesday and both the Cardinals and us had Monday off. The Cards would get into town late on Sunday so Branch Rickey, the vice-president of the Cardinals, thought it might be a good idea if the Cardinals played their Class D team in an exhibition.

Rickey believed in his ballplayers earning their money, so he didn't see why his major league club should have a day when they weren't working.

The visiting clubhouse at the Monessen park was having some work done on it and was closed off, so the Cards had to suit up in our dressing room. Meanwhile, we went across the street to the police station to dress. I remember coming out and there was Dizzy Dean, Terry Moore, Pepper Martin and all the players who made the Gas House Gang famous. We all were in awe of them. You have to remember we pretty much were still kids and these guys were bigger than life; ballplayers we used to follow on the radio and imitate. They were heroes to us, almost godlike. We had only seen pictures of them and now to see them up close was almost unbelievable. Of course they came to Portsmouth in spring training, but I was in the stands for that one.

The morning of the exhibition I went into Pittsburgh with Joe Mathes, a scout for the Cardinals, to buy me a new first baseman's mitt. The one I had was old and worn and I was embarrassed for the Cardinals to see me using it. That afternoon we were taking infield and I laid it down to go in for batting practice. When I went back out to pick it up, the glove was gone. I never did find it and I ended up using that old worn glove. Boy was I mad.

There was a good crowd at the ballpark for the exhibition on a damp and dreary day. The crowd and the Monessen players were really looking forward to this game. But no one was looking forward to it more than John McIlvain. McIlvain was 54-years-old and a local legend around Monessen and he had asked Lynch if he could start the game against the Cardinals. "Scissors", as everyone called McIlvain, threw the first pitch to Pepper Martin who lined out to centerfield. He then hit Stu Martin on the arm and, just as Don Padgett was stepping to the plate, the rain began to fall in buckets. We all went back into our dressing room to wait and see if the rain would stop and St. Louis manager Frankie Frisch was raising a fuss. He was cussing a blue streak. Frisch didn't want to play the exhibition in the first place because he wanted his Cardinals to have a day off before starting the series with the Pirates. And not only was his team playing an exhibition, but an exhibition against a lowly Class D team

Then to top it off, all that time wasted by the rain. Frisch was giving Rickey down the road in that clubhouse. It was a good thing Rickey wasn't there. There might have been some fireworks. Then again, Frisch might have bit his tongue. We fellows on the Monessen team just sat back, out of the way, and took it all in. We didn't say a word, as we all were too scared. We were disappointed we didn't get to play a full nine innings, but just seeing those guys was a thrill. It was something I had to brag about all winter when I went back to work at Ames-Baldwin.

Meanwhile, it was back to the season and we would start it with a new manager. Lynch, who was doing a good enough job, was moved up to Decatur in the St. Louis system as a player only and our new manager was Ollie Vanek, who also played centerfield for us. Ollie and I would become real good friends over the years and I would later play for him in Johnson City. The day after Ollie took over, a pitch broke the middle finger of his left hand and Ollie was out about a month, which didn't help our offense. But I was swinging the bat pretty good.

> *Lefty Shoals poled out a home run with two mates on the sack for the Redwings in the first inning to register three tallies. Shoals' drive, a tremendous wallop over the right-center field fence, went right smack into a moving boxcar on the P&LE (Pittsburgh & Lake Erie) tracks and the Monessen first baseman circled the bases with much gusto.*

> *– The Monessen Daily Independent,*
> *July 28, 1937.*

Maybe things were going too good. The very next day Lefty Jenkins, the manager at Butler, was pitching and struck out 16 of us in a 10-3 Monessen loss. In my last at bat, Jenkins hit me on the right wrist and I was on the bench for over a week. One game I missed that week, and so did everyone else, was against Beaver Falls as both teams were AWOL. There had been a carnival at Tin Plate and we had to switch some games around to accommodate the event. Well, the carnival left town and we were getting ready at Tin Plate to play Beaver Falls. We were on the field taking our usual pre-game workout and waiting on Beaver Falls to show up. It got to be 5 o'clock and still no Beaver Falls. Meanwhile, over in Beaver Falls, they were on their field taking pre-game waiting on us to show up at their place. After a few phone calls, it was decided to just cancel the game. I didn't like days off because there wasn't a lot to do in Monessen. But several of the guys went down to the Manos Theatre and saw Martha Raye in *Mountain Music*.

My wrist got better and my first game back I hit two home runs in an 8-4 win over Beaver Falls. The first one I hit against the back wall of the laundry building across the train tracks and then I hit another in the third inning, which was a line drive that cleared the right-center field fence by about a foot. Before that game I had a feeling I was going to do something real good.

> *"You know Chick, that Shoals sure can bust 'em when he's hot. Lefty told me this morning he was right perky and felt as if he was good for a couple of clouts. A new shipment of bats arrived and Lefty grabbed himself a 35-ounce stick. He took one look at that war club and said, 'Watch my smoke today.' "*
>
> *– Ollie Vanek in column by sports editor*
> *Chick Kramer of the Monessen Daily*
> *Independent on August 6, 1937.*

The weather got hot in August, and so did I, especially late in the month when I had two-home run games back-to-back. I was very happy with my first season as I hit .366 with 18 home runs and 74 runs-batted-in. That wasn't too bad for a big kid away from home for the first time.

I was a little disappointed at the end of the year when the PSA all-star team was announced. I was down there in the honorable mention category. I don't mean to sound like sour grapes, but I finished second in the league in hitting, second in home runs and wasn't too shabby with the glove around first base.

Joe Zagami of Beaver Falls was selected as the all-star first baseman. Joe was a good first baseman and a good hitter, I'm not trying to take anything away from him. But Joe hit .295 with six home runs. Defensively, I had a .980 fielding average with 16 errors in 100 games. Joe had a .976 fielding average, but he had 17 errors in 75 games. But, like a lot of things, it's water under the bridge. Joe, wherever you are, I don't hold it against you.

I said my batting average was second in the league, which it was, but it was a distant second. A little second baseman for Butler named John Russian won the title with a .393 average. Russian was a fine player. I often wondered what happened to him. He's like a lot of players I played with or against. I've moved around so much and played with and against so many, there's no way I could keep track. But, I still wonder oftentimes where they are, if they had long careers or who may have passed on.

I had a great time that season. From the first day I got back home to Parkersburg that's all everybody wanted to talk about. I couldn't wait to start playing ball again the next season.

I thought that by the year I had in Monessen, I'd move up another notch to Portsmouth, Ohio of the Mid-Atlantic League. Our minor league spring training was there and I arrived in Portsmouth fully expecting to be spending the season there.

But, Rickey had other ideas. There was another big first baseman by the name of Ed Sipay who had a good year the season before and Rickey wanted him at Portsmouth. Benny Borgman, the Portsmouth manager, and Sam Polatani, the general manager there, both wanted me, but they didn't have much say in the matter.

Rickey got word that I wasn't too happy not staying in Portsmouth, so Rickey called Polatani and told him he was coming to camp and that he would take care of the problem. The problem being me. Rickey wanted to send me to New Iberia, Louisiana of the Evangeline League. So when Rickey got to Portsmouth he asked me how much I had made last season at Monessen. Then he asked me how I would like to make $50 more a month playing at New Iberia. All of a sudden, for $50 more a month, New Iberia sounded like a great place to be.

Rickey picked up the phone and was calling Louis Jennaro, the president of the New Iberia club, to seal the deal. Meantime, Kelchner came into the office. As soon as Rickey got off the phone, he and Pop started talking about Dizzy Dean. Just a few minutes before I arrived in the office, Rickey had made a deal with the Chicago Cubs sending Diz there for $180,000. While Don Curtis, a part-time scout for Houston of the Triple-A Texas League signed Diz in 1929, Pop had scouted Dean some and Pop didn't care much for the deal with the Cubs.

42

Rickey was telling Pop that Diz was through. His arm just didn't have it anymore. Rickey was right. Diz had won 20, 30, 28 and 24 games from 1933 to 1936, but he must have blown his arm out because after pitching 315 innings in '36, Diz pitched only 197 innings and went 13-10 in 1937. Pop was thinking with his heart and you couldn't blame him.

I had been sitting in one corner of the room keeping quiet as a mouse as Pop and Rickey were talking when Branch suddenly realized I was there. Branch turned, looked over at me pointing a finger and said, "Shoals, you never heard anything. Not a word." I said, "Mr. Rickey, you're absolutely right, I didn't hear a thing about what you said about selling Diz to the Cubs."

The press hadn't even been informed yet and neither had Dizzy. So the only people who knew were Rickey, Pop and me, and of course the Cubs.

Rickey was a slick operator. He was selling me on New Iberia saying that it was just a short jump to Houston in the farm system and then to the parent club in St. Louis. He was using some psychology on me. In those days, guys like Rickey, Clark Griffith of the Washington Senators and Connie Mack of the Philadelphia Athletics were the big three at exploiting baseball players in the majors, as well as in the minors.

I used the word exploit but some people might call it being cheap. I never knew of a ballplayer on those three clubs that ever made any money. In fact, I had a friend, Bill Nagel, who played third base for the Athletics under Mack for a couple of years. Bill made $3,680 in 1939. I don't see how Bill lived in Philadelphia on that kind of money. Bill said Mack raised him $800 in 1940 after hitting 12 home runs. Bill argued over the money and, after the 1941 season, he was released. He ended up playing with the White Sox before returning to the minors.

Nevertheless, the only thing I was concerned about was that I had a contract for $50 more a month in my pockets and off to New Iberia I went.

Chapter Five

When I reached New Iberia, the season was already under way. But as soon as I got there the equipment boy issued me a uniform. I went in to play first base that night and struck out twice. It was a rough start for me. After 10 games I was hitting only .230 with no home runs. My frustrations were growing with each at bat. I wasn't accustomed to struggling like this.

The manager at New Iberia was Harrison Wickel. Wickel would spend over 50 years in baseball, finally retiring as a scout for the Houston Astros in 1985. It was Wickel who convinced St. Louis to convert Stan Musial from a pitcher to an outfielder and he would later serve as farm director of the Chicago White Sox from 1952-54.

Wickel had managed the last two years with Caruthersville in the Northeast Arkansas League and played shortstop. Wickel, only 25, had joined the St. Louis organization in 1935 after a career at Ohio State University. Harrison was a bright fellow with a degree in education.

I don't know what it was, maybe it was my inability to hit, but Wickel and I just didn't hit it off from day one. In most of the low minors, then as it is now, the manager of the ball club also coaches third base.

Our troubles began one day when we were playing Lake Charles. I got a basehit and the next batter smacks a drive down the right field line and it looked like it was a sure double. Wickel was waving me around third and toward home, but just as I got to third base he changed his mind and started screaming for me to get back to the base. "Back! Back!" Wickel was shouting. I slammed on the brakes about three strides past the bag and fell flat on my back trying to make the turn.

The throw came in from the outfield and I never got back to the base. I was an easy out. I was lying on the ground and Wickel is standing over top of me cursing with his face as red as the Louisiana clay on the infield. "You dumb S.O.B., where did you learn to play ball?" he screamed. That's all I heard him say and that was enough. I was high strung myself and I'd never been cursed like that by anybody and as far as I was concerned Wickel had no excuse in talking to me that way.

The stands were close to the field and there was a group of gamblers sitting right up on the first row. They were giving Wickel a pretty hard time. Not just on the play where I got thrown out, but just about every time something went against us, you could hear them up in the stands calling Wickel a dumb manager. Well, when I got thrown out, just like Wickel, they started screaming that I was a dumb ballplayer.

After I heard Wickel curse me, I jumped to my feet and went nose-to-nose with him, giving him a little shove backward with my chest. I was right in his face screaming at him, telling him nobody talks to me that way. I came awfully close to punching him right in the face I was so mad. But someone, I don't remember who it was, came over and separated us. I told Wickel I'd see him after the game. I fully intended to make him pay for how he humiliated me on the field.

After the game, I went into Wickel's office with my uniform still on and closed the door. I asked him what was the idea in trying to put the blame on me for being thrown out on a play that he himself was waving me around on. I told Wickel I didn't appreciate one bit being cursed, much less cursed on the field in front of my teammates and all those fans.

Wickel didn't back off, he got right in my face and screamed that he was the manager of this club and he didn't have to apologize for anything he called his players and that I was just another dumb ballplayer. I was getting hotter by the second and I shoved him backward over a bench. A clubhouse man came in and got between us before the fists started to fly. I was a lot bigger than Wickel and I probably would have hurt him bad if I hadn't been stopped.

It didn't take long before word made its way up the organizational ladder about what happened between Wickel and me. A couple of days later I was given a bus ticket that must have been three feet long with the destination Albuquerque, New Mexico of the Arizona-Texas League. The Arizona-Texas and Evangeline leagues were both Class D leagues, so the move was just more of a change in scenery than anything else. As for Wickel, he remained at New Iberia until early August and then the Cardinals sent him to manage at Daytona Beach.

I was still upset over what happened. I was mad at Wickel. I was mad at the organization. I was mad at the world. I was so mad I was ready to quit. As a matter of fact, I tried to cash in the bus ticket for money, but an official at the bus company said there was no way since it was bought by the Cardinals. So, I did the only thing I could do, I got on the bus headed for Albuquerque. I just kept thinking to myself that Albuquerque sure is a long way from West Virginia.

I've been told more than once that I've never met a stranger and I guess that's true. I like to talk and I like people. At the bus station I ran into this beautiful little Indian girl. We talked for a long time and she said she was a college girl heading home. It was time for me to catch my bus and she was going the opposite direction. Before we said goodbye to one another, she gave me a rosary and said that it was for good luck. I sure needed some good luck. As a matter of fact, that rosary may indeed have brought me some good luck when my life was on the line a few years later. But I'll get to that.

The bus hit Texas and made a stopover in Dallas. I was at the station and started talking to some fellows hanging around there. My next bus wasn't going to leave until the next morning, so I asked them what there was to do around Dallas. They said they would show me around the town. We hit about every bar there was and I had such a good time that I stayed over an extra day.

I didn't have much money to start off with, but by the time I was ready to move on all I could scrounge up was one lousy quarter. I got on that bus broke as a pauper. The bus pulled out of Dallas and in a few hours we made a stop for lunch and I was starving. So, I dug that quarter out of my pocket and bought two hot tamales, two for a nickel, and that lasted me until we got to Abilene. We had another long delay there so I searched out the Salvation Army because I knew I could get a square meal for free. By the time I got back to the station, the bus had already left. Just so happened I ran into a truck driver at the station and he said he was on his way to make a delivery in Albuquerque. I asked him if I could hitch a ride and he obliged me. I told him I was broke and he was kind enough to buy me a meal. It was a long haul and not the most comfortable ride in the world, but we arrived in Albuquerque the next morning at eight o'clock.

My instructions were to go to the Courte Café and meet the Albuquerque manager. I got to the café and was told the club just got off a tough road trip where they were 2 and 10 and that I might have a long wait. I was sitting there hungry as could be with only 20 cents in my pocket. It wouldn't have bought me much and, even if it did, I wouldn't have any money left.

I called the waiter over and I ordered up the biggest breakfast you could imagine. After I got through he brought the ticket over and I told him to just bill it to the Albuquerque baseball team. As I sat there drinking my third cup of coffee, I felt rather proud of myself that I was able to get from Dallas to Albuquerque on just 25 cents. To beat it all, I still had 20 cents left.

A couple of hours passed when in walked Albuquerque manager Bill Delancey and club president Sam Minces and they had a newspaper reporter with them. Minces wanted to know where in the devil I had been. I was supposed to have reported three days ago. I told him that I had lost my bus ticket and had to hitch a ride from Dallas. Part of the story was true anyway.

Delancey told me not to give it a second thought that New Mexico governor Clyde Tingley was supposed to have been there the night I was to report to be in a ball-throwing

47

contest with a city commissioner. The gov didn't show up either. Imagine, the governor and me both no shows.

Delancey and I seemed to hit it off right from the start. Bill had been a major league catcher with the Cardinals. He caught the Dean boys, Dizzy and Paul, in the 1934 World Series. But Delancey's career was cut short by tuberculosis and the Cardinals sent him to manage Albuquerque where the climate was dry. Bill went back to play a little with the Cardinals in 1940, but was still too sick. He died just six years later. Bill was a great fellow and he knew his baseball.

Bill and I got to be pretty close friends. In fact, I was the only guy on the club that sipped beer with him now and then. We were taking a chance doing that because Branch Rickey hated alcohol. He didn't believe in drinking. As a matter of fact, Rickey supposedly quit the Cardinals organization after the 1942 season because a brewery sponsored the radio broadcast of St. Louis games. But Bill and I would sit around after a game and down a few and he'd talk about his chicken farm in Phoenix and his family. He had two beautiful little girls. It was a shock when I heard he had passed away at the age of 35 in 1946.

Bill, who was born in Greensboro, North Carolina, would often say to me, "Leo, why me? Why do I have to get tuberculosis?" It was just one of those things I guess. He'd tell me that he used to hit the ball as far as anybody could and he'd get up to the plate occasionally during batting practice just to see if he could still make the fences. He always had Dizzy Dean stories to tell and he felt Dean was the greatest pitcher to ever live. He'd say that Dizzy's fastball moved so much that Diz would just rear back and fire the ball, not worrying about spotting his pitches.

I don't know what kind of report Bill gave the Cardinals on me. He told me later that he was skeptical of my story about losing the bus tickets, but he never questioned me about it. Bill wanted to put that little episode behind and he said he was counting on me to help the club get untracked.

Bill taught baseball the old way and the way of the Gas House Gang. It was hard, get dirty type of baseball. But he said I also had to keep my temper. One time in Tucson, I charged the mound after having been low bridged for about the third time in the game. Bill came running out and got me back in the dugout. He sat down next to me and told me a story about a time in Rochester that he charged the mound after getting brushed back and it wasn't long before every pitcher was low bridging him. Bill's point was that if the pitchers knew they could intimidate you, they all would start throwing inside to you. Bill was right. Pretty soon word got out that if you low-bridged Shoals you would get him upset. But, after that talk with Bill, I never charged the mound again and, after a couple of weeks, the pitchers left me alone.

You have to remember, back in those days we didn't have batting helmets like they do today. You got hit in the head when I played and it was very serious. Today, most of the time, you get hit in the helmet with a 100-mile-an-hour fastball and you might be stunned for a second or two, but the hitter is right back up. I've seen players that I played with seriously injured. Fortunately, I never got hit in the head.

Later on, when I was in the Southern League with Chattanooga, I had a friend with Atlanta, Charlie Glock, and we had a towering 6-foot-8 pitcher named Dick Wiek. Dick was a right-hander who could fire the ball about as hard as anyone I've seen. The only trouble was you didn't know where the ball was coming most of the time. The first time up against him Charlie walked. Down at first base Charlie told me he wasn't going to face Dick again, that he was getting out of the game.

The next time up Charlie took a pitch from Wiek right under the chin and Charlie turns around to the umpire and starts cussing and arguing and carrying on. He was trying to get thrown out of the game. The umpire just stood there smiling as Charlie kept on. Finally, the umpire said, "Charlie, you can cuss and spit all day long, but I'm not throwing you out of the game." Charlie got real quiet, stepped back in the box and on the next pitch Wiek plunked him right in the rear.

I was replacing Whitey Burleson at first base with Whitey was moving to centerfield, and I suppose the fans at Albuquerque were wishing Whitey was back after watching me that first week. The very first game I was in I fielded a ground ball wide of first base. I turned and threw to first but the pitcher wasn't covering and the winning run scored from second base in a 5-4 loss to the Bisbee Bees. Really wasn't my fault though. The pitcher should have been covering. I drew three walks in that game and flew out deep in my other at bat. The other games in that series I didn't get a hit and struck out a couple of times.

It was a rough start, but Bill defended me when he said: "Anybody would take Shoals on the record he turned in last year."

> *"Shoals looks promising and should be good for much more than he showed in the Bisbee series. A week's trip by thumb, after he lost his bus ticket, told on the new man, making his initial appearance a little disappointing to some of the fans."*
>
> *– Albuquerque Journal,*
> *May 27, 1938*

Everyone but Minces was patient with me. Sam had threatened to release me and put Burleson back on first base. But I really think, looking back, that he was just trying to motivate me. I got on track eventually and I enjoyed my season at Albuquerque. After all that happened, I had a decent year. I hit .327 with 10 home runs and 90 RBIs. Ray Alves, a first baseman from Tucson, beat me out for the all-star team, but he deserved it. Ray had 160 hits to my 112, but he had only one home run and 74 RBIs in 164 more at bats than me.

Our season was split into two halves. The first half we finished third and the second half we were second. Sounds like a great season, but I have to tell you there were only four teams in the league – Tucson, El Paso, Bisbee and us. We were 31-34 the first half and 36-31 the second half.

Our weakest link was in the pitching department. By today's standards of having one or two guys you can depend on our staff would have been an elite one. But in 1938 we were average. Bobby Whitlow was our ace going 15-11 with a 4.39 ERA, which was not too bad for our league. One time Bobby hit a home run and he asked the official scorer to break it up into four hits to fatten his batting average. Knowing Bobby, he was probably serious.

We had one interesting fellow who looked like he was going to help us out – Chief Littlehorse. Actually, his first name was Marcel but we called him Chief, for obvious reasons. He was a full-fledged Indian from out in Arizona. The first two games he pitched for us he won, beating Bisbee 13-4 on eight hits and no walks and then another 6-5 win over Bisbee with one walk and allowing six hits.

But then the Chief got shelled in his next start and, about a month after he won his first game, the Cardinals released him.

Sid Lawhon was a decent pitcher. He finished 14-16. Sid was a tall, lanky right-hander who always chewed tobacco. Sid was a terrible hitter, but in two straight games he had the winning hit. One time our regular catcher, Kenny Myers, got suspended and fined $25 by league president R.E. Souers for shoving umpire Charles Barrett at Bisbee. We had no backup catcher. It was always a volunteer thing for someone to come in as a backup. Sid told Bill he'd try it. So behind the plate goes Sid. He had that wad of tobacco in his mouth and he kept trying to spit through the facemask, but he didn't have much practice at mastering the art. Finally, Sid stood up, took the mask off and threw it towards the dugout. Sid said, "Either the Beechnut or the mask has to go and I ain't giving up my Beechnut."

Our troubles at Albuquerque just mirrored the pitching drought the whole St. Louis farm system was going through. Rickey came to Albuquerque in mid-July and addressed the problem. Rickey got on the PA system and told the crowd he was trying to get us some pitching and he also gave Bill a high compliment when he said that the Cardinals had never been able to replace Delancey behind the plate in St. Louis. There were some rumors that Bill might be going back to play, but Rickey dismissed any such notion.

The Albuquerque club was so hard up for pitching that they even had me out there on the mound. I didn't pitch that much, no more than 15 innings I suppose. I can't recall a lot about my pitching that year but I do remember coming in for Whitlow and pitching two innings in an 11-1 loss against El Paso and not allowing a hit.

There weren't a lot of home runs hit in that league and there would have been a lot fewer if it hadn't been for our pitching staff. Bill Creager of Bisbee led the league with 20 home runs, then Eddie Morris of our club was next with 14. I don't know the statistics, but I would have to guess our pitching staff gave up the most home runs. I'd be very surprised if it didn't. Even Eddie Baiocchi got one against us.

Eddie played shortstop for Tucson and was a little guy with absolutely no power. As a matter of fact, after about 400 at bats he didn't have one single home run, but Jeff Cooke of our staff took care of that. Actually, Cooke wasn't that bad of a pitcher. He finished 11-11 and had a decent ERA of 4.66. At least it was decent for that league.

It was toward the end of July and we were at Tucson, and Eddie was the leadoff hitter for the Cowboys. Baiocchi had great bat control. He made good contact and he had fouled off five straight pitches from Cooke when he put every bit of the wood on a fastball and sent it over the left field fence into a bunch of trees. Little Eddie wasn't used to hitting home runs and he took off after hitting the ball like he was beating out an infield hit. I mean he was streaking. He rounded first and I hollered at him, "Why you running so fast little man? Don't you know that when you hit 'em over the fence you can take your time?"

Well, Eddie got halfway to second, stopped and looked at me and came back to first base. He stood there and said, "Thank you Mr. Shoals for that bit of information." Eddie then got on his hands and knees and kissed the first base bag right in the center. He got up and said, "I may never get this chance again." He turned and went to second and got down again and kissed second base. He did the same at third and again when he crossed the plate. As it turned out, that was the only home run he hit in 491 at bats that year. I don't know if he ever played again or not, but that could very well have been his only career home run.

Of course we couldn't make it through the year without getting someone arrested, that's the type of club we had. We were playing a Sunday doubleheader at Bisbee when one of our guys got hauled off to jail. To back up, Bill Delancey was one of the nicest guys you'd ever want to meet – off the field. On the field, he was competitive. He'd do anything if it meant winning the game. I guess that's how he played with the Gas House Gang.

This particular Sunday we were getting beat and beat bad. A large group of fans was sitting close to our dugout and they were cursing every other breath. A couple of sheriffs, wearing those big old hats and huge badges and looking like Wyatt Earp, came down to try and calm the situation, which was festering. We had been cursing back to the fans and it was beginning to get a little tense.

One of the sheriffs leaned over into the dugout and asked us to stop the foul language. From the far corner of the dugout someone yelled to the sheriff to take his tin badge and shove it. Of course there were a few adjectives thrown in. The sheriff, I.V. Pruitt, turned red in the face and came down into the dugout. He marched across to the other end and grabbed Bill Shewey, our center fielder and one of the nicest boys on the club, and marched him back to the clubhouse before taking him to jail for inciting a riot. As it

53

turned out, Shewey hadn't even opened his mouth through the whole incident. It was Delancey who had yelled at the sheriff to shove it. We all had a big laugh out of it. We sent flowers down to the jail to Shewey. After the game, Delancey went to the jail and got Shewey out.

It wasn't unusual to have the police come down on the field. Like the time that Eddie Morris, an outfielder for us, went after Bisbee manager Charlie Moglia. Eddie and Moglia had been bickering over something from the start of the game. Along about the ninth Moglia was standing in front of the dugout and Eddie was just coming to bat in the ninth. Moglia said something and Eddie went charging on a dead run towards Moglia. They got into a knock 'em, sock 'em fight. Moglia came out on the worst end with a busted lip. The police had to intervene.

There was another time in Albuquerque in a game that we beat Bisbee 9-8 in 10 innings that I won with a 360-foot home run. In that game, in the ninth inning, Shewey was called out on a play at home. He jumped up and started beefing and then out comes Delancey and he was immediately ejected for saying the wrong thing. The crowd went crazy and I thought some of 'em were going to come down on the field. So did the umpires who ran to the dugout. A couple of the policemen came down and stood around so we could finish the game.

But, despite all the troubles, you could feel the love at the park as well like when Tiny Hansen, another outfielder, married Nellie Garrison at the stadium. As a wedding present Geddes McIntosh, our 10-year-old batboy, went through the stands to take up a collection.

The worst thing about playing in the Arizona-Texas League was the travel. We went from city to city by a chartered Greyhound bus and in those days there was no air conditioning, unless you consider putting down the windows a form of air conditioning. Believe me, if you've never been to that part of the country in July and August, it can get hot, real hot. Our longest haul was about 500 miles to Tucson and about the same to Bisbee, Arizona. There were very few days we had off.

Often we would ride all night, sleep cramped up on the bus and get to the town in time to play a game. I don't know how it is now, but then the highway was a two-lane, bumpy road. In between our destinations there wasn't a whole lot except barren land. We'd pass our time singing and when we would hit a little town we'd stop for a cool drink. Usually, Bill and I would find a beer joint around and slip off to have a fish bowl or two, which made the trip a little more relaxing.

I liked to play at Bisbee and Tucson because neither one of those places had lights. We'd play our games about 3 o'clock and that left plenty of time to make the rounds at night.

But El Paso was my favorite stop. We'd catch the streetcar across the Rio Grande River into Jaurez, Old Mexico. We'd wear an old pair of shoes over, buy a new pair there real cheap and wear the new ones back. That way, they couldn't tax you coming back across the border at customs. It was a rough place down there though. A week before we finished the season four of us took some girls down there for a good time. We all got loaded and got in a brawl in a nightclub. The Mexican police came in to break it up and it only got worse. They were swinging their clubs and we were swinging chairs and we did a lot of damage. Finally, they called in more police and they got us separated.

The owner of the club assessed the damage and we had to not only fork over all the money we had on us, but the girls had to give them their rings. The girls weren't too happy about that. We promised we would get their rings back when we got paid the next time. The nightclub owner said he would hold the rings until we got him the money. I really thought all hell would break loose when management found out about it, but the lucky thing for us was that no one ever found out about that brawl. We knew to keep our mouths shut – until now.

It never failed that when we pulled into a town, the women always seemed to show up. There was some type of infatuation I guess with ballplayers. I think the word for them today is groupies. I enjoyed their company. After all, I was single with no ties and a baseball season can get awfully long when you spend April to August with a bunch of guys. You appreciate female companionship.

One time we arrived at the Santa Rita Hotel in Tucson and a friend of mine on the club, Jack Hall, a pitcher from Long Beach, California, and I ran into two girls. We asked them what there was to do around town and the girls wanted to know if we'd like to go swimming at a place about 20 miles out in the desert. There wasn't anything there except a man-made lake, no trees, no nothing. We told them we didn't have any swimming clothes and they said don't worry about that.

The girls had their own car and said they would pick us up after the game on Sunday. We met them and drove out to the lake. Jack and I stripped off our clothes and jumped into the water and swam a little ways across to a sandbar. After diving a few times we started to swim back. We looked up and the girls had grabbed all of our clothes, threw them into the car and took off. The only thing they didn't take was a jacket of mine. Jack and I watched as the car went out of view. We just looked at each other wondering what in the heck we were going to do.

We waited and waited and thought the girls might have had their laugh and come back to get us, but they didn't. About an hour later a boy and girl happened to drive by. I put the jacket around me and explained our situation. They agreed to drive us back to the hotel for five dollars. I told them we'd pay them when we got back. Luckily, they had a blanket in the car and Jack put that around him.

We got back to our hotel and put on some clothes and decided to go get something to eat. We went in this restaurant and who do you think was sitting there? Those same two girls. We came up behind them and started letting them have it, screaming and yelling. We had them so scared they were ready to cry. They were just young girls looking for a little fun and I guess maybe we were asking for a little trouble.

It wasn't too long after that that Jack retired. He was 4-7 with a 6.44 ERA and his arm had gone bad. I hated to see Jack quit. We had a lot of fun running around together.

Delancey used to talk to us about women. He gave us advice on the dos and don'ts. He said you never know whether a woman is married or not. If she is the husband might have the notion of killing you if he thought you were fooling around. Then Bill would talk to us about venereal disease. He said if you ever got VD, your baseball career would be over. He told us about a member of the Gas House Gang, whom I won't mention, who got VD and the Cardinals lost the pennant one year because of it.

As for Bill, I could tell he was itching to get off the bench and into a game. It was around the first of August that Bill put himself in as a pinch-hitter and delivered a single. It was his first appearance in a game since he came down with TB in 1935. A few weeks later Bill pitched two innings, giving up a hit, in a 14-1 loss to Bisbee. Bill then went to shortstop moving 17-year-old Bobby Sturgeon to the mound.

We were on a pretty good roll at that time going on a binge where we won 14 out of 17 games after getting off to a 1-8 start in the second half. One of the reasons we were doing so well in the second half can be credited to Paul Piscovich, a right-handed pitcher who joined us in mid-July and won six straight games. He finished the year 9-2. I wished we had him from the start.

Of course, there was the stellar pitching of Ducky Shoals. Yeah, they called me Ducky because of my physique. I kind of waddled when I walked. Bill didn't put me in games just to mop up. There was the time we beat Tucson 2-0. I forget who our starter was, but in the ninth inning he put a couple of men on with walks. Bill came out to the mound and motioned for me to come over. I got the first batter on a popup and finished the game by fanning the last two batters.

I said earlier that one of the worst things about the Arizona-Texas League was the travel. Well, playing our games at Tingley was no picnic. You look at the minor league parks they have today. They're palaces compared to Tingley. We played in a park on the corner of 10th Street and Stover Avenue built in 1932 that had folding chairs for box seats and didn't even have a grass infield. It was nothing but dirt. It was a tough park to hit home runs in too. Center field was 480 feet and down the sides it was 348 feet.

There was one game where the wind was blowing up so much dust that the game was called after six innings. When Rickey made his stopover in Albuquerque, he was appalled at what he saw. He promised that the Cardinals would make sure the infield had sod on it in 1939. Bob Litton, our groundskeeper, was talking with me one time and he told me that they would have put sod down at the start of this year except for the fact the club was too cheap to spend $50 for a watering system.

As the season wound down we had a crucial series with Bisbee at home in early September. Bisbee had a three-game lead over us and we had a doubleheader set for Tingley Park.

We had the largest crowd of the season jammed in there, around 5,200 it was estimated. It wasn't a very good day weatherwise because it had been raining off and on. Just before the game started the umpires decided it was too muddy to play and Minces protested because the umpires said we'd just play three games the next day. He didn't want to lose the gate, of course, and there was the chance the games wouldn't be made up. We were upset because we wanted the chance to catch the Bees.

Minces did all he could to get the field in shape. He had 16 men working on it since six o'clock that morning and they used 110 gallons of gasoline to try and dry it up as well as 12 truckloads of dry dirt and eight bales of straw. They even dug ditches to drain the water and had water pumps going non-stop.

Well, the next day they decided to play two games and there were close to 6,000 fans on hand. We ended up splitting the twinbill by 8-3 scores. The umpires caught a lot of heat from the fans and there was extra security to make sure nothing happened. It was an active night as Delancey got thumbed and Bisbee manager Charlie Moglia protested the first game because he counted 19 players in uniform in our dugout and we were supposed to have had only 18. Turns out we had a kid who was only 13 or 14, Clarence Beers, who was in uniform just for the heck of it.

We won the first game and I hit a three-run home run and I came away with a wad of bills from the crowd as big as my fist.

My lasting memory of that season came in our last game played at Tingley against Tucson. Willie Reyes was called out at first base by umpire Jim Henry and Tucson pitcher Art Slette, who was on deck, rushed over to argue. When all else failed, Slette fell down acting like he had passed out over the call. A Tucson player ran from the dugout with a cup of water to throw on Slette but, by that time, Delancey had made his way out to see what was going on. Just as the Tucson player was getting ready to splash Slette, Delancey grabbed the cup and drank the water.

Albuquerque was a great place to spend some time. I had a room at the Savoy Hotel down on South First Street and I'd take the short ride to the ballpark in a Radio Cab. There were a lot of movie houses around like the Rio, the Mission, the Kimo and the Mesa. I remember seeing Errol Flynn in Robin Hood at the Lobo. And the nightlife wasn't bad in Albuquerque either. One of my favorite spots was the El Rancho Inn where I went as often as I could because you could dance for free and there were always single girls hanging around.

There was one girl who I started keeping regular company with – Georgia May Peterson. Somehow she got the idea I was going to marry her and that was the last thing on my mind. I wasn't ready to get married to Georgia May or anybody else for that matter. One day I was eating breakfast

59

and one of the guys came in and started congratulating me. I asked him what he was talking about and he opened up the paper and there was the headline: SHOALS WEDS LOCAL GIRL. I just about choked on my ham and eggs. There was a writeup and everything.

Leo (Ducky) Shoals became the fourth player from the Albuquerque Cards' lineup to become married here this season, it was announced Thursday night. Shoals was reported to have married Miss Georgia May Peterson of Albuquerque at Los Lunas Thursday afternoon. The first baseman was not in uniform for the last fray, replaced by Bill Garbe.

– Albuquerque Journal,
September 16, 1938

I tried and tried to find Georgia May all day, but never could. I finally had to go to the ballpark and everywhere I went people were shaking my hand and patting me on the back. I finally just had to go along with it because I couldn't stop to explain to everybody that it was a mixup. I don't know how that story got in there. I finally found Georgia May and we had a long talk and I told her I couldn't marry her now. My life was baseball and I was married to it. I told her it just wouldn't work out.

Georgia May was really hurt. It was the final day of the season when I found out that Georgia May's mother was coming in from Sante Fe. I knew I had to get out of town quick. I was going to catch a ride to Kansas City with one of the other players and instead of staying at my apartment where Georgia May's mother could find me, I stayed at my teammate's apartment and left at the break of dawn the next morning. I was afraid to go to the ballpark.

I kinda hated that I missed that last game against El Paso. Delancey and Bud Malone, one of our pitchers, umpired the game while regular umpire John Henry took over for Jimmy Zinn as El Paso manager and umpire David Barrett took over for Delancey. And one thing I know I really hated I missed was when Bill put on the catching gear in the second inning and caught the rest of the game. It was the first time he caught since leaving St. Louis and people I talked to said Bill was pegging it down to second pretty darn good. Even Sam Minces got in on the act when he went down and coached third base.

A few years later I received a letter from Georgia May and she said she now understood why we never married. She said I was right, that she had found someone else and was very happy.

One thing's for sure, I'll never forget Albuquerque.

Chapter Six

I found out a long time ago that if you can't have fun at what you're doing, then why do it? And that's the way I tried to live my life. Sometimes people misinterpreted my personal life and the way I liked to have fun away from the ballpark as not caring. But I always gave 100 percent on the field. Sure, I liked to have my fun, all ballplayers do. The season's long and you're playing ball about every day and you look for diversions. A ballplayer's life can be very boring. There's a lot of hours to fill away from the ballpark and if you're in a city or town which has some vices to offer, then more often than not a ballplayer is going to discover those vices. It wasn't like I was into spending my spare time in libraries.

I don't deny that I liked a drink or two or three. I also don't deny that I liked the ladies, at least when I was single. After I married Helen, that part of my life changed. I always tried to be a good husband to Helen. But when it came time to play baseball, I was there and ready to play. However, off the field was another matter, and in 1939 my shenanigans just about did me in.

When the 1939 season rolled around I went to Albany, Georgia for spring training. There were a bunch of players there who would be sent out to Albany, Johnson City, Tennessee or Gastonia, North Carolina for assignment. I was one of three first base candidates pegged for the Albany club of the Georgia-Florida League and managed by Johnny Keane, who would later manage the St. Louis Cardinals in the 1964 World Series. Myself, Russell Leach, a 19-year-old who had been with Houston of the Texas League, and John Streza were the three vying for a spot on the club.

Heinie Mueller, a scout with the Cardinals, told me later that Mr. Rickey held a meeting with the managers and scouts and my name was brought up. Mr. Rickey told them that whoever selected me had better be able to handle me or their job would be in jeopardy. Mueller and Ollie Vanek, who was the manager of the Johnson City Cardinals in the Appalachian League, then a Class D league, were good friends and Mueller asked Ollie if he would take me in Johnson City. Of course Ollie and I had been together at Monessen and we had gotten to be pretty good friends. Ollie had no qualms about having me on his club.

I was a little disappointed to be going to Johnson City, because after two pretty decent years I had hoped to move up a notch and get out of Class D. But, I didn't beef about it. I was still young and said, "OK, I'd give Johnson City my best shot."

Spring training can be very monotonous. I mean you run and go through drills every day for about six weeks. After the first couple of weeks you're ready to go and play ball. The Cardinals realized this so they decided to liven things up for us and hold a long-ball hitting contest at the stadium we practiced in at Albany. I called the place "The Bowl" because that's what it looked like and it was a big place too. I may be exaggerating, but it took about 600 feet to knock a ball out of there.

> *If you want to see a boy really hit that ball, take a look at one of the first base candidates for the local outfit, now working out at the bowl. He's Leo (Muscle) Shoals and he really lives up to his name. A left-handed batter, he follows through like a golfer with the result that the apple usually lands in fair territory.*

> – *The Albany Herald,*
> *March 31, 1939*

The big league Cardinals came to Albany for an exhibition and before the game there was scheduled a home run hitting contest which included Joe Medwick, Pepper.

Martin and Johnny Mize from the big league team. Russ Leach and myself were selected to represent the minor league contingent.

"The Bowl" was so big that all you could hope to do was plant the ball on the bank, which led up to the fence. It was almost impossible to knock one out and no one did. I know that Medwick and myself were the only ones who reached the bank. I thought I was keeping pretty fair company there with Medwick.

We then hooked up in a game against the Cardinals. It was a nine-inning game, but I only played three. However, I was in long enough to get a hit off the great Lon Warnecke. The Arkansas Humming Bird they called Lon and boy could he do things with that ball. He'd coil up that 6-foot-2 frame of his and cut loose with one of the sharpest curves I had ever seen, at least up to that point in my career.

Me being a left-handed hitter and Lon being a right-hander gave me a slight advantage I guess. I know my hat size expanded a couple of inches after getting the hit. I was feeling more confident than ever that I could hit good pitching.

I'll admit that Warnecke had seen his better years, but he could still pitch. Over the next three years with the Cardinals Lon would win 13, 16 and 17 games. You've got to have something going for you to win that many games.

Later that evening I went to downtown Albany to this little nightclub that the players liked to congregate at and there was Warnecke at the bar. I went up and introduced myself. He said, "Oh yeah, you're the lefty that got the hit off me. Well, son, you hit the best curveball in the major leagues." Lon wasn't bragging, he was just stating the truth. He was just telling me in his own way that I hit a very good pitch. We each got a bottle and sat down at a table where we talked until about 2 o'clock in the morning, well past curfew.

Lon introduced me to Terry Moore and Clyde King and there were a couple of girls we danced with through the night. We had been running up a pretty good size bar tab, but Moore, when he got up to leave, plopped down a $100 bill and told us to have fun. He didn't have to tell us that. It gave me a good feeling to be around stars like that. They made me feel like one of them. Even though I was just a busher, they had accepted me into their fraternity.

The next morning I saw a paper on the home run hitting contest and the reporter, using his imagination, called me "Muscle" Shoals. That was the first time I saw the nickname and it's a name that stuck like glue. The reporter took into account my big arms and the fact that Muscle Shoals, Alabama was just over in the next state. Everybody just about quit calling me Leo and began calling me "Muscle" or sometimes it came out "Muscles".

I guess while I'm on names, I might explain also that Shoals, at least the spelling of Shoals, was not the name I entered baseball with. As far back as I can remember I had, and my family had, spelled our last name Sholes. The very first time I ever saw my name in the paper was at Monessen and my last name was spelled S-H-O-A-L-S, not S-H-O-L-E-S as it should have been. I guess once it was misspelled the first time people just thought that was the correct spelling. I did try to point out back then that my name was Sholes, but whenever I saw the paper or a roster the name was spelled Shoals.

I finally just gave up and accepted the Shoals' spelling. At the time, it was just a lot easier to go along with that than it was trying to change everything. But officially, my name would always be spelled Sholes.

However my name was spelled, it didn't seem to affect the way I played baseball. I had a good spring training, hitting the ball as well as I felt I could. When camp broke, I was still disappointed that I wasn't selected to play at a higher classification. I was hoping to make the Class A Columbus club or, at the very least, the Class B Asheville team. I often wondered whether the reason I was still at Class D might have been because of what happened in New Iberia between Wickel and me.

While I wasn't too thrilled about going, I went to Johnson City ready to play. I felt I owed that much to Ollie

65

who stood up for me and wanted me on his Johnson City club. I hadn't been in camp more than a couple of days when I got hit by a line drive on my ankle. I suffered a bruise and was on crutches for a couple of weeks. To add to my pain, I was watching the other guys going through drills and I happened to see someone walking across the diamond. It was Harrison Wickel. Wickel was managing the Cardinals farm club in Williamson, West Virginia in the Mountain States League and he came over to Johnson City to help conduct a tryout camp. No, we didn't get into it again. You've got to let bygones be bygones. I hobbled over to Harrison and apologized for the way I acted and he in turn apologized to me for calling me names. We shook hands and that was that.

Even though I wasn't able to participate in our spring workouts at Keystone Field in Johnson City, Ollie expected me to be there observing. I don't guess I did Ollie right because there were a few workouts I decided not to attend and Ollie would fine me $10 each time. I didn't mind that fine because I was having a good time running around. I found that Johnson City, even though it was a small town, had a night life. Sometimes that night life would run into the wee hours of the morning and it was tough getting out of bed and making a workout at 9 a.m.

Ollie never really got upset with me. Aggravated, yes, but never really angry. I think maybe he understood my personality and gave me some leeway. Heck, all the guys liked to run around. Even Ollie liked to have his fun. He was only 25 and single. One thing about Ollie, he believed in working his ballplayers.

One of the drills Ollie conducted in early spring practice was to put a man at shortstop, another at third and leave the other positions open. A batter gets four or five balls and pops them up halfway between first and second. The shortstop has to race over to catch the ball and then throw to the third baseman, who relays it home. Almost the instant that the shortstop throws to third, the batter hits another ball to the opposite side of the infield. The shortstop has to run back, catch it, flip to third and immediately be ready to run back to the second base side of the diamond to catch another pop up. By the time Ollie ended the drill after several repetitions, the shortstop would have his tongue hanging out. But it just wasn't the shortstop getting this drill. Every player on the team had to go through this routine.

Ollie did another drill with the pitchers. I don't know if it was original or not, but it was the first time I'd seen it done. Ollie would fix strings vertically and horizontally between two posts at home plate. The top string is about as high as a batter's shoulders and the lower string was about knee high. The vertical strings were the width of home plate.

The catcher would get behind the plate and the strings and call for low outside pitches, low inside, high inside, high outside and the pitcher would try and hit the string which designated each of those pitches. The pitcher would throw ten fast balls, then ten curves. He would follow with five more fast balls and five more curves. It was a way to work on the pitcher's control.

I made some good friends early on. One of my best friends was outfielder Mills Tabor, who everybody called "Mule." "Mule" always had a chew of tobacco in his jaw so big that a fan in Newport asked him one time how he could fit a baseball in his mouth like that. Another fan one time in Elizabethton came up to "Mule" and asked him if he had to use a crowbar to get it out of his mouth.

"Mule" had one of the most unusual stances I'd ever seen. He'd come up to the plate and actually face the pitcher. Then, as the ball was delivered, he'd turn around. He reminded me a little of Arky Vaughn, only "Mule" was more exaggerated.

Another friend was Harry "Rube" Merchant, whose father was also named "Rube" and who had played in the old Appalachian League years before. Our "Rube" was one of the smoothest fielding shortstops I'd ever played with. He wasted very little motion in fielding the ball and then throwing it to first.

Over the years I kept the jersey that I wore while playing for the
Johnson City Cardinals in 1939.

(Photo courtesy of Sholes family)

If there was a contest for the biggest feet, then Ray
Yardley would win every time. Ray was a pitcher on our
club and he had the largest feet I've ever seen. They must
have been size 20. But one thing I remember about Ray, who
had worked in the zinc mines before signing with the

Cardinals, came when he was pitching at Pennington Gap. Ray, through four innings, was pitching great.

Ray also swung a pretty good bat and when he came up he connected for a long drive to left. The thing about the park in Pennington Gap was the left field fence was about 400 feet away and I really mean 400 feet. The ball rolled to the fence and Ray was dragging those size 20s all the way around and finally beat the throw home for an inside-the-park home run. When Ray took the mound he was still huffing and puffing. He was so tired that the Bears jumped all over his pitches.

Ollie comes out to the mound to check on Ray and Ray tells him he's tired from running. Ollie told Ray the next time he hit a home run to do it in a park where he could hit it over the fence and walk around the bases.

Like a lot of leagues over the years, some of the teams in the Appalachian League were having financial problems – Pennington Gap and Newport, Tennessee in particular. The two organizations were trying everything and the owners thought having lights might help. Greeneville had put in lights in 1938 and that city was doing well at the gate and we had lights in Johnson City. Kingsport was planning to install 120,000 watts of light, so Pennington and Newport decided to follow. Pennington planned on putting in 150,000 watts at Leeman Field at a cost of $4,000, which was big money back then.

League president Ray Ryan even came up with the idea of holding a special North-South all-star game with the proceeds to be divided between the Pennington Gap and Newport clubs to help them pay for the lights. The game was held at Kingsport and the gate netted close to $500 with $200 dollars going to each of the two clubs.

Both Pennington Gap and Newport were doing terrible at the gate, but they were also doing terrible on the field. As a matter of fact, they were so far out of the pennant race the league directors met on Monday, July 3 and decided that on Tuesday, July 4 they would split the season and start a second half to give those two teams a chance at making the playoffs.

The first half we won going away, but the second half we started to fall apart. It seemed like we couldn't buy a win. The club just absolutely went into a tailspin and most of it was because nobody was hitting the ball except for me and Ollie, who was a 5-foot-9, 190-pound sparkplug and a very good outfielder.

It was about that time that the rumor started that I was going to Asheville of the Piedmont League. If I was, I didn't know anything about it. It would have been a promotion, but I was having fun in Johnson City. Anyway, there was nothing to it but the fans had taken a liking to me in Johnson City and when the rumor started up a few of them began calling the front office. Walter Pattee, our business manager, called the newspaper up asking to get something in the next day's paper stating that I was staying in Johnson City and not going to Asheville.

Pattee told me, "Leo, if we got rid of you now we'd have a riot in this city." That made me feel good.

I stayed in Johnson City and got to see firsthand some horrible games we played. One of the most humiliating losses was on a hot July night at Keystone Field when we lost 10-3 to Greeneville and 40-year-old pitcher Red Walker. Walker threw a three-hitter against us and I had one of those hits. We were in such a dive that Ollie called on me to pitch in an 11-2 loss to Kingsport, but I think I even surprised Ollie as I pitched one and two thirds innings allowing no hits and striking out three while walking three. I pitched more that year, but I only mention this game because it was my best. I won't talk about the other appearances I made. I wasn't the only position player to pitch. You have to remember we only had 15-man rosters. It wasn't like we had a bullpen full of pitchers waiting to come in.

Our losing skid lasted so long that Ollie had to do something, so he came up with all these rules and regulations to tighten down on the club. He'd have bedchecks and curfews and all that. My roommate, Sammy Lamitina, would cover up for me whenever there were bedchecks. Sammy, who later played in the high minors and later became a fine minor league manager, would put pillows in my bed to make it look like I was there. Of course, in the dark you couldn't tell. If there was a bedcheck, someone would poke their head in the door and see something that looked like a body under the covers and go on to the next room.

Despite all of Ollie's rules, we were still playing horrible a month later. Ollie began to think now that maybe his rules might not be such a good thing. He started thinking that maybe the club was too tight and not relaxed enough. Ollie called a meeting one morning and said that maybe we were sleeping too late, so he had us getting up at 7 a.m. That didn't seem to help. Later he called another meeting and suggested we go out and have a few drinks after a game and maybe find us a girl friend to help us relax.

Ollie, without mentioning my name, and he didn't have to because everyone knew it was me he was referring to, said that one of us is hitting the cover off the ball and that person was the only one who seems relaxed game after game. Ollie decided to ditch the curfew and bedchecks to see if that relaxed the guys, but the second half never got any better for us as a team.

We finished third behind Elizabethton and Kingsport winning 69 and losing 51. I would certainly hate to think what would have happened if we did not have a fine first half. We made the Shaughnessy Plan playoffs, but we lost in the first round to Kingsport in three games. Elizabethton eventually beat Kingsport for the championship.

The Appalachian League was a good league then with a lot of fine talent, some of it on the way up, some of it on the way down.

Lew Flick played for Elizabethton and would get a cup of coffee with the Philadelphia Athletics. Beattie Feathers never played in the major leagues, but after what I saw of him with Pennington Gap, he sure had the talent. Of course, he went on to a great career in football with the Chicago Bears after an All-American career at the University of Tennessee. Beattie was also head baseball and football coach at North Carolina State from 1944 to 1951. A couple of other guys in the league with major league experience were Burton Hodge of Elizabethton, who had a call up with the Phillies, and Art Ruble of Newport, who had played with Ty Cobb in Detroit.

I ended up leading the Appalachian League in home runs with 16 and won the batting title with a .365 average. What's more surprising was that somebody as slow as I was could have 14 triples, not to mention 22 doubles. Of course, I had the help of that Johnson City park, the same park they use today in the rookie league, which had a very deep center field at 420 feet. But, the season ended prematurely for me and it came within a hair of being my last season ever. Actually, I was just lucky to have seen my 24th birthday in October.

Like I've already pointed out, and this isn't bragging on my part, but I did have the reputation of carousing. This point has already been made earlier. If I could go back and rerun my life, I couldn't say I wouldn't do it again just the same. However, my advice to ballplayers today is be careful and don't let your extracurricular activities get out of hand. If you are serious about a career in baseball, do things in moderation.

OK, the sermon's over, but the only reason I get on the soapbox is because my shenanigans almost caught up with me. There's a joke about these two players who make an agreement that whoever passed away first would contact the other and tell him what Heaven was like. Well, years later when they both were old, one of them died. A couple of days later the one who passed away contacted his buddy and said Heaven's great. He said they even play baseball there and as a matter of fact they have a game scheduled tomorrow and guess what? You're pitching old buddy.

Well, that was almost my story and it wasn't a joke, believe me. It was perhaps the scariest time of my life.

It was late in the season and after a game one night in Johnson City my girlfriend and another couple went out for a little entertainment at a roadhouse out on the highway which connects Bristol with Johnson City. Little did I know that in a couple of hours I would be lying on an operating table with the doctors trying to remove a bullet, which passed through my liver. They really didn't know if I was going to make it.

Here's what happened according to an article which appeared in the JOHNSON CITY CHRONICLE on August 18, 1939. It tells the story.

Leo "Muscle" Shoals, hard-hitting first baseman of the Johnson City Cardinals baseball team, last night waged a gallant battle against death from a bullet wound suffered early yesterday morning in an altercation at a tourist camp and filling station on the Johnson City-Bristol highway.

Hospital attendants said he was resting well as could be expected and that his condition was satisfactory. They added, however, he was not yet out of danger.

They said a .38 calibre bullet passed through the center of his abdomen, punctured his liver and emerged on the right side of his spinal column.

An operation was necessary to suture a liver wound, surgeons said, adding Shoals rallied well from the anesthetic and, barring complications, "stands a good chance to recover."

Sheriff Earl Sell, who investigated the shooting, arrested Dick Dunavent, about 21, an employee of the establishment who told the sheriff Shoals attacked him and menaced him with a knife. Dunavent posted $2,000 bond pending a hearing on the charge of felonious assault.

The shooting occurred shortly after 2 a.m.

Shoals, a 24-year-old Parkersburg, W. Va., 180-pound athlete and an idol of Appalachian League baseball fans, entered the place in the early morning hours with a woman companion. Sheriff Sell, who signed the warrant for Dunavent's arrest, said Dunavent told him the couple produced a bottle of liquor and sat down in a booth.

"Shoals became quarrelsome," Dunavent continued in his account to the sheriff. "We kept asking him to quiet

down and behave and he finally called a taxi. Before the taxi came, however, he started chasing me with a knife and when he was almost on me I shot him. I had to save myself."

Sell said he had so far been unable to find a knife, which Shoals allegedly had in his hand at the time of the shooting.

Charlie Johnson, one of the roadhouse proprietors, gave a more extended account.

Johnson said Dunavent told him Shoals was asked several times either to calm down or leave and that, when one of the employees attempted to mop up a spot where Shoals had spilled something, he grabbed the mop and broke it into small pieces. He did, however, phone for a taxi to take him and the woman away, according to Johnson's version.

Before the taxi arrived, Dunavent was quoted by Johnson as saying, it became necessary again to ask Shoals to be quiet with the result that Shoals allegedly got up and knocked Dunavent down. The young man then ran behind the counter, pursued by Shoals who, Dunavent said, had pulled out a knife.

"I ran from behind the counter," Johnson quoted Dunavent as saying, "with Shoals following me. I shot him when he was close enough to stab me."

The taxi, which Shoals had called to take him to his residence, arrived a few minutes later and he was carried in it to the hospital (Parker-Budd Hospital).

Sell, notified by the Johnsons of the occurrence, then went to the hospital to make an investigation. City officers Jim Broyles and Les Greer also investigated.

For the most part that's what happened. My girlfriend and I and another couple did go to a nightspot called the Country Kitchen after the game one night. We started to leave the club and I bought a pint of Crab Orchard. On the way back home we stopped at a lodge called the Broadway Camp. My buddy and I were playing a nickel racehorse machine. I walked toward the back of the establishment where I had my coat hanging with the pint in it.

I took the pint out and turned around to take a nip when this guy grabbed the bottle away from me and I went after him. Before I realized it, he had a gun and shot me in the stomach.

He ran out the door and I went after him, but I didn't get far before I keeled over. I can remember grabbing my side and feeling something warm oozing through my fingers. I really thought I was going to die right there in that roadhouse parking lot.

The story in the paper mentioned me breaking a mop. That didn't happen and it also said I had a knife. I didn't even own a knife. The bottom line, though, was that I was shot and the doctors really didn't know whether or not I would live, much less play baseball again.

Reports on the radio said I only had a 50-50 chance to live. But, in a couple of days, I was getting better. There was a picture of me in the paper, in the hospital bed wearing some rosary beads the Indian girl had given me back in Kansas City. Well, some Catholic priest, thinking I was Catholic because of the beads, came by and was ready to give me my last rites.

I was eventually out of danger, but the radio kept reporting that I was in serious condition and flirting with death. I couldn't figure out why they kept reporting that when doctors told me that I was going to make a full recovery.

There was another fellow in my room at Parker-Budd Hospital whose first name was Ezra and he'd been shot too. The room was divided by a great big curtain. One morning when I woke up, I got out of bed and walked past his bed and Ezra wasn't there. When the doctor came by I asked him about Ezra and the doc said Ezra had died. I kinda figured that maybe the radio people were getting reports on Ezra instead of me.

But, I never heard the radio report me dying and I'm glad I didn't. No way I wanted to be like the guy who checks the obituaries in the paper each day just to make sure his name isn't there.

I felt bad about the whole incident. I was embarrassed by it. There's some things to this day I don't remember about it. I felt worse that I had let the ballclub down. While I was in the hospital recovering, I received a letter from Carl Jones Jr. who was the president of the Johnson City club and later became publisher of the Johnson City Press-Chronicle. It reads as follows:

Dear Leo,

Perhaps you won't feel like reading this now. If this is true, lay it aside until you feel more in the mood because I do hope you will be able to digest it for your own benefit.

You are now at the critical point in your career. If you have learned the lesson we all hope that you have from your recent escapade, the fans (most of them young kids that idolize you because you meant professional baseball to them), your employers, your manager, your teammates, your family and friends and last, but not least, yourself, will be willing to give you another chance at life as a gentleman, a ballplayer worthy of being connected with a game that no stone has been left unturned to keep cleaner than any other American sport.

What you do to take advantage of this opportunity will depend solely on yourself. You will have the chance to repeat the same disappointing experience you so miraculously escaped with your life or of going on the other side of the road and being what you have meant in the eyes of hundreds of kids that have daily watched, listened and read of your exploits in baseball.

Your natural ability will not be impaired if you are willing to take care of yourself during your recovery and because you have followed some semblance of training you are in pretty sound physical condition. Mentally, you are probably distorted and mad with everyone, including yourself. The first thing you should do is to get this out of your mind because it isn't true. No one has it in for you or tried to take advantage of you. Unfortunately you got what you had coming to you. Everyone regrets that it had to be as brutal and harmful as it was.

The second thing for you to do is to make an apology to your teammates and your employers and to your fans. This can be done either by a written statement or by your honest effort to do what is expected of all young men in life – not only in baseball – start over and go the right way.

Everyone will think more of you for admitting that you were wrong and making an honest effort to come back than if you just figure everyone is down on you and won't give you a break. It is better to have gotten off the right track and admit to it and to get back on the straight and narrow than to get off and make no effort to recover.

Sincerely,

Carl Jones

I appreciated Carl's concern and the concern of the fans. If I didn't say it then, I'm saying it now. It was a mistake for me to be in a place like that at two in the morning, drinking and carrying on. I guess I was asking for trouble. If it weren't for the support of people like Carl Jones and my teammates, it would have been a tough road back.

As I began to recover enough to move around, I would visit the Veterans Hospital and I'd sit there on the side of the beds of World War I vets and listen to them tell of their experiences. Most of them were baseball fans and they knew who I was from listening to our games on the radio. I would have some of the guys from the team slip me some baseballs – I say slip because the Appalachian League had a rule that if a player took a baseball he would be fined $2 – and I would autograph them and give the balls to the fellows there. Pattee found out I was being slipped the balls and he confronted me about it. I said yes, it's true. I told him I gave out six or seven balls and how much did I owe. He said don't worry about it and the next day he brought me a dozen balls to sign to hand out to the veterans.

Toward the end of the season the Johnson City Cardinals and several players from other clubs played a benefit game for me on the field at Soldier's Home. They collected $150. I watched the game from inside an automobile and I couldn't believe they were doing this for me.

I never thought that 41 years later I'd be lying in that same ward, but I would be. I had a mountain bike accident which led to degenerative arthritis which dried up the joint cartilage in my hip and I had to have a hip replacement in 1980.

As I lay there in the hospital, I kept thinking back to 1939 and how I almost died from that bullet. I just thought how young and how foolish I was back then. But, you learn from your experiences. At least you should learn from your experiences.

Chapter Seven

There were plenty of questions on my mind when I finally got well enough to leave the hospital. At the time I really didn't know if I would be healthy enough to play baseball again. And, knowing Branch Rickey, I didn't know whether the Cardinals would want me back.

As the days and months went on, I began to feel much better and I knew I would be physically fit to play the 1940 season. But, as it turned out, it would not be for the Cardinals. St. Louis had enough of me, so I was peddled off to Tyler, Texas of the East Texas League. Tyler was an independent team, which about midway through the year was able to get a working agreement with the St. Louis Browns.

I was a little miffed at the Cardinals at first, but I guess I really couldn't blame them. I caused my share of problems to the organization. St. Louis had been good to me by giving me my first start in pro ball. But, at least I was still going to be playing baseball and I was moving up to a Class C league.

Tyler, being independent, had no affiliation. It was a feeder to the higher leagues. If Tyler got a player who looked like he might have potential, then Tyler would sell the player and make a few bucks. You don't have that today in pro ball, but back then it wasn't uncommon.

Tyler was an East Texas oil field town and it would entertain baseball off and on from 1924 to 1955. For some reason, baseball just wasn't popular around Tyler as we never drew any fans, despite the 40 cents admission price. I guess it might have been because of its independent stigma with players coming and going all the time that baseball didn't seem important to the folks there or it could have been the weather which was hot as a firecracker in July and August.

Ty Cobb played for Tyler that season and not even he could get the fans to come out. Of course it might have been

79

because this Ty Cobb was a pitcher, not the Hall of Fame outfielder for Detroit. This kid's dad was a great baseball fan and when he was born, with the last name Cobb, he was slapped with the name Tyrus. He got real tired of people kidding him about the name.

Bobby Goff, a former minor league second baseman who pinch hit a few times that year, was the manager at the start of the year before giving way to Sam Hancock. Tyler's general manager was Johnnie Maher, who was very innovative. Maher used every promotional idea he could imagine to entice people to come out and watch us play.

Maher would bring out a big bucking bull and invite fans down to ride this beast. If the fan stayed on for a certain amount of time that fan would win $25. They did this a couple of times before one fellow got thrown off and nearly got trampled to death. One time they pulled this 1935 coupe out on the field as a giveaway to some lucky fan. They pulled the lucky winner's number and this gal comes down to collect her prize. When she started the engine something went pop and fire started coming out from under the hood. The players started filling buckets with water to put it out.

None of these promotions seemed to bring in more people, but we still played ball anyway. I didn't get off to the greatest start ever. I struggled at the beginning, but then things began to fall in place. It was at Tyler that I got my first chance to play the outfield. As a matter of fact, it was my first and last.

Roy Zimmerman, a first baseman on option from the New York Giants organization who later would get a cup of coffee with the big club, was told he would be playing right field. Well, Roy told Goff no way because he was a first baseman and first was where he was going to play. I could see trouble brewing, so I told Bobby I'd play right.

Bobby asked me if I ever played right field. I said no, but it can't be too hard. I was willing to give it a try. I might as well as had a blindfold over my eyes and weights on my feet. I soon found out that right field is a tough position to play. When the ball was hit, I just never knew where it was going. If it was hit by a right-hander, the ball would slice and I would be chasing it to the fence or down in the corner.

Fortunately for me and fortunately for the Tyler pitching staff, Zimmerman got off to a slow start and it wasn't long before he was sent back to the Giants farm system and I was mercifully put back at first base where I couldn't do too much damage.

I was hitting over .300 and feeling real good, but then disaster struck. I don't remember the pitcher, but it was at Marshall that I got hit on the fingers with a pitch and I was out almost two weeks. When I did come back I wasn't comfortable, the fingers hurt like heck when I made contact. As a result, my average dropped and I didn't hit many home runs from that point on. I wasn't the only one suffering, so was the league. Just like the year in the Pennsylvania Association, the East Texas League was having trouble keeping its head above water. What started out as an eight-team league went to a six-team loop after Palestine and Jacksonville dropped out.

Our Tyler team was struggling at 22-24 up to the point of the league losing those two teams but, when Palestine dropped out, we picked up a couple of their players. It improved our club so much that Tyler finished second in the league that year going 57-32 the rest of the way. We picked up a couple of good pitchers in Grover Miller and Mike Barbella and we added some good sticks in George Kovach, who hit .316, and Dick Valencia, who finished at .299.

I was hitting .290 for Tyler with 11 home runs and 66 RBIs in 414 at bats and I was happy with the way things were going, especially considering the fact just a few months earlier I was lying in a hospital bed with a bullet wound. My 11 home runs didn't sound like a lot, but the leader that season in home runs was Tom Jordan of Marshall who hit 19. However, it took Jordan 100 more at bats to hit his 19 than it did for me to hit my 11 – 514 to 414. I made the all-star team but then, to my surprise, I was sold to El Dorado of the Class C Cotton States League. After it was announced I was sold I still played one more game for Tyler. At first I wasn't going to go because there was only two weeks left in the season and I figured why bother?

> *The game last night was a tribute to Leo Shoals, the Trojans' hustling regular first baseman who was sold yesterday to the Cotton States League. Shoals will leave immediately."*

> *– Tyler Morning Telegraph,*
> *August 13, 1940*

Also amid all this was the fact that the threat of war was looming. Hitler had been quite busy in Europe and the United States was on the brink of getting into the fray. I had received my notice for a pre-induction exam for the draft. Everyone was expecting us to get involved before long as the pieces were being put in place. But I wasn't worrying, baseball was the only thing on my mind.

I really didn't want to go to El Dorado, but Hancock, who was the manager then, and Maher convinced me that if I wanted to stay in baseball I'd better report. Maher even offered to drive me to Hot Springs, Arkansas, which was where the El Dorado club was playing. I relented and told Maher OK.

We hopped in Maher's car and we drove all day and we get to the Eastman Hotel just as the El Dorado club was leaving for the ballpark. We check in and I get to the park just as the game was getting under way. I sat on the bench for a couple of innings and I was about half asleep when along about the third inning our manager, Guy Sturdy, hollered out, "Shoals!" I kinda looked at him as if to say, "What do you want?" Guy said, "Grab a bat, you're hitting next." I thought to myself that I'm in no shape to hit. But I go up and all I know there was a right-hander on the mound. I didn't even know what the score was or who we were playing. The first pitch came down the pike and I swung and

It wasn't too long after this picture was taken that I went into the U.S. Army. Maybe that's why I was looking so serious.

(Photo courtesy of Sholes family)

the ball went sailing out over the right field fence for a three-run home run. I got back to the dugout and Sturdy said, "Son, it looks like you've found yourself a home."

But I wasn't through that day. I stayed in the game and I ended up with two home runs and a single and I also had five unassisted putouts at first base.

For the short time I was with El Dorado I hit .347 with three home runs and 21 RBIs in 20 games and I liked playing for Sturdy. Guy was an old first baseman who had played with the St. Louis Browns in the late 1920s for a couple of years. He didn't see a lot of action because he was playing behind George Sisler, who owned a couple of batting titles.

Guy said he didn't mind sitting on the bench because it gave him more time to drink whiskey. Guy liked to drink and he didn't mind us doing the same as long as we didn't come to the field loaded or with a hangover. On Sundays, when you couldn't get a drink anywhere around town, Guy would give me the key to his locker where he kept a bottle of Jack Daniels just in case I needed a little pick-me-up. If any of us ever came to the park a little wobbly, then Guy would have us run until we sweated the alcohol out. Guy and I became great friends. He would tell me that I reminded him of himself back in his younger playing days because we had the same stance.

We made the playoffs and beat Helena three out of four. In the one game we got beat I had the worst luck. I was robbed of three hits at home at Rowland Field. The first time up I hit a little looping fly behind third base and Helena third baseman Dexter Savage made an over the shoulder catch. In the fourth inning I hit a long drive to center field and Mike Speas backed all the way up to the flagpole and pulled it in. Then, in the ninth inning, Al Zarilla in right field speared a line drive with one hand on the run.

But our season ended in the next round of playoffs as we lost in five games to Monroe. It was time to go home. Guy asked me before I left if I would like to come back next year. I said, "Guy, that would be OK by me" Guy said he was going to try and get me back and, sure enough, when the 1941 season rolled around I was back in El Dorado but Guy wasn't. It seemed as if the front office was trying to get someone else in to manage and Guy just told them to forget it and take his name off the managerial list.

The new manager was Ray Rice, who also caught. Rice had hit .330 with Lenoir of the Tarheel League the year before and he was a tough customer. Rice was 26 years old and he had been the bullpen coach under Bill McKechnie with the Cincinnati Reds. One of his favorite phrases was: "Button up your lip and keep your ears open when somebody who knows his stuff is doing the talking."

We held our spring training right there in El Dorado at Rowland Field and I thought we had a pretty decent club. But, we got off to a 4-10 start and that was enough for management to get rid of Rice and bring back Guy to manage. We were still without a catcher but Wally Kopp, who was managing and catching for the Texarkana Liners, was fired and we signed him.

I was really happy that Guy was back with us. I even gave him a present his first game back with a first-inning home run against Texarkana and then put the icing on the cake with a 10th-inning home run for a 6-5 win.

> *Shoals had put the Oilers back in the money with a terrific four sack clout over deep center field fence that probably unroofed half the houses in St. Louis addition.*
>
> *– El Dorado Daily News,*
> *May 14, 1941*

A couple days later Woody Head and I teamed up for a 5-4 win over Hot Springs. It seemed me and Woody were coming through in the clutch. As a matter of fact, we were being called the "touchdown twins", which I really don't understand. In the win over Hot Springs, Woody had singled in the eighth and I followed with a game-winning home run. The very next day against Hot Springs, Woody hit a two-run home run in the ninth to tie the game 9-9 and I followed with a home run to win it 10-9.

Leo looked over a couple, brandished his war club around his head and rode one over the right-center field fence for a home run. That, gents, was the ballgame.

– El Dorado Daily News,
May 18, 1941

I don't know if having Guy back loosened us up or what it was, but we were playing better. If not for Guy, I'd been somewhere else. Even though he was 42 and I was 24, Guy and me got along great. Guy introduced me to a lot of people and a lot of things I had never been exposed to before. That 1941 season, Texarkana and Vicksburg replaced Pine Bluff and Greenwood in the league. When we'd make a road trip to Vicksburg, which was right on the Mississippi River, Guy would take me with him on the gambling boat anchored on the river.

This was one of those boats where you had to know somebody to get aboard. We'd go down to the end of Pier Street and board a motor launch, which would take us out to the boat. There would be a couple of big brutes there to meet you and Guy would tell them who he was and they'd let us on.

I wasn't much into gambling because I didn't have that much money in the first place. But, while Guy would head for the crap tables, I went to the bar and usually found a girl there. There would be times when Guy would spend all he had and I'd have to lend him some money, but he would always pay me back.

We had a pretty good club at El Dorado, but the fans weren't turning out, which bothered Guy. So Guy thought he would liven things up a little and maybe get more fans to come out to the park. We were having a series with Monroe and Guy talked Monroe manager Poco Taitt into staging a free-for-all between our two teams.

We were playing a close game in the first of the series and Monroe had a runner on second. Poco goes out to talk to his runner while Guy goes out to say something to our third baseman Woody Head. Guy comes back to the dugout and says, "This is it fellows. Be ready to charge." We knew what he was talking about. The next Monroe batter bunted to the mound, the pitcher throws to third where the runner, Red Pruitt, slides in hard on Head. Head and Pruitt jump up and pretend to be slugging it out. Both dugouts, on cue, cleared and the teams were putting on a pretty good show, ripping shirts off each other and wrestling around on the ground.

I had been playing first base and I had somebody pinned on the ground when the guy on the ground hollered, "Oh no, Muscle, look coming here." I looked around and the fans began pouring out of the stands rushing the field to get in on the fracas. There wasn't any security to stop them and before we knew it the whole situation had turned into a real free-for-all. The fans were going for the Monroe players and we were trying to protect ourselves and the other team from those crazies. I was scared the fans might head for the bat rack and then we would be in trouble.

It took a few minutes, but a couple of police cars show up at the park and they were able to get the situation under control. Nobody was hurt real bad, just a few bumps and bruises and Pruitt got a bloody nose when Head swung and accidentally landed a punch. The next day in the paper was a quote from Taitt saying that if there wasn't enough police protection at the park the next night, he was going to take his players home.

The umpires reported the free-for-all to the league president who wanted a full report from Guy and Poco. Well, neither confessed to staging the fight between the players and neither ever got the blame. Guy promised he would try and keep his players in line in the future.

Well, the next night, that park was filled with fans, our largest crowd of the year.

In the Cotton States League, there were teams all up and down the Mississippi River. Along with Vicksburg there was Greenville, Mississippi; Helena, Arkansas; Clarksdale, Mississippi; Hot Springs, Arkansas; and Monroe, Louisiana.

We'd cross back and forth across the river on a ferry boat and these ferries were floating casinos with slot machines. Fellows would drop money in those machines like they were eating peanuts. It wasn't unusual for a player to lose what money he had, even his meal money. Guy was a gambler, but he didn't like the slot machines. Guy sometimes would walk up to a player who he knew would spend his money on those one-armed bandits and ask for the player's meal money, which he would hold until the ferry got across the river.

We had fun and this team was a lot of fun to be around. One fellow on our team who I will never forget was our center fielder Harry 'Crazy Horse' Schmeil. We were in Helena for a game and we had all taken our positions about the fourth or fifth inning when the umpire raised his arms to call time. He went over to Guy at the dugout and asked Guy where his center fielder was. Guy looked around the dugout and back on the field and still no sign of 'Crazy Horse'.

There was a gate near the outfield fence which went out behind the stadium where a small stream flowed past. Well, the gate was open so our right fielder went over to check it out and there was 'Crazy Horse' sitting on the bank of that stream with a couple of little boys fishing. 'Crazy Horse' comes back to his position and when the inning was over came trotting back to the dugout and he was the first batter up for us. He goes up to the plate and the umpire calls time. "Mr. Schmeil," the umpire says, "would you please take that fish out of your back pocket?" He had caught that fish and stuffed it into his back pocket. Guy was coaching third and didn't know what was going on so he comes down to the plate to find out. 'Crazy Horse' pulls out the fish and says, "Guy, hold this for me until I get through batting." He slaps the fish into Guy's hands and Guy takes it, puts it in his back pocket and goes back to coaching third.

Our paths would cross again in 1948 when we both ended up with Charlotte. Harry and I had something in common and that being our last names. Neither one of us could ever get anybody to spell it right. Like I finally just gave up and let it go at Shoals instead of Sholes, Harry's last name was actually Chmiel, not Schmiel. Harry, who was Polish and born in Chicago, didn't have a middle name, but when he signed his contract they asked what his middle name was. So, since he was born on George Washington's birthday, he put down George.

As for his name Crazy Horse, well he liked to horse around and he acted crazy, thus the nickname.

Harry, who was a great center fielder, was with Decatur, Illinois one time and his manager was a center fielder, so Harry got moved over to right field. There was a low fence in right and a bunch of kids climbed up on it and through the first few innings would throw pebbles at Harry. Harry told them to quit or there would be hell to pay. Well, they kept on and finally Harry took off after them. Harry didn't stop at the fence, he jumped the fence and chased them two or three blocks. He caught one of the boys and marched him back to the park. The poor kid was trembling. Harry took him to the dugout and bought him a soda and hot dog. Those kids never threw rocks again.

Another time Harry was playing in the Nebraska State League and he was on first and his manager was on second. There was a hit-and-run and the batter hit a short single. Harry was running hard and was right behind his manager as both crossed the plate. Harry ran on into the dugout ahead of the manager and took a seat. The manager came in, sat down next to Harry, looked around and never saw Harry and said, "Where's Schmiel? I thought he was on base."

Players back then were a lot closer than they are today, even with players on opposing teams. I had a friend with Monroe who was released and he asked me if I thought there was a chance he might catch on with El Dorado. I asked Guy, and Guy in turn asked our owner Doc Rushing and he told Guy that he wasn't making any money and that he couldn't put another player on the payroll.

We went on a road trip to Texarkana, Texas, a new team in the league, and I talked to its manager Tex Genes and asked him if he needed a good defensive outfielder. Just so happened he had an outfielder who was injured. Genes told me to tell my friend to come by for a tryout. As it happened that friend of mine, Charlie Metro, turned out to be a pretty good ballplayer. He would play in the majors for a few years and even managed the Kansas City Royals.

"I got to know Muscle when I was with Palestine and Texarkana in the East Texas League in 1940. In 1941 I was with Monroe of the Cotton States League and Muscle was with El Dorado. I was released and was picked up by Texarkana. I don't know if I would have caught on with someone or not if Muscle had not recommended me. I'm indebted to him for that. I went on to have a good year and eventually moved up.

"I respected Muscle's ability a great deal. I would rate Muscle as one of the most feared hitters over my years of evaluating players. He was powerful. Today, Muscle would be a DH making a million bucks. The best hitters I ever saw for power and for making contact were Muscle and George Vernon of Washington.

"I don't know why Muscle never made it to the majors. Sometimes it's competition within an organization, which holds a player down, and it's also being in the right place at the right time.

"I know in 1950 or 1951 I was managing Montgomery in the South Atlantic League and we were looking for a first baseman. I wanted Muscle, but we ended up getting a young kid on option who had lots of potential. Turned out that kid, Jim Ray Hart, played quite a few years in the majors.

"I know one thing, if I had Muscle on one of my teams he would have made me manager of the year. Muscle was just a great player."

– Charlie Metro,
outfielder, Texarkana

One of the highlights of that year was when Al Schacht came to El Dorado. Schacht would dress up in a top hat and long-tailed tuxedo and clown around on the field making the rounds of all the minor leagues across the country. In later years Max Patkin would do the same sort of thing, but Schacht was the first. It just so happened that Schacht visited us the day after Lou Gehrig passed away and he told us a story about the time he was pitching against Gehrig in the minor leagues. This is how I remember Schacht tell it: "I first met and discovered Lou in Hartford, Connecticut in 1924. I was pitching for New Haven under Clyde Milan. We came to Hartford and it was my turn to pitch. When that big kid came up, I asked my catcher what to throw him. He said to throw one high and inside that Gehrig didn't like them there. So, I threw it there and a second later the ball was high and outside – over the right field fence."

When Schacht visited Rowland Field, it was one of the few times the fans actually turned out to the park. If only we could have booked Schacht for every home game our financial situation wouldn't have been so gloomy. The South Arkansas Athletic Association, which owned the Oilers, was in financial problems. We were getting ready to take a road trip and there wasn't enough money to go. There was some hope that the Detroit Tigers, who were interested in Woody Head, might come through with some money, but that didn't happen. Judge Emmett Harty, president of the Cotton States League, told the club officials to go ahead and put the club on the road and that the league would take care of the next payroll.

A group in Greenwood, Mississippi, which was out of the league in 1941, was trying to put together a group to purchase the franchise and move it from El Dorado. It was then that a civic group in El Dorado, headed by Dr. Shade Rushing, vowed to finance the team through the end of the season.

But that spelled the end for Guy as our manager. With about a month to go in the season, Guy was let go. Guy had opened up a stag club downtown to make a little extra money and to give him something to do in the offseason. Doc didn't like it one bit. He told Guy to either shut the club down or he was going to let him go. Guy told Doc he wasn't shutting the club down. Part of it too, I think, was that Rushing wanted a player-manager to cut down on expenses. Whatever the reason, Guy was gone.

They brought in Sam Hancock to manage the club. Hancock, who managed Tyler in 1940, was managing at Paragould in the Northeast Arkansas League. Hancock, who also played left field, made the deal look good right off the bat as he hit a two-run home run in the first game of a doubleheader sweep over Greenville and then, in the second game, he had a pair of RBI singles.

As for our attendance, it wasn't improving. The great minds who operated our club were trying to concoct some promotions to draw the fans in. We had a pretty good black population around El Dorado and I know the front office was trying to bring them into the park when they put together a black only watermelon eating contest and a black only beauty contest. Both events, by the way, were held just in front of the black section of the stands.

I was ready to get out of El Dorado and I did, thanks to Guy Sturdy. Guy was quick in finding another managing job with Marshall, Texas of the Cotton States, which on July 10 had been the Clarksdale franchise, taking over for L.L. (Cowboy) Jones. Guy had been on the job just one day when he put together a trade getting me from El Dorado. I was traded for five players and I took with me to Marshall 15 home runs, 62 RBIs and a .318 batting average. The morning after the trade I walked into the Hollywood Café in El Dorado for breakfast and those five players were in town for a game. The waiter called me by name and one of the players, sitting at a table close by, said out loud, "That's the jerk they traded us for." I turned around, looked at them, and said, "I don't know who's getting the better deal. Marshall getting one jerk or El Dorado getting five."

Before I knew I was going to Marshall, the great Rogers Hornsby, who was managing Oklahoma City of the Texas League, sent Red Boras up to El Dorado to see about getting me for his club. Red found me at the Howdie Club and I told Red I was having a good time and enjoyed playing for Guy. Red hung around a couple more days to try and persuade me to come to Oklahoma City. It would have been a move up, but I had my mind made up, I was staying. As it turned out, Oklahoma City was cutting things to the quick in the budget and Hornsby didn't even finish out the season, quitting because he got fed up with all the cutbacks.

I also got word that Montreal, Brooklyn's top farm club, was interested in me. But with my draft status at 1-A they didn't want to take a chance with the winds of war getting closer.

I really didn't have too many offers to move up and deep down I often wondered why, considering the stats I had been putting up. Then one night in Greenville, Mississippi I found out why.

I had had a great night at the plate and after the game in the hotel lobby I was talking to a couple of scouts. One of them said, "Muscle, tell me something. What have you done?" I looked at him not knowing what he was getting at. I said, "What'ya mean?" He said, "Well, to be honest, there's several of us scouts who have orders not to even bother making out a report on you." The scout went on to say that I was on a blacklist. That I was a troublemaker and wasn't even to be considered when it came to making a scouting report.

I know I had been in and out of some scrapes and I knew I hadn't made life easy on some of my managers, but to be on a blacklist just stunned me. I didn't know what to think of this. To this day I still don't know the full story because I could never find anyone who would level with me. Nobody in a front office capacity ever said I was blacklisted, but what other conclusion can I draw?

Anyway, I ended up with Marshall where I hit .275 with 11 home runs and 26 RBIs in 51 games and 167 at bats. I liked being back with Guy, even though our club stunk. Little did I know that when the season ended that I wouldn't be playing baseball anymore for a while. On September 10, 1941 I got a letter to report to the Army Induction Center in Huntington, West Virginia. Uncle Sam had some plans of his own for me. Unfortunately for me, I wasn't on his blacklist.

Chapter Eight

In Europe, Hitler was making the headlines every day and in the Pacific, while we weren't actually at war yet, we were preparing for the unavoidable.

Having been gone all summer playing baseball, I had a couple of days at home and I tried to tell Mom that I wouldn't be gone long in service. Actually, as far as my baseball playing days, I figured this was it. Ballplayers all over were going into service, even the major leaguers. Stars in their prime were turning in their cleats for combat boots. In 1941, 5,298 men were in organized baseball and in 1944 that number was reduced to 1,753 with only 12 of 44 leagues in business. When all was said and done over 5,000 men from the minor and major leagues served their country. I'm proud to say I was one. A lot of those guys never made it back. William John Hebert, who played ball with Merced of the California League, enlisted in the Navy and was wounded at Guadalcanal. Hebert died on Oct. 30, 1942 and became the first professional baseball player to lose his life in the war.

I didn't think about dying. I wanted to do my tour of duty and get back in one piece and play ball again. I told Mom to keep my glove. Who knows what might happen?

I reported to Huntington, West Virginia just like Uncle Sam ordered and I wasn't there long before they herded a couple hundred of us on several cattle cars at the train depot. We would be going to Ft. Thomas, Kentucky for a brief stay before going on to Camp Roberts in California for basic training.

There was no confusing Camp Roberts with any summer resort. There were barracks after barracks lined up and troops in uniform marching in every direction. We all were issued our gear and personal items and then assigned to our barracks. The barracks weren't that bad. I'd stayed in worse places while playing baseball.

We were putting our stuff away and picking our bunks when a booming voice called us to attention. There stood this stocky fellow who called himself Sergeant Batta. He said these were his barracks and that we would do as we were told while living in his barracks. He let every one of us know who was boss real quick. He asked us if we all had heard of God and he said that for us to consider him God while we were under his command.

We did have recreational time during basic where each day there would be some activity. Batta organized a couple of softball teams from our barracks and he pointed to me and said, "You, play first base." We began to play a game and in the first couple of innings I had a few fielding chances where I threw to second base without moving my feet, since I was left-handed. Batta came over and asked, "You ever play any ball, because you have some fine moves out there?" I grinned and told him I had played a little.

My first at bat I didn't hit the ball well at all, because in softball the timing is different than it is for baseball. But my second time up I ripped one hard over into the next diamond. Batta went crazy and, a few innings later after I hit another one just as hard, he comes running over to me and said, "Shoals, you're going to be a squad leader." I didn't know what that meant, but I found out later a squad leader doesn't pull KP and he doesn't do any details.

All I had to do was report whether my squad was present and accounted for. Batta, as it turned out, was a baseball fanatic. It wasn't long before he moved me out of the main barracks and into his room. We'd stay up to 2 a.m. on weekends drinking beer and talking baseball.

For eight weeks I was what was called an acting gadget which meant I didn't have to pull KP. Basic training was never so easy. The war was heating up in Europe but still quiet in the Pacific. Basic was about over and we were told to be ready to move out any day. We moved to Presidio, which was a distributing point in San Francisco, and in only a matter of days we boarded a transport vessel with our destination being the Philippine Islands.

We had been on the ocean a couple of days making our way to the islands when we heard that the Japanese had pulled off an early morning surprise attack at our naval base in the Hawaiian Islands at Pearl Harbor. Our destination changed. We were now going to Pearl Harbor.

We arrived at Honolulu on December 16th, only nine days after the bombing of Pearl. It was dark when we got there because of the blackout which had been implemented in case the Japanese decided to come back for a night attack. I can honestly say I was scared to death, because the talk was that the Japanese would definitely be coming back. When daylight came, we got our first look at the destruction at Pearl. We boarded trams which took us to Schofield Barracks where the Japanese entered Pearl and into Hickam Field. I've never forgotten the destruction I saw there. As long as I live I will never forget it.

The tops of some of those ships, which had been sunk, were sticking out of the harbor and other ships half blown away. The Arizona was at the bottom with over a thousand sailors still trapped, but you could still see the top of it rising out of the water. The divers were trying to salvage whatever they could on the bottom of the harbor. Those of us in the 24th Infantry, 34th Regiment, 4th Platoon, Company C, 1st Battalion suddenly knew the meaning of war. It wasn't a pretty sight at all.

We stayed at Pearl for several weeks waiting for the Japanese to pay another visit. We strung barbed wire from one cliff to another and we dug pill boxes and cut trees making fire lanes and brought in artillery to fire point range on the beach. At night we would take turns manning the machine guns, just waiting anxiously for that attack we all felt was coming. The Japanese had wounded Pearl and our Navy and surely they would come in for the kill. But, thank God, they never came back.

We were there several months before getting our orders to move out to Guadalcanal, the first island invaded in the Pacific. The Japanese occupied the island, but we were going to retake it. Then, at the last minute, another outfit was sent in our place. As it turned out, many lives were lost on Guadalcanal.

At the same time the battle of the Coral Sea was taking place and Australia appeared to be in jeopardy. If the Japanese navy had won the battle, then they would head for Australia. As it turned out, our navy wiped out the Japanese there so, when we hit Sydney, we immediately headed north to the Darwin area for jungle training. Our next destination was New Guinea, but first we landed on Good Enough Island to the east of New Guinea, a small island with a deep harbor where we received supplies for the planned invasion of Hollandia Dutch New Guinea.

In a few days we made our landing on New Guinea without any immediate confrontation from the enemy thanks to a smart move by General Douglas MacArthur who staged a fake landing at Port Moresby on the east coast. The Japanese took their main force across the mountain to repel the landing, but MacArthur withdrew.

The Japanese had left behind a lot of their supplies and, after the island was secure, we began building roads. And, since we had the bulldozers there, we made us a baseball diamond. I was asked to pick a team made up of boys in the regiment to play a game against a troop of special services ballplayers from the states headed up by Hugh Mulcahy, who had pitched for the Philadelphia Phillies.

Erv Dusak, an infielder for the Cardinals, was on the team and there were a number of guys who had played some in the minor leagues. After we had played the game a couple of players asked me to go up to their area for a beer, but I couldn't. Can you believe that? Me not being able to take time out for a beer. But the fact of the matter was that we were moving out at four the next morning. We were going to Biak, an island about 300 miles north. The 41st Division was pinned down there after making a landing and we were going to give them a hand.

The next morning we boarded the LSTs, which were transport ships, and made our way to Biak. We didn't know what we were going to get into up there. But from all we heard, I'd just as soon as stayed where we were and played some more baseball. I'm sure a few thousand more guys felt the same way as I did, but we also knew our fellow comrades were in trouble and needed our help and we were determined to get them out of it.

We had limited rations, which included plenty of coffee and baked bread and butter and two peach halves. We were told not to eat our type C canned rations because we would need it when we landed.

We reached Biak and went through the 41st line they had built up from the beach to the high ground. We then headed to the mountains. We spent 21 days up there. All we saw were platoon skirmishes and patrol action trying to pinpoint the enemy. One of our main missions was on a company combat patrol trying to contact a large unit of the enemy moving north in a valley. We were supposed to make contact and fight our way out.

We were preparing to go after the enemy when we ran into Company A heading for a ridge two or three miles away. About dark, we had dug in and we heard gunfire coming from that direction. We moved out quickly toward the ridge, but by the time we got there the action was over. Company A had moved up the ridge and found things quiet. They had unloaded their equipment and put their rifles down and just like that the Japanese were at the base of the hill ready to close in on them.

Company A tried to get out of there, but they had no chance. The day we ran into Company A before they went up on the ridge I had been talking with a red-headed lieutenant and I remember him saying, "See you guys later." That night, when we went up to the ridge, I helped carry that lieutenant down. It was very sad, but it made us more determined to wipe out the Japanese on the island.

Our job now was to hit the valley in search of the Japanese unit. We didn't know what to expect. It was very nerve wracking because we knew the Japanese were strong. As we moved up the valley with our flanks out and a platoon in the rear, we moved closer and closer to the enemy's

99

position. We could still see cigarettes burning where they had been just minutes before and there was the smell of mosquito lotion they used and it seemed to be getting stronger and stronger.

We advanced about a mile and stopped. We could actually hear the Japanese talking and we formed rather quickly a solid perimeter. We suddenly realized that we had walked into something and that the Japanese had closed around us and had us surrounded. They began moving in on our position.

We attempted to make radio contact for some assistance, but our communications were down. We had strung sound power wire to clip into with our phones since we were down in a valley to communicate with our forces on higher ground, but the Japanese had cut our wires. We were beginning to think this was the end for us.

We were in an area where kuni grass, a high grass, was all around. You couldn't see well at all in front of you. A bunch of Japanese would run in on us through the grass to test us, to get an idea on how close we were to them. We formed a tight perimeter and set up machine guns. They were getting closer on us and no doubt ready to launch an assault when shells began coming in on us from the rear. It was our artillery. It was ringing in almost right on top of us, but it was just ahead of where the Japanese were gathered.

Our guys were firing a bracket. A bracket is a round of fire and then, on the next round, it would be a hundred yards farther ahead and then on the next round another hundred yards ahead and so on. Our commander saw this as the way out for us and said, "Boys, let's follow this artillery out of here." As our guns would fire 100 yards beyond us, we'd run to just where it had hit. This scattered the enemy and gave us protection. Each time our artillery came in, we'd run the 100 yards ahead just where it had hit seconds before. It saved our necks. Later, we found out that we had been surrounded by over 4,000 Japanese.

There's no doubt they would have wiped us out, but we made it back to higher ground and to safety. As it turned out, the 41st Division knew our position and had ordered the artillery fire, which saved us. The boys in the 41st made an attack to where we had pushed the Japanese and it turned out to be a successful operation.

We returned to the coast and were put to work unloading supply ships. The sailors on those ships ate pretty good and we would trade our Japanese souvenirs for meat and potatoes.

A week or so later we left for Hollandia to stage for the Philippine mission, which MacArthur made famous by saying, "I shall return." Leyte was the first island we hit and later we spearheaded Luzon at Subic Bay, which the Eighth Army took over, and we withdrew to stage for the Island of Mindanao which was to be our last mission, but I never made it that far.

I was stricken with hookworm and was sent to Biak to one of the hospitals there, but they couldn't find anything. They finally came up with the diagnosis of Epigastric Hernia from the incision on my belly where I had surgery after being shot in Johnson City. I went to Letterman's Hospital in San Francisco and later went by train to Moore General Hospital in Swannanoa, North Carolina, which is not too far from Asheville, where I was operated on.

I was one of the fortunate ones to return home after World War II. This picture was taken in 1945.

(Photo courtesy of Sholes family)

101

That was an operation which may have saved my life. I ran into a truck driver in Roanoke, Virginia a few years later who was in our company. He said my unit was wiped out on Mindanao. They were mostly just kids. I wondered why I was saved and they weren't. I still think about it to this day.

It wasn't too long after that the war came to an end. I was overseas 40 months and 16 days and whoever said war is hell knew what he was talking about. There was nothing glamorous about it like some movies would have you think. A lot of good, young men died and I came back. I was just lucky.

One time, when I was playing for Reidsville, I had a surprise visit. A lieutenant whose last name was Gordon came to our house about nine o'clock one morning and I was sound asleep. He told Helen he'd like to surprise me, so Helen let him in. He ran into my room and jumped right on top of me, screaming his head off. I thought someone had broken in and was trying to rob me. I started tossing and turning and trying to get my arms out from under the covers so I could start swinging and protect myself. Then I recognized who it was. He said, "Remember the last time I jumped on you?" We were in the Philippines and were pinned down with crossfire and someone jumped right down on top of me in a shell hole. It had been raining and he shoved my face down in the mud. He was just like me, trying to find a place to get out of the line of fire. He had been working in Atlanta, read about me playing in Reidsville and decided to pay a visit.

Like a lot of our boys over in the South Seas, I had about all the diseases. I had jungle rot in my legs and feet. I had bilateral hearing loss and I had malaria. I was discharged from Fort Meade, Maryland in July of 1945, but had to go to a VA hospital with a bad recurrence of malaria. After a couple of weeks and with a bottle of aterbrin pills, I came home for a long rest.

While pondering what my next move would be, I started thinking about baseball again. I had not played seriously now for four years. I was 28 years old and I had some scars from service. I wondered if I had any baseball left in me and I wondered if I would get another chance. I hadn't lost the feel for baseball. It was still burning inside me.

Chapter Nine

When spring of 1946 rolled around, I wondered to myself should I or shouldn't I give baseball a try again? I had my doubts whether I could still hit like I did before I went into service. You miss four years in your prime, who wouldn't have some doubts? But I started thinking that I didn't want to work in a factory all my life. If I could find somebody willing to give me a shot, then I would take it.

I wrote a letter to Kingsport team owner H. Joseph Higgins asking him if he could use a first baseman. Higgins talked with Cherokees manager Hobe Brummette, who managed in the Appalachian League when I played in 1939, and Hobe told Higgins that if he could sign me that would be a boost to his club. I always admired Hobe. He was very successful as a manager winning the past two Appalachian League pennants with Kingsport and he had won six pennants over the past seven seasons, as he also managed Elizabethton. That seventh season, in which he didn't win a pennant, he brought Elizabethton in second. He was a fiery type. I used to hate to play against Hobe because at least once in a ballgame he would have one of his pitchers knock me down.

One time I was playing against Hobe and he had a pitcher named Rudy Parsons. When I stepped to the plate Hobe hollered at Parsons, "Knock him down, Rudy." The next pitch was right under my chin and I went down. I got up and the first thing I heard was Hobe yelling, "Knock him down, Rudy." Again, Parsons throws a fastball up and in and I go down. I dust myself off, get in the box and there's Hobe standing on the dugout steps yelling, "Knock him down, Rudy." I peered out at Parsons and about the time Parsons wound up I stepped back a little. The ball wasn't quite as tight this time and I swung and knocked the ball out of the park. After I crossed home plate, I looked over at Hobe smiling and said, "Knock him down, Rudy." Hobe started slinging his arms and yelling something back at me. I don't know what it was, but I don't think he was inviting me over for supper after the game.

Hobe was one of the greatest I ever saw at playing mind games with the opposition. Anything he could do to get an edge, he would.

Specs Garbee was managing Johnson City and he also pitched. In one game against us, Specs came in to pitch the ninth inning. Specs was taking his warmup tosses on the mound and there was Hobe raising cain with umpire Bernie Webb over the amount of pitches that Specs could take. Specs kept throwing and finally Webb approached Specs on the mound and told him he probably had thrown enough. Specs, who spoke in a slow southern drawl, said: "When you get that guy (Brummette) off the diamond and back in the coaching box where he belongs, I'll start pitching to the batter."

Hobe's attempt at upsetting Specs didn't work. Garbee pitched the ninth and set us down 1-2-3.

I always went to the plate knowing that I would be wiping dust off the seat of my pants at least once. I hated to play against Hobe, but he was my kind of manager. I told Hobe that if he was willing to take a chance on me, I was willing to put that uniform on again.

I got off to a slow start with Kingsport and I wasn't in danger of winning any of the prizes being offered. Several businesses around Kingsport were offering incentives to the players. For the first home run of the season J. Fred Johnson's clothiers was giving away a suit and for the first hit Sobel's was giving away a sport shirt. Then Harrison's was giving a pair of shoes for the first single, the Jewel Box a man's ruby ring for the first double and Hayden's a Seeland watch for the first triple. Too bad nobody was giving away a prize for the first strikeout because I might have got that one.

When we opened the season at J. Fred Johnson Stadium, the fans were ready for baseball. We had a lot of former servicemen among the crowd of 2,588, which was the largest opening day attendance in the league. We were facing Bristol and pitching for the Twins was Buck Zeiger who was coming back from the war after being wounded in France. I was hitting cleanup and took the collar against Buck as we lost the game.

The first few days you could count my hits on one hand. No one was confusing me with my teammate Claude Trivette who had 11 hits in his first 17 at bats. I was struggling, so Hobe moved me down to sixth in the order and I responded with a home run in the ninth to beat New River 2-1. I was barely hitting .200 toward the end of May and Hobe told me: "Muscle, I hate to do it but I'm going to have to drop you down in the order again." I told Hobe I understood and I didn't beef when he made out the lineup card and I was hitting eighth. It must have inspired me because the night that happened we were in Bristol at Shaw Stadium and I had a home run and three singles. After that, things began clicking for me and I got my stroke back.

The fans were patient with me through that first month. I was still taking the pills for malaria and the jungle rot had slowed me down even more than I already was. I remember after I hit that home run against New River, I was in the dugout and somebody brought me an army helmet filled with money. The helmet became a routine. I was making $350 a month and I got as much as $120 for two home runs in a game. John Parker, a local constable who was a really big fan, started passing the helmet, which was painted white, through the stands on home runs. Two girls handled the right field bleachers and two more the left field bleachers. They would count the money and announce it over the PA.

By the middle of July I was feeling like a kid again and was playing baseball the way I was capable of playing. By the league's all-star break I was hitting .327 with eight home runs and 46 RBIs. I wasn't picked for the all-star game and, because of my horrible start, probably didn't deserve to be. Although, my stats weren't that far off from Bluefield's

Tom Zikmund, who was picked to play first base. Zikmund was hitting .346 with 49 RBIs and only one home.

As a whole, we weren't playing very good baseball. The Cherokees were struggling, but it's always tough for an independent club like Kingsport was in '46. We didn't have the backing of a major league franchise to stock us with players. We had to get players wherever we could. Hobe literally had to beat the bushes to find guys who could play ball. We had a couple of injuries crop up around the middle of the year, so Hobe went to Atlanta to see if he could come up with another shortstop and a pitcher. Hobe's theory was that if you needed a good ballplayer, go to Atlanta.

Before he left he told me that I would be in charge of the team. Hobe was gone a couple of days when in comes this kid into the clubhouse and said his name was Carl Beringer. He was 5-foot-6, 120-pounds, if that. A real little guy. I thought, well, Hobe must have seen something in him to send him to play. Hobe called me and said put the kid in at shortstop that night.

I began to get a bad feeling about the kid when I showed him where his locker was and he began unpacking his gear. He pulls out a pair of short white wool socks. I told him that we had a box of long white sanitary hose we wore and to put them on. He then pulls out a red sweatshirt and I told him to put it away that we wore blue. Then he pulls out a pair of cleats that looked to be about four sizes too long. The toes were turned up and, believe it or not, he had yellow shoestrings on those things. I was able to find another pair that fit him better. Then he puts on this little ball cap with stripes on it. He looked like a Munchkin.

I said, "Beringer, you can't wear that cap." He said, "But I like this cap, I have a small head and it fits." I said, "Yeah, I noticed you've got a bullet-shaped head, but I can't let you go out with a different cap on then the rest of us." Then he just exploded. "What in the devil's going on around here? I can't wear a dadburn thing that I've got."

We finally get Beringer all suited up and we go out on the field. He went into the batting cage and kept swinging from the heels, trying to lift one out of the park, which he never did. He wouldn't get out of the cage. I was in the dugout and I heard the other fellows hollering for him to get out so they could hit. I finally went over and drug him out myself.

I started him at short, just like Hobe told me to, but I could tell this boy wasn't a ballplayer. The first ball hit was right to him and the ball kept on going right between his legs. He put his hands on his hips, then dropped his glove and began shaking his head.

The next batter hit another grounder to Beringer, which he stopped, but he threw the ball with a submarine motion and it sailed about 10 over my head at first base. The fans began screaming and hollering.

Well, just so happened we got out of the inning with only one run scored and in our half we scored six. So I decided to leave Beringer in to see what he could do at the plate. He gets up there and is carrying a 36-ounce, 34-inch bat. He was late swinging on the first three pitches to him. He throws down the bat and came back to the dugout kicking and cussing. He took off his cap and threw it down and said, "I told you I couldn't play with this blasted cap." I took him out of the game and after it was over I gave him a few bucks and told him to take the next Greyhound back to Atlanta.

It was a couple of days later that Hobe returned and he wanted to know where Beringer was. I said, "Hobe, you probably passed that kid on your way back from Atlanta." I went on to tell him everything that happened. Hobe said he never actually saw Beringer play, but was taking the word of a scout down there about what a good player Beringer was. I don't know whatever happened to Beringer, but I never heard his name mentioned again.

It was things like that which Hobe didn't like. A manager shouldn't have to leave his club to go look for players. Twice before the all-star game Hobe told Higgins he was going to resign, but both times Higgins talked Hobe out of it. As a matter of fact, Hobe had retired after the 1944 season, but Higgins talked him into coming back in 1945 and Hobe led Kingsport to the pennant, nine games over Bristol.

We didn't have an outstanding club and you could see the frustration building in Hobe. He couldn't hold it in any longer and Hobe blew his stack in one game. We were playing Pulaski and the umpire, Melvin Lashure, made a call on a pitch that Hobe didn't like. Hobe goes running out of the dugout and gets in Lashure's face and starts shaking his fist right under Lashure's chin. We all thought Hobe was going to punch Lashure, so a couple of the guys went out to get Hobe away. Hobe never hit Lashure, but he did bump him with his chest and it cost Hobe a three-day suspension and a $25 fine from league president Carl Jones.

It wasn't too long after a 25-10 loss to Elizabethton, in a game in which our center fielder Armando Traspuesto made five errors, that the man who everyone called "Uncle Hobe" called it quits. Hobe had been in the pros from 1921 to 1946, taking off 1943-44 for the war. Finally, just a few days after the all-star game, Hobe told Higgins he was resigning and retiring from baseball. He said he was going back to Knoxville and work for the wholesale meat house, which he had worked for in the offseasons. Of course Higgins thought he could change Hobe's mind, but Hobe said this was it and there was no coming back. Hobe told Higgins he would stay on at least another week so that he could find a replacement.

Higgins knew exactly who he wanted to replace Hobe – Russell Mincy who was playing left field for the Pulaski Counts. Mincy, who was known as Red for his carrot top, was leading the Appalachian League in hitting with an average of over .400 when Higgins traded catcher Joe Sullivan to Pulaski. I think there may have been a few dollars traded under the table as well because the Mincy for Sullivan swap just didn't seem right. But Pulaski was getting a very good catcher and a guy who would end up hitting over .300. We happened to be playing in Pulaski when the deal was made and Mincy, in his last game there, got five doubles in a 10-8 Pulaski win. As it turned out, Mincy's first game as manager of the Cherokees was back in Kingsport against the Counts and we won the game 8-2. Red even had a run-scoring single in that game and made a spectacular running catch off of Ray Trout's 400-foot drive to left field.

But our woes as a team continued. At one point we had lost 15 of 16 games against Bristol and I had a terrible time against lefty Paul LaPalme of the Twins. But I had good company, as it seemed a lot of people had trouble with LaPalme, who would finish the year at 20-2. Even pitchers had trouble with LaPalme, who swung a pretty good stick as he hit .341 with 61 hits. I guess I had more trouble against LaPalme more than some other guys because I swung left and he pitched left. Another guy who was trouble that year was Shannon Hardwick of New River. Hardwick, a right-hander, was 19-0 at one point and finished the year 23-3. There weren't a lot of guys pitching that year who gave me fits, but LaPalme and Hardwick, who had a nasty curve, were a couple who did.

Sometimes watching us play was like watching the Keystone Cops. One night we lost to Johnson City 6-4 in a Keystone Cop manner, but there was nothing funny about it to us. We were leading 4-2 in the fifth when the Cardinals got runners on second and third with two out. It looked like we were getting out of the inning when Jim Jacquot popped up and our shortstop, Bill Alhouse, was settling under it. The base umpire, a guy named Moneyhun, was looking straight up at the ball and wasn't paying attention to where Alhouse was. Moneyhun ran smack into Alhouse knocking Alhouse on his rear. The ball fell for a hit and two runs scored to tie the game. Mincy screamed interference and argued until he got thrown out of the game. Johnson City then went on to score two more in that inning, all after two were out.

The Kingsport Jewelry Company offered Red a Lord Elgin wrist watch and each player an extension watch band if we made the playoffs, but there was no danger in that. We finished sixth in the league with a 55-70 record. New River, which finished the regular season 83-40 for tops in the league, ended up winning the playoffs. New River was managed by Jack Crosswhite and the actual town the team was located was Narrows, Virginia, a hamlet of only 1,489 people. The only other place in organized baseball in 1946 with a smaller population base was Centreville, Maryland of the Eastern Shore League, which had a population of 1,141.

New River had such a good season thanks in large part to right-hander Hardwick. The 28-year-old Hardwick won 19 games in a row and finished the season with 23 victories. The thing about Hardwick was that he only pitched at home and cities close by like Bluefield and Pulaski. Hardwick sold insurance and he was also New River's business manager. He and Robert Woods of Pearisburg, who started the New River club, were insurance partners.

When Hardwick won his 19th straight, he broke Lefty Akard's mark of 18 straight wins set in 1945.

While he was only 8-7, lefty Jim Mooney of Johnson City was one of the most amazing fellows I've ever seen. Jim, who was the head baseball coach at East Tennessee State College in Johnson City, was playing for the Johnson City Cardinals in 1942 before entering the U.S. Navy. Before that, Jim had played with the New York Giants and the St. Louis Cardinals.

In 1942 Jim won 15 games for Johnson City, was never relieved in a game and did not issue a walk all season. Jim was pitching for the semipro Bristol State Liners early in 1946 before signing with Johnson City. Jim pitched 124 innings in 1946 and walked only nine batters. He had amazing control. To put that in perspective, you look at Dick Callison of New River who walked 123 batters in 198 innings. Also, Jim did not hit one single batter and he had only three wild pitches. Imagine three wild pitches over 124 innings!

Like I said before, I had a good season with Kingsport. When the season was finished I hit .333, led the league in home runs with 21, a new league record, and drove in 106. I even stole 10 bases. They had a vote for the team MVP and Melvin Nee, a right-hander who went 14-14, got the award and I was second. Nee, who pitched for Kingsport

111

in 1943 before going off to war, got a new Elgin watch and I was awarded a Schick electric razor. This was by vote of the fans and I had been leading in the MVP race until the final count.

Helen and I shortly after we were married in 1946.
(Photo courtesy of Sholes family)

Helen and I celebrated our 50th wedding anniversary in 1996.
(Photo courtesy of Sholes family)

Well, when it was announced that Nee got the award several fans were upset so they took up a collection and bought me an Elgin watch as well. It was great being back and playing again.

But the best thing to happen to me came after the season. I had met a girl from Kingsport early in the season, Helen Perry, and we began dating. I began to get the feeling that Helen wasn't like any other girl I had ever been with before. With Helen, I didn't have any desire to see any other girls. Before, I'd date several girls at a time. But not with Helen. For the first time in my life I had that feeling deep down and I knew it was love. When the season was over I popped the question to Helen. I asked her to marry me. I really didn't know what kind of answer she would give. I told her that if I played baseball, it would mean a lot of traveling and a lot of moving around and that part of the game wasn't much fun. Despite that, she accepted my proposal and we were married.

Well, we've been together ever since, so I guess it worked out pretty good. Along the way we've been blessed with five beautiful children – four boys and one girl.

Helen and I moved back to Parkersburg for the winter where I worked putting in awnings and insulation. Back then you didn't make any money, especially in the minor leagues, so you had to have a winter job to supplement your salary.

It seemed like that winter moved by quickly. Kingsport wanted me back in 1947 and I went to spring training in Ocala, Florida. On the way back from Florida en route to Tennessee, we would stop in a couple of towns and put on exhibitions with other minor league teams.

When we reached Kingsport we had a game with the Watertown Athletics of the Class C Border League. Watertown was training for 10 days up in Bluefield, West Virginia at Bowen Field because Bluefield's business manager, Jim Morse, was a friend with somebody on the Watertown club. Watertown was managed by Bob Shawkey, who pitched 15 years in the majors – 12 with the New York Yankees – and appeared in four World Series. Shawkey pitched the opening game in Yankee Stadium in 1921. He retired in 1927 and came back in 1930 to manage the Yankees that season finishing third. He dropped out of baseball until coming back to manage Watertown in 1947. I just remember that because everyone was excited about seeing Shawkey, who was a big name in the 1920s.

We also had an exhibition with the Homestead Greys, an all-black touring team. Before the game one of the Greys had a bat that looked like it might have been bought in a drugstore. It was painted black and wasn't a good quality of wood, but I thought it'd be fun to use it in the game, so I traded a Louisville Slugger for that dime-store bat.

On either my second or third at bat, I hit one out of the park. The bat didn't have a good ring to it, but I hit it out anyway. When the season started, the fans wanted me to use that black bat. They remembered the home run. So I started using it, but all I was doing now was popping the ball up. Then one night I broke the bat on a pitch and I was glad. I went back to a Louisville Slugger and started hitting the ball again. As a matter of fact, I led the Appalachian League in hitting with a .387 average and led in home runs with 32 while driving in 124.

One of the strangest exhibitions we had that year was against the House of David team at J. Fred Johnson Stadium. This was a group of touring players who all had these long beards and they'd cut up and act crazy, but they were pretty good ballplayers. Charlie Allen, a good friend of mine on the team and a good friend many years later, hit a couple of home runs and his second tied the score 9-9. I came up in the eighth inning and hit a home run to win the game. Afterwards, one of the fellows asked me if I'd like to join the team. I started thinking how I would look in a beard and decided against it. It wouldn't have been a pretty sight.

Kingsport got a working agreement that year with the Washington Senators and the organization put in Dick Bass, a former pitcher for them in the minors who did get up to the majors for one game in 1939, as our manager. Bass was still active as a pitcher and the year before had won 13 games for

Gainesville in the Florida State League. Bass was 38 years old and a native of nearby Rogersville, Tennessee. Bass had signed with St. Louis in 1930 and worked his way up the system and was considered the best relief pitcher in the American Association in 1935 going 18-8. He was sold to Washington and then the war came along and he settled for his long career in the minor leagues.

Dick, a right-hander, still had plenty of zip on his fastball, but control was his strong point. Dick was rolling along with 14 wins when, in mid-August, he hurt his ankle. He came back about three weeks later and suffered his first loss in 15 starts, 13-11, to New River. He won two more, his last and his 16th win was at home, 6-3 over Elizabethton. I remember that night because it was the last day of August and we were waiting around for the Elizabethton team to show up, but their bus had broken down on the highway. When they finally got to Kingsport this hound dog kept getting out on the field and delaying the game.

Early in the year Dick would sometimes take off for Chattanooga to look at possible players for us and he'd leave me in charge of the team, so I got some experience at managing which would prove beneficial later in my career. When Dick got hurt he was out for that long spell but, at the same time, I took a line drive off my leg and I was out of action. Well, Higgins told Jimmy Morgan to take over and I ended up quitting baseball and leaving the Cherokees.

"Shoals was under the belief that he was acting manager of the club but at a meeting of the players it was brought out that Morgan was the acting manager. The meeting was held Monday night at the clubhouse and I didn't know that there were any ill feelings until I delivered Shoals his regular paycheck on Tuesday.

"I went to see Shoals because he said he had something to discuss with me. After a

*conference that lasted about an hour, he
informed me that he had decided to quit.*

*"I told him that I was sorry that he took
that attitude, but if he wanted to quit there
was no way for me to keep him on the team."*

*– Higgins as quoted in
Kingsport Times-News,
July 16, 1947*

Well, that was part of the reason I quit. But that's not
the whole story. At the time I had 20 home runs and was
leading the club in average at .386. I had been home taking
care of my foot, so I couldn't manage even if I had wanted
to. When I got back Morgan came up to me before the game
and handed me the lineup card and asked me to manage the
club. He said it was OK with Higgins. But I told Jimmy to
keep on managing because he was winning and I didn't want
to upset the applecart. But Jimmy insisted that I go ahead
and fill out the lineup for that night and manage until Dick
got back.

Well, I did and we lost three games to Welch, and in
the last game I used Charlie Allen, a 19-year-old rookie
outfielder. For some reason Higgins didn't like Charlie and
that's when Higgins held the team meeting. I didn't quit
because I wasn't named manager. I quit because of Higgins
second-guessing me.

Dick came back and we had a conference that lasted
five hours. Dick tried everything to talk me into coming
back. During this time I had missed the all-star game in
Pulaski to which I had been selected the starting first
baseman, but I didn't even care about that now. As far as I
was concerned, I had retired from baseball.

But everyone kept trying to talk me into coming
back. After about a week I began thinking that maybe I let
my pride get in the way of good sense. And, too, I was
letting down Dick, my teammates and the fans who wrote
letters in my support.

About a week after I had quit, I told Dick I'd come back.

> *Leo (Muscle) Shoals returned to the Kingsport lineup Tuesday night and collected a double and two singles in five times at bat, but still the Cherokees bowed to Johnson City, 15-5, before, 2,500 fans.*
>
> *Shoals, who resigned from the Cherokees a week ago, was greeted by wild applause when he took his position at first base. In the ninth inning the fans were still on his side as he slapped a ball over the right field fence. The umpires ruled that the ball landed in the bushes, however, and limited him to a double.*
>
> *– Kingsport Times-News,*
> *July 23, 1947*

I was back and I was glad. I wanted to put all that behind me and get on with playing ball again.

Some of the attention was taken off me just a few days later when the league directors met to discuss what they were going to do with what they thought was a problem with the umpires. One of the directors at the center of this was Higgins. Apparently, several of the league directors felt their teams were being chastised by the umpires and they went to league president Carl A. Jones Jr. with their gripes.

Oh, there were some run-ins with the umpires by some of the teams, but overall I thought the umpires were doing a pretty good job and the umps were taking some abuse.

There was a night in Elizabethton on July 4 when umpire Jeff Puckett was knocked unconscious and had his nose broken by an irate fan. The Elizabethton team was then fined $75 for allegedly permitting money to be taken in the stands the next night to pay the fine of Puckett's attacker. Elizabethton manager Lew Bekeza was fined $20 and

117

suspended for three days for starting the initial argument over a call on the field, which led to the attack.

Some of the owners didn't feel like the umpires had any control on the field. One of those times was when Bristol manager Charlie Fox and Elizabethton manager Jack Crosswhite exchanged punches during a game.

Well, the situation with the umpires got nastier. Jones pretty much said he wasn't going to do anything with the umpires. He said he thought they were doing a good enough job. The board of directors of the league met with Jones to floor their complaints and when Jones stood his ground John F. Clarke, director for the Bristol Twins, said: "Gentlemen, it's about time we got down to business and do what we came here to do – fire Carl Jones."

One by one the directors rose to back up Clarke. They asked Jones to resign and Jones refused. Jones said that if they wanted to get rid of him, they'd had to fire him. It didn't take long for that to happen. Jones' parting words were: "I wish for the league every success. I shall continue to be a fan and will buy a ticket now instead of going through the pass gate."

The umpires, by the way, were attending the meeting. While the directors met in executive session to decide what they would do about a president, the umpires left and held their own meeting. Seven of the umpires resigned and two more, who were not at the meeting, were soon to follow.

So here's the Appalachian League with a month to go with no president and no umpires. The directors all congregated in Wytheville, Virginia the next day to decide what they were going to do. The first thing they did was name league vice-president Chauncey DeVault as acting president. Chauncey said he didn't want it, but said he would fill in until a permanent successor was found. DeVault, who owned a sporting goods store in Bristol, ended up serving as president until 1979

Meanwhile, the league found amateur umpires around the towns and cities to umpire the remaining games and the season went on. We weren't playing that great but I was doing OK. I held the Appy record for home runs with 21 in 1946, but already passed that mark in mid-August. I was getting some competition in that department from Homer Moore of the Bluefield Blue-Grays, which was a farm club of the Boston Braves. They called Moore 'Homering Homer.'

Moore was a rookie in pro ball coming back from the war where he was awarded the Bronze Star and the Purple Heart. He was a right-handed batter and was a sturdy-built fellow. He was 23 years old and stood 5-foot-11 and weighed 190 pounds. I never got to know Homer that well, but I enjoyed watching him hit the ball.

A reporter was asking a catcher on another team how to pitch to me and Moore: "Do anything but throw Shoals the disappearing ball – a fast one around his knees. They said to pitch Shoals high and outside. So we pitched him high and outside. The last time I saw the ball it was still high and outside the park. As for Moore, give him nothing inside and feed him curves."

Whatever they tried throwing us didn't work all that well because we both had pretty decent years.

I ended up leading the league with 32 home runs and Homer had 31. So I beat my old record by a pretty good margin. A fellow by the name of Cochran had held the record hitting 20 in 1913 for Rome, Georgia. There were some familiar names who had led the Appy in home runs. Andy Seminick, who played for the Philadelphia Phillies, had 15 in 1942 for Elizabethton and Gil Coan, who played in the majors with Washington, had 13 in 1945 for Kingsport.

It also turned out to be a pretty good year for our second baseman – Bill Polston – as well. It was in late August and we were hosting New River. It was a game where I went 4-for-5 and we won 10-0. But after the game Bill got married, right there on the field. Bill married Mary Neil Adkins at homeplate with both teams staying to watch. When the ceremony was over both teams lined up opposite one another and made an arch with crossed bats and the couple left the stadium by walking under those bats. Sounds like something out of the movie Bull Durham.

One of the most unusual situations that season came in a game we won over Bluefield 8-7 when, in the sixth inning, Jimmy Morgan scored from the dugout. This is what happened. Morgan was on third and on a hit somehow missed the plate and ran into the dugout. Bluefield's catcher, Frank Baldwin, ran to the dugout to tag Morgan but instead tagged Charlie Anderson thinking Anderson was Morgan. Morgan, meanwhile, ran back out onto the field and tagged home plate.

The umpire, Vincent Moneyhun, who just happened to be from Kingsport, called Anderson out, but reversed his decision when he found out it wasn't Morgan and then called Morgan safe after he touched home plate. Well, Bluefield manager George Lacy went crazy. He was jumping up and down and stomping on his cap and slinging his arms.

Lacy ended up protesting the game and he won his protest. We had to replay the game but I don't even remember who won the game the second time around.

I didn't end the year on a very positive streak as I went 4-for-21 in the last week and barely hung on to win the batting title over Larry Kinzer of Pulaski – .387 to .381.

A long and, in some ways, troublesome year was over. At the end of the year, Washington had the option of taking players away from Kingsport and moving them to another club. Me, pitcher Gene Howell and outfielder Jimmy Morgan were sold to Chattanooga of the Class B Tri-State League. Another adventure was about to begin.

Chapter 10

In the spring of '48 I went to train at Winter Garden, Florida in the Washington Senators minor league camp. The only problem was that winter I had put on some weight. Mike Garbark, who later would catch with the Yankees, and I both were ordered to shed some pounds. We had to put on this split inner-tube and then zip our sweatshirts up. That tube would burn you up and it wasn't long before those pounds came off.

I had been assigned to the Chattanooga club of the Class AA Southern Association and during camp we worked out with the Charlotte club of the Class B Tri-State League. We would play the big league Senators twice in Orlando and twice in Winter Garden and I faced a staff comprised of Early Wynn, Mickey Haeffner, Walt Masterson and Sid Hudson. I hit one home run off Haeffner in Winter Garden and that's the only time I ever hit a home run against major league pitching. I almost had one off Hudson, though. Sid had come down with a sore arm, so he went to a sidearm delivery, which I didn't have much trouble with. In one game I had a single and double off Hudson, but the double came close to being a home run. I hit that ball about 375 feet to right field and that sucker hit at the base of the wire fence and scooted underneath for a double.

Overall, I didn't hit that well against Washington's pitching. They had a bunch of junk ball pitchers and I had a little trouble with that. But, our manager, George Myatt, stuck by me.

"Slow stuff was bothering him. Yet he had hit a change-of-pace for a homer in Winter Garden. I don't see how slow, or fast, stuff bothers him, for with those quick wrists

121

of his, he doesn't swing at the ball until it is right in front of him."

– George Myatt,
The Chattanooga Times,
April 11, 1948

In one of those games at Orlando against Washington, we knocked Wynn out early in the game. We had a lot of left-handed hitters on the club. It was toward the end of spring training and the Senators were about ready to break up camp and they wanted Wynn to go as long as he could in the game.

There was a table set up along first base where Clark Griffith, the owner of the Senators, and Wirt Gammon, a sportswriter from Chattanooga, were sitting. Wirt was a character and Early was about as tough of a guy you'd ever want to meet.

Wynn was having his problems and wasn't in the best of moods. Wirt starts yelling at Wynn, "Hey, Early, the FBI's after you." About that time, boom, somebody would hit one out. Wirt would shout again that the FBI was after him. Again, somebody hit one out. Wirt just kept on badgering Wynn. Finally, Wynn came off the mound and headed to where Wirt was sitting. You could see the veins bulging in Wynn's neck. Wynn slammed down his glove on the table and got down to Wirt and said, "What in the blazes are you talking about, the FBI's after me?" Wirt leaned back with a big smile and said, "For impersonating a major league pitcher." Wynn threw up his hands and you could hear him cussing all the way back to the mound.

Washington was managed by Joe Kuhel, who was a pretty fair first baseman in his day. Before one of our exhibitions, Kuhel came over to where I was at first base and said he wanted to show me a little quicker tag on the pickoff play. He said I was taking the throw, looking around and making the sweep tag. Joe said I should take the throw and make the sweep without looking, that I would save a split second. Well, the game started and right off the bat Mickey

Vernon got on base with a hit. I saw the pickoff sign and the throw came over, I made the sweep without looking, but Vernon wasn't there. He had jumped out of the way and was on his way to second. I could hear Myatt's loud, bullfrogish voice coming from over in the dugout: "That was a very lucious play Leo." Myatt's favorite term was "lucious." A home run would be a "lucious" home run.

George could never remember anybody's name. He called everybody "Stud" and everybody called Myatt "Stud." I began noticing that every time somebody broke a bat, George would retrieve it and put it in the corner of the dugout. After the game, he'd collect however many he may have gotten throughout the game and take them to his little office in the clubhouse. As the bats began piling up I asked him one day what he was going to do with all those cracked bats and he told me he was going to build a fence around his home in Orlando. I'm curious as to whether he ever did.

I had a very "lucious" spring training, hitting around .400, which I think surprised a lot of people who thought I was water under the bridge at my age. A column in the paper said I was a member of Alcoholics Anonymous, but that I had settled down since getting married. While I wasn't a member of AA, I had settled down a whole lot. I was looking forward to the season and we opened in Nashville at the old Sulphur Dell ballpark.

There were over 9,000 fans in that park, the most I ever played in front of. And, to help open the season, they had Minnie Pearl, Eddie Arnold and Ernest Tubb perform before the game. They capped it off with Minnie on the mound pitching to Eddie while Ernest was umpiring behind the plate. Just as Minnie wound up to throw the pitch, Eddie was cutting up and ran behind Ernest. But Eddie came back out of hiding and stood at the plate and missed the first pitch thrown by Minnie. Minnie threw a second and Eddie swung and missed again. Then, on the third pitch, Eddie swung and popped the ball up. Eddie could sing, but he couldn't hit. The crowd loved it and the players did too.

123

That was some ballpark in Nashville. It was built near the city dump. If you were in the park and the wind was blowing right, especially on a hot day, the odor would knock you over. It was a most unusual park, too, in that right field had a slope which began just a few feet behind first base and went up on a 45 degree angle. The slope leveled off at 235 feet and went to an area that was level and was about 10 feet wide. The slope then continued to the fence located 262 feet from home plate. Outfielders were referred to as mountain goats because they would "graze" on that level terrace so that they could run downhill for short flies.

In that opening game, I went 3-for-4 and one of my hits almost went out, but it bounced off the fence and rattled around. I was running like the devil and was able to leg out a double.

A couple days later we opened our season in Chattanooga at Engel Stadium, named after club president Joe Engel. Chattanooga was excited about baseball. Mayor Hugh Wasson declared a half-holiday with city hall and the courthouse closing down and we packed them in for that opener with almost 13,000 at the game against Nashville. The club got this huge army searchlight and put it on top of the stadium roof and it was lighting up the sky to let the fans for miles know there was a game going on. They ended up leaving that light there for the rest of the year and every home game it would streak across the sky.

Engel was a pioneer of sorts in baseball. He was the first to install a hit and error light on the scoreboard. But one time, years earlier, a Chattanooga player got on base and then got picked off while he was looking up at the board to see if he had been credited with getting on by a hit or error. Engel got so mad that he had the lights torn off the scoreboard and it was a few years later before he put them back.

It was Engel who signed 17-year-old Jackie Mitchell, a female, to pitch in an exhibition against the New York Yankees in 1931. Mitchell was called in from the bullpen and struck out Babe Ruth on a called third strike, fanned Lou

Gehrig on a curve and walked Tony Lazzeri before leaving the game. Everyone swears that Ruth and Gehrig were giving it their all. Ruth, by the way, hit the first home run at Engel Stadium in an exhibition in 1930.

There was one year that Engel stored baseballs in a freezer the night before a game in which he was expecting a huge crowd. The plan was to rope off an area around the outfield to squeeze the fans into the ballpark. Engel wanted to make sure he didn't lose any balls in the crowd, so he froze them.

Engel was a character of which I've never known before or since in baseball. One time during a game at Chattanooga there were these two umpires sitting in the stands. They were supposed to have been umpiring a game in Nashville, but on their way they got word that the game was rained out so they drove back to Chattanooga just to watch. Engel found out these two umpires were in the stadium, so he had the boy doing the scoreboard to hang up a first-inning score of the Nashville game. Joe had his eye on these two umpires and when that score went up they said those two umpires jumped up and went running to the nearest phone.

I really thought Engel Stadium was going to be a great place for me to play. The year before the right field fence was 330-feet, but in '48 they cut it down to 317 feet. As a gimmick, they cut a hole in the fence about the size of a basketball and any player hitting a ball through that hole would get $50. I never came close.

The club overall was pretty lousy. It was mainly because we had no pitching. We'd lose games 9-8, 8-7 and it only got worse as the season went on. Myatt was long past his prime as a ballplayer, but we were so bad he was playing second base. Sammy Meeks was scheduled to play second but, just before we left Florida, Sammy was called to camp by the Senators. I remember the first ball hit to George at second, he reared back and flung that ball into the first couple of rows in the stands. It didn't get a lot better.

I'll say one thing about Myatt, he could be a cunning manager. He got the idea of picking off the runner at third just like you would a runner at first. I had never seen the play before but he pulled it off one time when we were playing Atlanta at Ponce De Leon Park. Ki Ki Cuyler was the Atlanta manager and he was coaching third with a runner on third. Our third baseman cut behind the runner as he breaks off the bag and the pitcher, a lefty, wheels and picks the runner off third. The runner was flat-footed and didn't know what happened. The next day we were sitting in the stands waiting for the rain to stop. Cuyler wanted to know where did that play come from and how we executed it so perfectly with the third baseman breaking and the pitcher wheeling and throwing to the bag before the third baseman ever got there. Myatt said maybe one day he'd tell him how it worked.

As we went into May, I was in a slump hitting only .190 and I wasn't hitting anyone whether they threw right or left. It usually didn't matter which side they threw from, I could usually hit lefties as well as righties. Nobody could figure out why I was struggling. After a tough series in New Orleans, it was said that maybe I was afraid of flying. It's true, I didn't like flying and we had to fly from Atlanta to New Orleans to play, but that didn't have an affect on my hitting. Anyway, a day or two later we faced a lefty and I went 0-for-4 and Myatt decided then he was going to sit me against all lefties. We had another left-handed hitter on the team, Babe Ellis, who wasn't hitting either, but Myatt left Babe in.

I didn't like this one bit. I was in a slump and I knew I couldn't break out if I wasn't playing every day. I confronted Myatt about it and he said he had to play the percentages. I pointed out to Myatt the good average I had against lefties over my career and he wouldn't listen to what I had to say. He said I was going to be benched against lefties and if I didn't like it I could leave.

The next day I got four singles and it was the same day that Johnny Rizzo joined the club from New Orleans. About a week later the club brought up first baseman Bob Reid from New Orleans. A story in the paper said that I might be leaving Chattanooga with Reid reporting to the club. Sure enough, I was told I was heading to Charlotte, which was where I was supposed to have started the season in the beginning.

> *You never did see the Shoals that made sports writers' jaws drop in this year's spring training until his dramatic homer in his last time at bat, two strikes on him, Tuesday night. In Florida he had murdered the ball. He never struck at a bad ball. Not until the last game in Florida was there any inkling of his weakness. It was against Washington, and Sid Hudson and Early Wynn worked on him. They gave him a lot of slow stuff. It worked. But slow stuff hadn't worked on him in previous games, so it was dismissed with a wave of the hand. Just a bad day.*
>
> *Back home, he lost his timing, went for bad balls. He even was sluggish afield. A war-injured foot, which bothered him a little, slowed him up more.*
>
> *Incidentally, a writer friend in the Appalachian League tells me that last year in that loop Muscles hit only .280 the first six weeks; .400 from there out.*
>
> *– Excerpt from*
> *Wirt Gammon's column in*
> *The Chattanooga Times,*
> *May 13, 1948*

Helen and I was in our room packing when there's a knock at the door and it's Myatt. He said Rizzo was sick from food poisoning and he wanted me that night against Little Rock. I was teed off at Myatt, but I knew I had better stick around or my name would be on more blacklists. Along about the fifth inning that night, with a lefty on the mound, I hit one out of the park and we won the game. The next morning Helen and I were headed for Charlotte where I would be on a 24-hour recall. Joe Engel knew I wasn't happy to be leaving. As a matter of fact, I tried to talk Joe into keeping me. But, the roster had to be cut down to 17 and we were at 19 and I couldn't say a whole lot because I was only hitting .222 with three home runs and 15 RBIs. Joe said he pretty much had to go along with what Myatt wanted, after all he was the manager. So Joe told me that if I went, he would see that I'd get a $150-a-month raise. After he told me that, I was ready to see what Charlotte looked like.

I wish things could have worked out at Chattanooga. I looked forward to playing some more in Atlanta's Ponce de Leon Park with those billboards stacked four high in right field where fans could sit on each level. I think it would have made a good target for me and I often wondered if I could have gotten one to go over that fourth row of signs.

Scott Cary, a pitcher who went 3-1 with Washington in 1947, was also assigned from Chattanooga to Charlotte and we joined the Hornets, who were second in the Tri-State League with an 18-13 record behind Asheville at 22-7. The only uniform they had big enough to fit me was No. 13, but I wasn't superstitious. If anything, it turned out to be a rather lucky number. When I got there one of the first players to greet me was Larry Kelchner, Charlotte's shortstop. Larry was from Bethlehem, Pa. and had gone to the University of Georgia on a baseball scholarship and his uncle was Pop Kelchner, who I knew from my Cardinal days.

My first game was a home game at Griffith Park against Florence and in the stands was Washington farm director Ossie Bluege. I didn't get off to a great start as I struck out twice and popped up in my third at bat. Then, in the eighth inning, I hit the first pitch over the right-center field fence, which was 375 feet away and 30 feet high. Ossie came up to me after the game and said, "You hit many more like that and we may have to get you up to Washington." I didn't know if he really meant it or not.

I kept going pretty good and even put together an 11-game hitting streak, but the club wasn't playing all that well.

128

Then I hit a little slump. Joe Bowman, our manager who had played for Pittsburgh, and I got into it one night and I was ready to walk off. Our club was losing bad and when that happens managers look for scapegoats. Bowman had put a midnight curfew in effect on the road. Well, one night in Florence, South Carolina about a half dozen of us came straggling in on the porch of our hotel just five minutes after midnight and Bowman was sitting there keeping watch.

Joe jumped up and wanted to know what I was doing out after curfew. I told him it was only five minutes and what was the big deal. He jumped all over me and didn't say a word to the other five guys who had been out with me. We actually almost came to blows. If it had not been for Rocky Spatacennie, our trainer, who came between us, we might have. I told Joe to shove it and that I was through and I walked off. The next morning I went to the clubhouse to get my belongings and ran into Phil Howser, our business manager.

Phil tried to talk to me and asked me to reconsider leaving. He wanted me to talk with Joe and see if we couldn't iron things out. I cooled down and agreed to stay and talk to Joe. The three of us met and Joe apologized saying that he picked on me specifically the night before because I was a veteran and he thought by targeting me that it might shake up the rest of the guys. Joe and I shook hands and, as I was heading out the door, Phil handed me a $50 bill. I asked him what that was for and he said for taking Joe's apology so gracefully. After that, Joe and I got along great. I guess there's a moral in there somewhere that problems can be ironed out.

But our losing continued. We had been making our road trips on a charter bus and Phil thought maybe we would be better off with our own bus, so he shelled out $4,000 for a blue and white 1948 model bus which we nicknamed "The Blue Goose." But even with the Blue Goose, we didn't play much better, especially when we had to travel to Knoxville and face two guys who I absolutely hated to face – lefty Jim Constable and knuckleball pitcher Hoyt Wilhelm, who would throw that flutterball even on 3-1 and 3-0 counts. We could always expect to see those two pitching. Constable pitched me tight and it took a lot of quickness to get around on him. He just kept the ball in on my knuckles. Of course everyone had trouble with Wilhelm. That ball would flutter up there and you'd swing and be way out in front and that ball would be all over the place. He was tough.

The season seemed to be rolling along when, out of the blue, we were in the middle of a gambling scandal.

I will set up the story by explaining that earlier in the year Bernard DeForge, the pitcher-manager at Reidsville in the Carolina League, and Ed Weingarten, general manager and stockholder with the Florence, S.C. club in the Tri-State League as well as with Leaksville, N.C. of the Blue Ridge League, were banned for life from baseball for gambling. According to George M. Trautman, president of the National Association of Professional Baseball Leagues, DeForge admitted throwing a game between Reidsville and Winston-Salem on May 14. Weingarten played a role in that scandal in setting up the scam in a meeting with DeForge and a gambler by the name of W.C. McWaters.

Winston-Salem, which won the game 5-0, had bets placed that it would win by three runs or more. Supposedly, after all this came out, DeForge had been seen talking with McWaters while warming up before a game. In the game mentioned, Winston-Salem was leading 2-0 going to the eighth inning when DeForge removed pitcher Tal Abernathy and put himself on the mound. DeForge walked four straight and then hurled a wild pitch resulting in two runs. DeForge told Trautman he had received $300 from McWaters.

Anyway, that sent a shockwave through baseball. The day after this became news, Charlotte police chief Frank Littlejohn assigned two detectives to check on reports of alleged betting during the Florence-Charlotte game at Griffith Park on May 16.

There were rumors of huge sums of money passing hands between gamblers and players but the police investigation never turned up anything. I can honestly say that I personally never knew anything about any gambling on our club. And, I would think that if something like that was going on, I would have heard about it. The players might keep it hush-hush from getting outside the clubhouse, but inside the clubhouse it would be hard keeping something like that a secret. But there was gambling going on in the minor leagues and had been for many years. It was just hard to catch somebody at it

The black cloud of a gambling scandal passed and, in the meantime, I began hitting the ball pretty good.

> *Leo Shoals, the minor league journeyman with the barbell biceps, who in three weeks has lifted the Hornets to their highest post-Estallela slugging peak, reached an apex of his own at Griffith Park yesterday afternoon.*
>
> *No matter what The Muscle does of a similarly sensational nature for the remainder of the summer, his 400-foot grandslam home run in the sixth inning to beat the front-running Asheville Tourists, 7 to 4, will probably remain tops in the minds of the 3,016 sweating fans who saw him do it.*
>
> *The blow which lionized Leo was his sixth since he pulled on a Charlotte uniform May 14. It came on the first offering from Asheville's Tom Lakos.*
>
> *Some might argue that the sock which streaked over the Tucker-Kirby sign in right centerfield was the longest home run ever hit in a Tri-State league game here. At any rate, one almost expected to see a jet blast trailing behind it.*
>
> *– Excerpt from story by Eddie Allen in*
> *Charlotte Observer,*
> *June 7, 1948*

Eddie Allen was always giving me those flowery writeups in the paper. I'm glad I gave him reason to. Like the long *double* I had at Griffith Park in an 8-4 win over Florence.

> *The Muscle's mighty maul came with two on in the seventh inning, and if it had been .aimed in almost any other direction it would have gone for his 14th home run. As it was, it crashed against the top deck of the last sign to the right of the green planks in centerfield, a good 425 feet distant. If the Pettit Motor company doesn't feel moved to give Shoals a new Ford for hitting their ad, they can at least award him appropriately for coming through in the "clutch." The blow went only for a double, thanks to the power with which it was tagged and agile retrieving by Oscar Garmendia.*
>
> *– Excerpt from story by Eddie Allen in*
> *Charlotte Observer,*
> *July 13, 1948*

I was hitting the ball so good, in fact, that I was selected on the league's all-star team. The all-stars played the Asheville Tourists, the league leaders, at McCormick Field in Asheville and baseball commissioner Happy Chandler was there. It turned out to be a great game, although the stars lost 6-5, but the Charlotte contingent made a good showing. The stars had 12 hits and six of them were by Hornets as I had three hits, Bobby Deal had two and Sammy Meeks the other. I came close to getting another at bat in the ninth inning. There were two out and I was on deck with Oscar Garmendia at the plate. Oscar sent a screeching liner to right field, which sent Sammy Sporn running back toward a bushy bank. As Sporn reached out with his glove to snare the ball, he fell flat on his back into the bushes, but hung on to the ball for the final out. Boy, I was hoping for one last shot.

The second half of the season was pretty uneventful. I finished the year hitting .287 with 21 home runs and 82 RBIs. One of those home runs, however, almost caused a brawl. We were in Rock Hill, S.C., which isn't far from Charlotte, and I hit a home run to win a game for us. Well, the ball was right down the line and there was no question that it was a home run. I could see it as plain as anybody as I was running down to first. But the fans thought otherwise. Well, the two umpires that day – Red Simpson and Glenn Cooper – met between home and first and both agreed that it was a home run. When they gave the home run signal the fans began throwing eggs, rotten tomatoes and even a golf ball at the umps. The police had to escort the umpires to the dugouts while the Rock Hill club tried to calm the fans down. I often wondered why fans would bring eggs, rotten tomatoes and golf balls to a baseball game unless they were anticipating pelting the umpires or opposing team at some point. Anyway, the Rock Hill club ended up with a $500 fine for the ruckus.

My split season between Chattanooga and Charlotte wasn't the best year I ever had, but I wasn't unhappy. Actually, I was now looking ahead to 1949 and what a year it would be.

Chapter 11

Before the 1949 season, Charlotte and the Senators wanted to get a look at some younger first basemen, so I was the low man out and was sold to Reidsville of the Carolina League for $600. I could see the organization's point. After all, I was 32 years old and that's getting up there for a minor league player. I was no longer a prospect and the fact was Charlotte had some young kids they wanted to put under the test and see if they could hack it.

However, I did make the statement to a reporter for a newspaper at some point later in the season on how I felt being let go by Charlotte and I replied: "I just didn't fit in with their plans. By the way, I see that Charlotte is in seventh place. We're sixth in our league."

I wasn't disappointed to leave Charlotte. When I was younger and not married, Charlotte would have been my kind of town. But I was happily married and didn't carouse around anymore. Well, not nearly as much as I used too. My vice was still a stiff drink now and then. As for changing leagues, the Tri-State and the Carolina were both Class B leagues with the Carolina being a little faster.

Reidsville was a small town of around 12,000 people. Like a lot of towns in North Carolina, it was tobacco which kept Reidsville's economy flourishing and Reidsville's main industry was a Lucky Strike factory. The team itself was independent when I first got there, but in early May it signed a working agreement with the St. Louis Browns. The team was owned by Tom Smothers, who made his fortune operating the tobacco warehouses around town. He also owned an auto dealership. Tommy Clark, the team's business manager and a former newspaperman in Martinsville, kept everything running smoothly. Fittingly enough, our nickname was Luckies.

I liked Tom Smothers. He was someone you could talk to on equal terms. Tom liked to take a nip now and then,

134

which didn't go over good with his wife. In fact, she didn't like me a whole lot because Tom and me would often have a drink together. One time I was supposed to be given an appreciation night at the ballpark and Tom was going to present me with a car. Tom's wife found out about that and put an end to that notion. I wound up getting a set of luggage instead.

Reidsville was a typical rural town of the 1940s. There was a main street and running parallel to Main was Scales Street. It was on Scales that I would get my hair cut at Service Barber Shop, which boasted that it was Reidsville's only air-conditioned barber shop. The Sanitary Café was on Scales and it was a good place to get a bite to eat. Then, if you went shopping for clothes, the place to go was Belk-Stevens.

Also, like many small towns in the deep south, Reidsville had two funeral homes – one for the whites and one for the blacks. I always thought that if you were going to the same place after you died, why did you have to have segregated funeral homes? I lived in a boarding house next to the white funeral home. The family who ran the funeral home lived next door and they had a little boy. I asked him one day how business was going and he said his father was having it a little tough because there weren't enough people dying.

The Luckies played their games at Kiker Stadium, which was on the opposite side of town to where I lived. I usually took a cab to the game and by the time it got to the stadium there would be a load of kids we'd pick up along the way. The cabbie would never want to stop, but I'd tell him to pick up the kids. I remembered how it was being a kid back in West Virginia and seeing those ballplayers, who I looked up to. I'm sure these kids felt the same way.

Kiker Stadium sat in some bottom land and it was where the Reidsville High School team played its football games. There was a wooden scoreboard in right and behind the scoreboard was a high clay bank. There were cement

I was usually a picture of concentration before I batted.
(Photo courtesy of Sholes family)

bleachers on the third base side and a covered wooden grandstand on the first base side. There were two entrances to Kiker – one on Morehead Street and the other on Franklin Street. I always had the cabbie let me off at the Morehead entrance because it was closer to our clubhouse behind the left field fence.

Kiker would be my home for the 1949 season. Around the league the Burlington Bees played at Elon College's park; the Danville Leafs at League Park; the Raleigh Capitals at Devereux Meadow; the Winston-Salem Cardinals at Southside Park; the Martinsville Athletics at English Field; the Greensboro Patriots at Memorial Stadium; and the Durham Bulls at Durham Athletic Park.

I got very familiar with Kiker Stadium because we even held our spring training right there. Not everybody went to sunny Florida to get in shape. Burlington and Greensboro trained in Bartow, Florida, Raleigh in Titusville while Martinsville went to Moultrie, Georgia and Winston-Salem to Albany, Georgia. Us, Durham and Danville did our training at home.

The Luckies were a group of older players and, in all honesty, we weren't that good. We had some pretty darn good hitters as we led the Carolina League in hitting in '49 with a .278 team average. But our pitching was horrible. Other than Mike Forline, who went 19-9 that year, we just didn't have anybody who could get outs.

We'd lose games 12-11, 14-13, 9-8. We hit the devil out of the ball, but so did the other clubs against us. We went 63-80, but we didn't finish last thanks to Martinsville, which outdid us 52-92. Some guy wrote a letter to the paper one time requesting the paper print the standings upside down so his Luckies could be at the top just once. We were so bad we couldn't keep managers around. Johnny George began the season as our manager, as well as our catcher but, on May 2, he was released after a 2-7 start and George Souter, our third baseman, took over.

Souter and I were about the same age. He was a real quiet fellow. George never had a whole lot to say. He was a student of the game though. If you were doing something wrong at the plate, like uppercutting on the ball or jerking the bat, George could spot it right off. I always went to George when I started having problems and he'd usually find a little hitch that I may have developed in my swing.

But George didn't want to manage and he told Tom Smothers. So Tom contacted the Browns and the Browns came up with a third baseman in their farm system by the name of Harry Hatch. So, eight days after Souter took over the reins of the club, he gave them up to Hatch.

> *"Nothing cocky about Shoals at all. He is a small team player and does not have a big head at all. I am glad he is on our club and the Reidsville fans like him a lot, but those folks in Danville, Greensboro, Raleigh, Winston-Salem, Durham, Burlington and Martinsville shouldn't expect good old Muscles to hit one out of the lot every time he comes up."*
> *– Harry Hatch,*
> *Charlotte Observer,*
> *July 1, 1949*

We didn't play well for Harry, just like we didn't play well for any of our managers. But poor old Harry, things just didn't go his way sometimes. Like the time we were in Durham for a two-game series. We were leading the first game of that series when Harry decides to walk Ralph Caldwell to load the bases to get to Earl Richmond. Richmond proceeds to smack a double off the wall to clear the bases as Durham scored six runs for the win.

Well, the very next night we were tied with Durham at 2-2 in the last of the seventh inning. There were two outs, but Durham had runners on second and third. Lefty Merkle was pitching for us and Harry told Merkle to walk Jack Graham to load the bases to get to Barney Cook, Durham's pitcher. On the surface that seemed like a good move until

Barney smacked a 400-foot double to clear the bases and give the Bulls a 6-2 win.

So, on July 23, Zip Payne, who had managed the past three years at Winston-Salem and who was managing Fayetteville of the Tri-State League earlier in that 1949 season, replaced Harry as manager and finished out the season. Zip had had some kind of operation and was out of baseball at the time, but he had recovered and we were lucky to get Zip who had a pretty good reputation as a manager.

We had a hard-hitting lineup in Reidsville with Dick Sipek, left, George Souter, center, and myself.
(Photo by Raleigh News and Observer. Courtesy of North Carolina Department of Cultural Resources)

We may not have been very good on the field, but we had a great bunch of fellows on that team. It was a fun club to be with. Of course back then we had a roster of only 17, so you got to know one another pretty good.

I might explain, too, that while we had 17 active players, we also had 10 "under control" players who were not active. The "under control" players were those who were disabled, suspended, temporarily inactive or on option.

A few of the guys I still keep in contact with – like Cart Howerton. Cart still lives in North Carolina. Cart was under contract to the Browns, but he was unassigned and was

139

playing semipro ball for Hertford, N.C. of the Albemarle League. Cart didn't get to Reidsville until early August. He was a lot younger than most of us other fellows. He was a left-handed hitter and he was a hustler if there ever was one. He wanted to win and he took it hard when we didn't.

Glenn Rawlinson was our second baseman, a scrappy player. He was our leadoff hitter most of the time but ended up hitting only .235. It seemed like he was always on base though. Late in the year we were at home against Martinsville and Glenn must have had the best day of his career. In the first game of a doubleheader he had two hits and in the second game picked up four more. There was another doubleheader that Glenn hit a grand slam home run in each of the games and everybody started calling him "Little Muscle."

"Muscle Shoals could hit the ball further than any hitter I've ever seen. Fans used to come out just for batting practice to watch him hit. The biggest crowds around the league was when Reidsville came into a town and that was because of Muscle. I played with Muscle in 1949 and I played against him in 1950 when I was with Raleigh.

"I remember one time, and I don't know who we were playing, but I was on first and Muscle was up. If you went by the book, a bunt would have been in order. Well, I doubt Muscle ever bunted in his life. But the opposing manager was going by the book despite it being Muscle at the plate. The manager told the first baseman to play in for the bunt on the grass. I heard the first baseman let out a stream of cuss words. He turned around and told his manager that if he wanted someone to play in on Muscle, then why don't he come out and do it. Can you imagine playing in on the grass with Muscle

batting up there left-handed? If he hit a line drive towards that first baseman, it would have killed him."

– Glenn Rawlinson,
second baseman, Reidsville

Our right fielder was James Miller, a steady ballplayer, who was real quiet and kept to himself. But a likeable fellow. Our center fielder was Dick Sipek. Dick was a real good athlete. One of the friendliest guys you'd ever want to meet. He overcame a lot of obstacles, the biggest one being the fact he was a deaf mute. I got attached to Dick. I even learned some sign language, so that I could communicate with him.

But imagine a guy like that playing baseball and he played the game well. Dick was a left-handed batter, he walked bow-legged, but he was fast. He led our Reidsville team in hitting in 1949 with a .321 average and for a little guy, he was only 5-9, had surprising power, hitting 14 home runs. Dick set a Carolina League record with eight straight hits, breaking the record of 7-for-7 by Winston-Salem's Louis Sanders set in 1945.

It's a real testimony to Dick that in 1945, as the war was ending, he got called up to the Cincinnati Reds. Dick didn't let his handicap stop him from his goal of playing professional baseball. He was a fine example and a role model for a lot of people who had handicaps.

"It's hard for me to write because I have had surgery on my hand. But I remember in 1949 we had a good team. Wow! Muscle Shoals could hit the ball over the fence and made it look so easy. He was a slugger and he was such a nice guy. He was extremely nice to me. We even communicated in sign language. Nobody will ever beat his home run records in the Carolina League."

Robert Denson, who also went by Alton, was our shortstop and we had John Morris at third and a great catcher in Charles Ferrell, who was with Raleigh in '48. Charles was the nephew of Wes Ferrell who spent 15 years pitching in the big leagues. Wes, who was managing at Greensboro, wasn't a bad hitter either. In 1948, he played and managed at Marion in the Western Carolina League and ended up hitting .432, which was the second highest average in organized baseball that season. Wes didn't last the season at Greensboro. The papers came out and said that Wes resigned, but Wes said he was fired. Either way, he was out.

As for Charlie, who we signed when Johnny George was released, we hung out together quite a bit. Charlie, who had already played for three other teams in the Carolina League – Burlington in 1945, Durham in 1947 and Raleigh in 1948 – was a diabetic. He had told me once that his uncle Wes had spent a lot of money on him, sending him to hospitals trying to find out what was wrong before his disease was diagnosed.

We'd be riding the bus after a game and Charlie would pull out his diabetic kit and load up that needle with insulin and jab it in his arm. He'd say, "Boys, I'm going to have me a big steak and a couple of brews when we get back to town." I got a kick out of Charlie the way he jabbed that needle in his arm. I called him "The Shot Man". He had a good sense of humor. I used to get Christmas cards from him signed by "The Shot Man."

One night we were playing in Raleigh and we were taking infield before the game. Charlie came toward the dugout staggering. If you didn't know better, you'd say he was drunk, but we all knew what was going on. A couple of us led him down the steps to the bench, stuck a bottle of Coca-Cola to his lips, got him to drink some and he raised right up. Turned out he had taken too much insulin and I guess getting out there in the hot sun made him have a reaction.

Another time, we were in a restaurant in Danville. A couple of us had gotten up to play the jukebox and the waitress yelled at us to come over quick. Charlie had slumped over on the counter. We got the sugar bowl and put some in his mouth. He came right out of it.

I got off to a good start in 1949. Opening day we were at home in Kiker Stadium playing Martinsville in front of over 1,700 fans. I hit a home run off a guy named Neidowicz. Bob Downing and Bill Howell had three hits each for us and Melvin "Lefty" Adams hurled a four-hitter.

We were all happy with that first win, but things went sour very quickly. We lost our next six games. In our third game we didn't have a hit against Danville's Rob Twarkins going into the ninth. Then, with one out in the ninth, Jim Miller pinch hit for our pitcher Red Gardner and got a single.

Where Kiker Stadium once stood is now an empty field. Notice the bank that once was behind right field is still there.

(Photo by George Stone)

143

The next day I hit a home run, but Danville scored seven runs in the sixth to beat us 10-7. The next night against Raleigh at Kiker I got four hits, including a home run, but we lost 7-6 in 10 innings. We then hit the bottom of the standings in a 19-9 loss to Durham in a game in which we got 17 hits off Jerry Sheehan, who went all the way.

So, off to a 1-6 start, we were glad to see some rain come in Durham so that we could head back home for a day off to collect our senses. We were back at Kiker and hoping to change our luck, but it was damp and cold and the construction on a new $8,300 roof to cover the grandstand was still under way so it was a mess at the stadium. I still wasn't hitting the ball like I should have been. Take away my 4-for-5 and I was hitting only .200.

But we finally got our second win by beating Winston-Salem 3-2. I scored the winning run in the eighth inning. I walked, Miller singled and Johnny George singled me home. It's ironic that George got the winning hit because it was the next day that he was let go.

No one ever said it didn't rain in Carolina. For four days it rained. Too bad it didn't keep raining, because in our first game after having the rainouts, I went 0-for-5 in a doubleheader at Greensboro, both losses of course. I went 0-for-4 the next day at Martinsville in a game we lost 14-2 in which we were tied 2-2 as late as the seventh inning.

Martinsville manager George Staller, who had a cup of coffee as an outfielder with the Philadelphia Athletics in 1943 and had managed Portsmouth, Ohio in 1948, hit a home run down the left field line. Everyone knew it was out of the park, but it was just a matter of whether it would go fair or foul. The umpire ruled it fair and Red Gardner, who wasn't even pitching for us in the game, went berserk in the dugout. Red went charging out onto the field and went nose-to-nose with the umpire, whose last name was Rich. A couple of our guys had to drag Red back to the dugout, after he was ejected of course.

I finally ended an 0-for-9 string against the Athletics with a single, but we still got beat. As a matter of fact, we

144

sent three pitchers to the mound in the first inning as Martinsville scored eight runs and 11 batters reached base before the first out. Remember what I said about our pitching being bad? I wasn't lying.

Souter, who had taken over for George, must have wondered what he had gotten into.

We went back home to meet Danville in the first of two games and I had a hit in my second straight game. That may not sound like a big deal, but the way I was swinging the bat a two-game hitting streak was monumental. We outhit the Leafs 17-10, Bob Downing hit a grand slam in the ninth and had six RBIs for the game and guess what – we got beat 11-10.

Danville's leading the league at 12-4 and they didn't hurt themselves any the next night at Kiker Stadium. We lost 8-3, but I extended my hitting streak to three games and did it with my fourth home run, a two-run shot off Fred Guilliani.

I had finally stopped my 0-fors, but now we'd lost seven straight. I wasn't having a whole lot of fun.

Chapter 12

In 1988 there was a movie called *Bull Durham* starring Kevin Costner as a character named Crash Davis. I thought it was a pretty good movie. It showed minor league life pretty much as it was. I can't say from experience whether guys and gals got together in the clubhouse like the movie showed. However, there was one fellow, who I won't name, he got caught in an embarrassing situation with a girl one night in the dugout. He thought everyone was gone, but George Souter was still in the clubhouse and caught the two. Nothing happened. George just told the player to lock the gate when he left.

But I was talking about Crash Davis. A lot of people think that's a fictional character, but there really was a Crash Davis. Now the Crash Davis in the movie and the Crash Davis I knew didn't have a whole lot in common.

The Hollywood Crash Davis had spent his entire baseball life in the minor leagues waiting for his shot at "The Show." The real Crash Davis played from 1940 to 1942 with the Philadelphia Athletics.

If Crash could have just hit, he would have stayed a long time in the majors. Crash was the best second baseman I ever saw, bar none. I don't believe the ball ever touched his glove on a double play. At 6-feet and around 175-pounds, he was pretty big for a second baseman, but he was as agile and smooth as a little man. He would make the quick pivot at second and make the quick throw to first and he had pretty good speed.

Of course, Crash wasn't his real name, but it stuck to him better than Lawrence. Crash came back to the Carolina League after his release from service signing with Durham in 1948 and hung around until 1952, when he finished up with Raleigh. Crash was from somewhere down in Georgia called Canon, which is east of Atlanta, and moved to Gastonia, North Carolina early in his childhood. One time I asked

Crash how he got his nickname and he told me that there was a comic strip called "Freckles" and some kid said that he resembled the character Crash in that strip.

Crash had played college ball at Duke University under the legendary Jack Coombs and then went on to serve in World War II.

I don't know what Crash hit against us in 1949, but it seemed every time Raleigh and Reidsville played, Crash was always scoring a run or driving somebody in. It seemed like I was always having a conversation with Crash at first base. But like everybody who plays the game, he did have a little slump when we were playing a series against Raleigh. Crash was in a 1-for-10 funk and I said, "Crash old buddy, you've hit the skids haven't you? Think maybe you're over the hill?"

The next day Raleigh was making its second trip into Kiker and in the first game we get beat for the eighth straight time, 5-4, losing in 10 innings as Crash doubled in the winning run. As Crash ran by me he said, "Still think I'm over the hill Muscle?" Of course, I never thought he was over the hill.

Crash was a competitor on the field, but was such a nice guy off the field. We had our battles, but when we were able we sometimes got together after games and talked baseball. I still see Crash now and then when we have our old timer reunions. He's always trying to get me on the golf course just so he can beat me.

"Muscle was the most powerful hitter I have ever seen. No question. He was simply a great hitter. As a second baseman, I respected his power so much that I would play him deep and to the left. I mean way back, almost to the grass. Those shots he hit would come up on you so quickly. If you played Muscle as you did other hitters, you more often than not couldn't react to the shots hit at you.

"Muscle was a unique character, too. I played in the major leagues and I had the opportunity to play against Ted Williams. There are two players who, when they came out to take batting practice, everyone else would stop what they were doing just to watch. One was Ted and the other was Muscle. When they got through taking their licks, then everybody would go back to whatever they were doing before.

"I don't know why Muscle never made it to the majors. The money they paid major league players wasn't like it was now. When we were playing, you made about as much money playing in the Carolina League as you did playing in the majors. I made $3,000 with Philadelphia and that wasn't much more than I made with the Caps.

"I just know that when I played with Muscle in that 1949 season, he was the terror of the league. He was well coordinated with good, quick hands. He had no weaknesses that I ever saw. He had all the attributes of a great hitter. And not only could he hit, but he was probably the best fielding first baseman around. You would take a look at his build and think no way, but he was sure-handed and had good feet around the bag.

"More than anything about Muscle that I will always remember, more than the home runs, was the type of guy he was. You see a big guy like that and you'd think he'd be as mean as a snake, but Muscle would give you the shirt off his back.

– Crash Davis,
second baseman, Raleigh

Our losing streak went to nine the next night in a game we lost 8-1 and my troubles continued as I went 0-for-3 and now I was 13-for-56. But, we didn't lose our ninth straight without a fight, literally. I don't know what precipitated it, but Raleigh outfielder Tom Martin was at the plate and I saw him step out of the box and start jawing with our catcher Charlie Ferrell.

Charlie gets up out of his crouch, slings off the mask and the next thing I know the two are trading punches. The home plate umpire, a little fellow, was trying to break it up as I ran in from first to keep them from killing each other. Both Martin and Charlie got tossed from the game. After the game I asked Charlie what happened to cause the fight and Charlie said, "When that SOB stepped into the box, the first thing he said was that Reidsville was the most pathetic team he'd ever seen. I didn't have to take that crap."

We had a rainout the next day to help cool the tempers, but news was made for the Luckies as for the third time in the season we had a new manager. Souter stepped aside as Hatch took over. Not much was made of the change. George just didn't want to manage. We had several war vets and one of the more decorated was Harry. Harry, who had spent a couple of years playing for San Antonio in the Texas League, was in the Marines and saw lots of action in the Pacific, including Iwo Jima. Harry received the Purple Heart, two Presidential Unit Citations and the Asiatic Pacific Ribbon with four battle stars.

The rains were relentless and we had a second straight rainout. To get back to Bull Durham, there's one scene where some of the players turn on the water hose one night to soak the field so they could have a night off. Nothing like that ever happened with us. For one, Mother Nature was doing it for us, and two, we wanted to play.

The only time I recall players using a water hose was the time when I was with Albuquerque and we were staying at the Copper Queen Hotel in Bisbee which, by the way, had the longest bar in the world that was a block long. Anyway, the players took a waterhose that hung in the hotel hallway and stretched it down the hall to the room of some old fellow who had been complaining about us making noise.

One of the guys got on a chair, another poked that hose through a window up over the door and another player knocked on the door. When the old fellow stepped to the door to see who was there, another of our guys turned the water on and the guy got soaked. We also got kicked out of the hotel because when the guy came to the door, our guys ran and left the water running and the water began dripping on the floor below.

I was swinging a pretty good bat back in 1949 for Reidsville.
(Photo courtesy of Sholes family)

But the two rainouts were what the doctor ordered. We were back at Kiker and ended our nine-game losing streak beating Durham 8-4 in Hatch's managerial debut. In the process, we stopped Durham's six-game win streak. Mike Forline threw a complete game eight-hitter and I hit my fifth home run coming off Eddie Neville.

Then, for the first time on the year, we won our second straight. Harry must have been feeling good about the job he was doing as manager. He was undefeated at 2-0. We beat Durham 10-9 in 10 innings as Lew Hester, a left-hander, pitched the 10th inning for the win. As for me, I had two hits, both home runs. The first was a three-run shot in our five-run fifth and I won the game with a solo home run in the bottom of the 10th. It was too bad I wasn't wearing a Durham uniform. Joe Robbins, who owned Robbins Department Store in Durham, had a sign to the right of the scoreboard in right field and he gave away $15 to a left-handed batter who could hit the sign and $25 to a right-hander. I know during the course of the season I hit that sign at least twice. Beyond right field was the Uzzle Motor Company building and I hit one up on the roof.

Anyway, Lew's appearance was his first of the year and the night before he got a standing ovation when he came out to coach first base. Lew was selected the MVP of the Carolina League in 1948 after he had won 25 games for a seventh-place team. Lew was sold to Baltimore of the International League, but came back to Reidsville just a few days before the night he coached. The fans worshiped Lew and we hoped he could regain the form that won 25 games in '48.

We're rolling now. Two in a row and I'm hitting the ball, so chalk up win number three in a row. It was a typical game for us. We're in Burlington for a doubleheader and we won the first game 17-16. Funny, but with all the runs we scored, I was 0-for-2. We came back down to earth as our little streak ended 8-4 in the second game.

Tom Smothers felt we needed some help so he was able to purchase pitcher Mike Dattero and shortstop Alton Denson from San Antonio of the Texas League. We also picked up Donald Pope, a first baseman, from Springfield of the 3-I League. I don't really know what old Tom was thinking in getting a first baseman, since I was there. I guess he just wanted insurance.

"That 1949 season Muscle was hitting every pitcher. It didn't matter whether it was a fastball, curveball or what, he was hitting the ball hard. In my opinion, Muscle should have been playing in a higher league. Boy, could that guy rip 'em down the right side. I remember one time I reached first base and Muscle comes up. The manager tells the first baseman to play back on the grass, as if he had to. At the same time I yell over to our dugout and ask if it was OK if I played back too.

"He had those huge arms and shoulders. He was a lot older than most of us. I was only 20 or 21. The thing I recall about Muscle, other than his power of course, was that he was such a nice fellow. He never showed anger. He kept to himself a lot, of course that was because he was married and most of us other guys were single, but everyone liked Muscle.

– Alton Denson,
shortstop, Reidsville

We put together another three-game win streak and I had hit my eighth home run. I was still struggling though. I was only three for my last 16 at bats, but then I began to take off. In a 6-0 win over Winston-Salem, Forline had a complete game victory and I hit my ninth home run.

The next day we went to Durham for a twinbill and in the first game we won 22-6. I went 6-for-6 and was one hit shy of the Carolina League record for most hits in a game. But the seventh time up, I didn't get anything close to the plate and ended up getting a walk. But my batting line was: AB 6, R 5, H 6, RBI 5. I also had a double that night. Then, after that game, what do I do? I go 0-for-3 in the second game, which we lost 11-5 as Durham scored eight runs in the

152

third inning. I remember Ed Komisarek hitting a 425-foot triple off the Cary Lumber Company sign in center field. I also recall our catcher that night, John Morris, getting thrown out of the game when he argued a call with umpire Bill Hearn. Morris didn't like one of Hearn's calls so John kicked dirt on the plate. Hearn pulled out his brush, dropped it on the plate and told John to brush it off or he was out of the game. John took the early shower.

We fell to 10-21, losing 5-4 to Durham as the Bulls scored twice in the bottom of the ninth in the third game of the series. We then moved on to Burlington where, in 1948, the Luckies won just one game there at Elon Park. We got beat the first game, but Forline, who was pitching outstanding for us, had another complete game and we won 14-5 over the Bees in what they called the "Bee Hive." We had made a visit to Burlington right after Tal Abernathy, a left-handed pitcher for the Bees who would move over to Greensboro later in the year, had been fined for throwing a ball out of the park in Raleigh after getting upset over a call. Tal was an easy-going type and he apologized to his teammates and promised to buy each one a $2 steak if he was ever fined again. After that, every time that Tal would go to the mound against us we would start razzing him. "Hey, it's Tal pitching. Come on guys, let's put some steaks on the grill."

We were just hoping to get our record up to the .500 mark and we were making progress, but not enough. We were still trying to bolster our roster. We had added Dattero and Denson and we sold Okey Flowers, a right-handed pitcher, to Tyler, Texas and Earl "Snake" Norton, who occasionally caught for us, was optioned to Kinston of the Coastal Plains League.

We had been playing without Charlie Ferrell who was hurt and on the disabled list for 10 days. Charlie came back and we added Harold McKinley, a right-handed pitcher, who came from Springfield, Illinois of the 3-I League.

Our pitching was actually starting to look pretty good. At least it was looking better. Lefty Adams gave us a boost when he beat Martinsville 8-1 on a one-hitter as Antonio Campos spoiled what would have been a no-hitter with a first-inning single.

At the end of May and the first of June, it seemed as if the home runs were flying out of the parks at a rapid pace. We swept Raleigh in a twinbill and I had a home run off Gene Kelly in the fifth inning. It went 365 feet over the right field fence. We lost the next day to Raleigh, but I hit another home run and on June 1 we beat Greensboro 9-8 and I had two home runs.

> *"It seems I saw a lot of Muscle's home runs going over my head. One night at the stadium he had already hit two home runs and then he hit a line drive and I caught the ball against the fence. It was in my glove, but the umpire said that the ball hit the fence first and then hit my glove. I know one thing, it just about took my hand off and then about knocked the fence down."*
>
> *– Emo Showfety,*
> *outfielder, Greensboro*

That's me on the right signing autographs alongside Crash Davis.
(Photo courtesy of Sholes family)

The next night we couldn't buy a run as Greensboro's Luis Arroyo held us to five hits in an 11-0 loss at Kiker. Arroyo was a starting pitcher, but he later earned his fame as a relief pitcher for the New York Yankees from 1960 to 1963. He led the American League in saves in '61 with 29. But Luis was a crafty left-hander. He had some mean pitches even back in '49. Luckily for us he wasn't around the league too long.

Maybe one of the best athletes overall in the league was Chuck Hummell of Martinsville. Chuck was a former Penn State fullback who led them in the Cotton Bowl one year. I got on a roll in early June where I hit home runs in three straight games and one of them was off Hummell, a two-run job in a 6-2 loss in which he three-hit us.

The second home run of the streak was off Martinsville's Archie Templeton and the third came at Devereux Meadow in Raleigh off Chuck Cronin. The writers there were saying that it was the longest home run ever hit in the Meadow. There were two fences in right field and the ball cleared them both and landed in the parking lot.

> *"The strategy we always used in pitching to Muscle was to pitch him away and to change up on him as often as we could. Most of our pitchers didn't have a lot of trick pitches back then, but they would throw him slow curves and offspeed stuff so that he would have to supply the power, which he often was able to do. Muscle was so hard to pitch to."*
>
> *– Earle Brucker,*
> *catcher, Martinsville*

The next day Souter hit a two-run home run to beat Raleigh 3-2. George and I were keeping pretty good company in the home run hitting department. He had hit his 15th and I had 18. George had more RBIs than I did at that point – 49 to 39 – and I was just a few points ahead of him in

155

batting – .329 to .322. So I guess it was appropriate that we hit back-to-back home runs in a 14-4 win over Durham as we were still trying to get our record somewhere close to .500. We now stood at 19-28.

> *Reidsville batting power broke loose again last night as the Reidsville Luckies defeated the Durham Bulls 14-4. The Luckies rapped three Durham hurlers for 17 hits as third baseman George Souter batted in seven runs with two doubles and a home run.*
>
> *The "Boom Boom Boys," Souter and Shoals, put on their old one-two act as they hit consecutive homers in the fifth inning.*
>
> *Souter's blow, which sailed over the right-center field fence, was his 15th of the season. Shoals' roundtripper was "a mile high and a mile long" over the right field scoreboard.*
>
> *– The Reidsville Review,*
> *June 11, 1949*

We went on to win two more games and our record was up to 21-28 with a 5-2 win over Winston-Salem at Kiker. I went 0-for-4 as Hal McKinley had a four-hitter and Souter hit his third grand slam of the year. I guess we just couldn't stand success though. We dropped a pair in Winston-Salem and another against Greensboro. We're back at 10-under .500 at 21-31.

One good thing about us losing was that not many people were listening to us on the radio. Back during the winter the Carolina League directors voted to place a ban on radio broadcasts figuring that broadcasting the games was costing them at the gate, which was stupid thinking. Danville and Reidsville were the two clubs instrumental in leading this fight against radio broadcasts. But later, the league lifted the ban, which they had no right in enforcing anyway.

But Tommy Clark, our business manager, was totally against the broadcasts. However, the pressure was on him to allow the radio broadcasts to continue and he said OK, but that no broadcast would be permitted at Kiker Stadium until after 9 p.m. About halfway through the season Danville said no to radio and so did Martinsville.

Radio or no radio we weren't playing well. Maybe it was just as well that our pathetic play at times wasn't broadcast all over the state. The one thing we had to put up with wherever we went were the fans giving us a hard time asking us if we wanted to place a bet. The way we played sometimes people would yell at us wanting to know if we lost on purpose. It may have looked like that sometimes, but we never lost on purpose. Of course all that went back to the year before with that betting scandal. I must admit, sometimes that talk got under my skin, but I tried to block it out.

But, tomorrow's another day.

Chapter 13

If you look at most home run hitters, they get into streaks. Long spells where they don't hit home runs and then, all of a sudden, they go on a binge. I got into one of my hotter streaks when I hit those three home runs in Greensboro. Over a seven-day period that included those three, I had a total of five home runs. Actually, one of those days was a rainout, so I guess you could say I had five home runs in six days.

I don't know why I got hot. Maybe it was because the weather had been a little cool and now it was just beginning to turn warm. I felt good. I felt loose. I felt confident when I stepped to the plate. It's funny, you get in a groove like that and it seems everything that comes up you can hit. Then, there are those times they could throw a basketball up there and you'd swing and miss.

I know when I hit those three home runs that night at Greensboro, it didn't seem like that big of a deal to me. I was just glad to be swinging the bat good.

The headline in the paper the next day said: **SHOALS CAN SET NEW LOOP HOMER RECORD.** It was only June 13, there were still two and a half months left in the season and they were talking about me going for Gus Zernial's record of 41. I didn't think much of it before that. I wasn't concerned with records. I didn't know Zernial had the record. Heck, I didn't even know what the record was. But when all the talk started, I admit I got a little interested.

We split a twinbill with Danville at Kiker, winning the second game 3-0 as Forline had a five-hit shutout and I helped him with my 23rd home run. While the home runs seemed to fly off my bat, we were winning. We swept Burlington in a twinbill and a couple days later we beat Winston-Salem in a doubleheader as I went 6-for-7 with my 26th homer coming off Goose Gosselin. All of a sudden, we were looking at .500 with a 30-33 record.

Remember we were talking about streaks? Well, just as the home runs seem to be coming, the well went dry just as quickly. From June 21 to July 2, I didn't hit a single home run. That was nine games. I was still getting my share of hits (8-for-28), but just wasn't hitting the long ball. I collected my 27th home run on June 20 and my 28th and 29th home runs came on July 3 as we beat Martinsville 16-4.

Charlie Ferrell had a pair of home runs that night and Ray Hardee, who started the season pitching for Danville, picked up his first win with us after signing just a few days before.

On July 4 we had Martinsville at Kiker for a day-night doubleheader. I wasn't too fond of that. You'd play in the afternoon, leave and come back to play a night game. I went 0-for-4 in the day game and 0-for-3 in the night game. We had gotten within two games of .500 before dropping those two. The All-Star break was approaching and we wanted to get to .500 before then. As a team, it would have been a great morale booster to start the second half at .500 after being so far down.

We split a twinbill in Winston-Salem, losing the second game 9-0 as a kid pitcher we had by the name of Hernandez went into the stands after a fan. It's a wonder he didn't get killed and I don't know why he didn't get thrown out, but he came back in to pitch three innings. I don't remember his first name, but he didn't speak any English so I'm not sure what he heard that got him upset. But as he was leaving the mound at the end of an inning he started running toward the stands, jumped in and went after some guy. Several of our boys were right behind and drug him out before the fracas got out of hand and somebody got hurt. The kid wasn't with us long after that.

We won our last three games before the break and stood at 37-40 following a 19-3 win over Durham. I went 4-for-5, but was overshadowed by Dick Sipek who went 6-for-6 with two doubles and an inside-the-park home run. We followed that with a 4-0 win over Durham and finished the first half with a 10-4 win over Greensboro. We were 39-40 at the break. It wasn't .500, but it was close enough.

The next evening was the Carolina League All-Star Game in Danville. That place was packed with 5,337 fans. Without a doubt the biggest crowd I'd seen all year. The All-Star Game was a nice touch and I was honored to be picked.

The way the game worked was that Danville was leading the league, so it hosted the game and the Danville team would play another team made up of the league's all-stars.

Danville had a pretty darn good team and was managed by Woody Fair. They had guys like Bill Brown, who would eventually end up leading the league in hitting with a .361 average. Fair at shortstop hit .325, Hugh Taylor was one of the best catchers I'd seen in some time, Bill Nagel was at third and a tough pitching staff led by Adam Twarkins and Pete Angell. Twarkins would win 22 games and sport an earned run average of 2.07, while Angell would win 20 games.

Fair was the one who made that club go. Woody came to the Carolina League in 1946 and set it on fire with 161 RBIs, 161 runs scored and had 52 doubles while batting .349. Woody had left the Carolina League to manage his hometown Carthage, Missouri club of the Kansas-Missouri-Ohio League in 1947, but quit midway through and went to Winston-Salem to finish out the year.

In 1948, with Danville, he hit .336 with 29 home runs and that came while missing a month after breaking a bone in his leg. If not for that, Woody might have broken Zernial's home run record. Woody, a quiet person, was a swell guy and a great player.

The all-stars went into League Park and the Leafs did a number on us. We got shut out 2-0 as Twarkins, Angell and Fred Guilliani held us to just three hits. I played three innings and went 0-for-2. We made two errors in the first inning when they scored both of their runs. The rest of the way it was nothing but goose eggs. Believe it or not, we played the game in one hour and 23 minutes. After the sixth inning, we had a rain delay, which was about that long, of one hour and eight minutes.

But, we had fun and that's what all-star games are for. We especially had fun with the home run hitting contest before the game. There were 10 players in the contest – five from the Leafs and five from the league, including me. We were hitting against Danville right-hander Thump Lowe. Each batter was to get five fair-hit balls and the man hitting the longest ball was the winner and would get a check for $15.

Earle Brucker creamed a pitch into a clump of trees about 50 feet beyond the right field fence, which was 303 feet from home plate. Brucker ended up with three home runs. Bill Nagel followed with one, Jim Halkard was next and didn't get any out, the same with Woody Fair. Emo Showfety came up and hit one about 10 feet behind the 363 mark in left center. It was a wallop.

Willie Duke followed and didn't get one out, Carl Linhardt hit one over the scoreboard about 345 feet away and Bill Brown hit a line drive off the scoreboard in right. Then it was my turn. I had got to the park late, along with George Souter, and missed batting practice. I got two warmup swings against Lowe. I missed the first couple of pitches and then I hit two balls over the right field fence and a third hit the fence.

The $15 went to Emo for his long drive. Emo picked up a few more dollars as we had a friendly wager among us as to who would hit the longest ball. I'm not sure how much Emo walked off with, but it was more than the $15. I guess you might say we were betting, but it was all friendly and nothing under the table. Nobody ever said anything to us about it, so I guess it was OK.

Everyone had the day off after the all-star game but I, for one, was ready to get to playing again. After winning our final three games before the break, I was anxious to get back out and pick up where we left off.

But we just couldn't seem to get over the hump. Whatever momentum we had, we lost. First game back we

161

fell to Raleigh 5-1. Raleigh had only five hits, but three were home runs by Don Siegert. I hit my 30th off Charlie Miller, but that was my last one before we went on a 0-6 skid and dropped to 39-46.

We couldn't seem to get a break. We had lost four straight and were at Kiker against Danville. I had a decent day, going 3-for-3, but we lost 5-0. In the game I was on second and Angell whirled around to try and pick me off. Eddie Gallagher was playing shortstop for the Leafs and he comes running over to cover the bag. I get back, the throw comes from Angell and it gets past Gallagher and goes about four or five feet past the bag. Well, the umpire, a guy named Staley, called me out. I couldn't believe it. I was too stunned to move.

Harry comes running out of the dugout screaming and carrying on at Staley and calling him every name in the book. He was so red in the face I thought he was going to have a stroke. He didn't win the argument and got thrown out of the game to boot.

Shoals is just as greatly respected by Carolina League umpires as by the pitchers, largely because he is hardly ever known to raise a howl over a call. It's easy to work behind him, the arbiters say, because nine times out of ten when Shoals doesn't swing, the ball isn't over.

Shoals is always the gentleman on the field, a genuinely affable fellow who hasn't got any enemies, except for several hundred pitchers around the minor leagues.

– The Raleigh News and Observer,
August 31, 1949

Fortunately our losing streak ended when we beat Greensboro 5-4 in 13 innings exactly nine days after we had won our last game. I didn't win the game with a dramatic

162

home run, but I did have a two-run single in the top of the 13th which made me just as happy.

Harry drew a bases-loaded walk to give us a 5-2 lead and it's a good thing he did because the Pats scored twice in the bottom of the 13th and we came close to losing our seventh in a row.

But we suffered a bad loss of a different kind as Bob Downing fractured his leg sliding into second. Bob was hitting .307 at the time with seven home runs. I think he had hurt the ankle before that when he rammed into the fence trying for Ed Ellis' triple. Anyway, Souter moved from third to the outfield and Harry Hatch took over at third.

> *"Boy, I remember that like it was yesterday. Luis Arroyo was on the mound for Greensboro. I slid into second breaking my leg. I remember Muscle being one of the first ones out there to see how I was. He was such a nice fellow.*
>
> *"We had this black fellow who drove our bus and he was also the one who made sure we had our uniforms ready before a game. But, he also made sure we had a tub of beer on the bus after a game and the first one to that tub was usually Muscle.*
>
> *"He had that reputation, but I don't know if he drank any more than the rest of us. That's just the way it was back then. It's a wonder we all weren't arrested for DUI because everyone on that bus would be tanked, except the driver of course.*
>
> *"Muscle could hit that ball though. I know one thing, if they'd used the ball then that they use now, Muscle would have hit 100 home runs in 1949."*
>
> *– Bob Downing,*
> *outfielder, Reidsville*

Our whole season at that point was like a snowball going downhill. After playing so hard and getting within one game of .500, we lost another five straight and we were now at 40-51.

I guess we all could see it coming, but on July 23 Cecil "Zip" Payne replaced Harry as manager. Payne had managed Winston-Salem for three seasons and started the 1949 season managing Fayetteville of the Class D Tobacco State League. Payne suffered a bruised thigh, resigned his post and went home. Meanwhile, he began coaching the Madison American Legion team at his home in Mayodan, North Carolina. He began to heal and was ready to get back and that's when Tommy Clark approached him and he accepted the job. We gave him a present of a 10-4 win over Raleigh, but then the party was over as we lost a twinbill to the Caps before reeling off a four-game win streak.

The first game of that streak I remember because I went 5-for-6 and hit my 33rd and 34th home runs, but again some of the joy was taken out of that because just before the game Lefty Adams, a good friend, was sold to Greensboro. Lefty was a good pitcher but he just couldn't get untracked for us. I told him that I'd be pulling for him unless he was pitching against us.

Then, a few days later, we picked up a young outfielder by the name of Cart Howerton. Cart was a nice fellow and turned out his life was in baseball as he coached a few years with the Boston Red Sox and later scouted and ran the Winston-Salem club.

Right about the time he came, I hit home runs in three straight games and went 7-for-13. But, we lost all three. We had 45 games left in the season and I had 37 home runs and needed five more to set the record. I don't mean to sound cocky, but I figured I had that record in the bag as long as I didn't get injured. People at that point were speculating as to how many home runs I would end up with.

I moved one closer on August 1. We were at Kiker for a doubleheader with Burlington. We won the first game 4-0 and I went 0-for-2, but we lost the second game 9-6. In that game I hit the longest home run I believe I ever hit that season, coming against Larry Hartley. Those at Kiker that night said it was the longest they've ever seen hit there. It went over the center field fence and must have gone 450 feet.

Durham came in for a two-game set and we lost the first 9-1 and the second 12-9, but I had three hits in the second one, two of them home runs – my 39th and 40th.

When I first came into pro baseball, the experts said, "Change up on him. You'll get him on his front foot." They said that because I had an open stance. The only thing you can do is show them they can't change up by not getting out on your front foot. I had pretty quick and strong wrists. I'm not bragging, but I was a pretty good hitter with two strikes on me.

Two of my favorite people were Crash Davis, left, and Willie Duke.
(Photo courtesy of Sholes family)

I could get the bat around. I would try to wait on my pitch and often times I might take a strike or two. The theory was during some of my hot streaks was to pitch me away. I saw a lot of bad pitches and they seemed to come more and more the closer I got to the record. No pitcher wanted to be the one who threw the ball to break the record.

I guess if it was down to the last game of the season and I still needed one home run to break the record, it would have been more dramatic, but we still had 40 games left. Unless I fell and broke my leg, the record was going to me mine.

We went into Winston-Salem on August 4 and I went 2-for-4 as we beat the Cardinals 6-3, but I didn't get close to sending the ball out of Southside Park.

To be honest, I was hoping to be able to set the record at Kiker in front of the home fans. Those fans had been unbelievably nice to me. It would have been great to pay them back. I know they were making a big deal about the record. I'm sure being one away from tying the record that we would have had some big crowds at Kiker. But, you can't choose where you're going to hit them. You just go out each night and swing the bat. If the home runs came, then they came.

While I'm talking about the Reidsville fans, we had great fans and they were orderly. And we had a lot of kids come to the games and they usually behaved, not like in Greensboro. Some of the kids there at the park weren't there to watch baseball. They were causing some big problems. One night we had just lost to Greensboro and after the game the boys, who were probably between the ages of 14 and 18, rushed to the top of the grandstands picking up left behind seat cushions. When they got to the top, they began throwing the cushions into the departing crowd. I'm sure they were thinking they were having some harmless fun, but those seat cushions don't feel so soft if you get hit in the side of the head from a distance. As a matter of fact, a week or so before some boys stole some cushions before the game was over, threw them to some waiting kids outside the park who ran off with the cushions. One of the boys ended up getting arrested. And it wasn't uncommon for those kids to run out to the parking lot and start jumping from car to car and putting dents in the autos.

Well, the club came up with the Knothole Gang. There was a barricaded area in left field for the boys who were admitted free. But the first night a lot of the boys left their designated area, went through the main gate and began running all over the grandstand. One night several of the Knothole Gang kids tore the backing off some of the wooden bleachers and began fighting. The kids were a problem. Carolina League president Ted Mann made a plea to parents to help curb these "juvenile delinquents." Finally, the Greensboro club put some extra police in the park and that pretty much solved the problem.

Anyway, we were back in Winston-Salem the next night. Lee Peterson, a right-hander, was the starting pitcher. He was about 5-11 and 175 pounds and had a pretty decent fastball.

Lee was a veteran of the St. Louis farm system and had been obtained by Winston-Salem on option from Rochester of the International League. Lee had pitched for Winston-Salem in 1946 after serving three years in the war and went 16-12 with 180 strikeouts. In the off-season Lee lived and worked in a jewelry store in Winston-Salem.

Willie Duke didn't have a lot of pitching on his club and when Peterson came aboard Willie put him right to work during an eight-game Winston-Salem losing streak. Lee stopped the Cardinals' skid by hurling a 3-0 win over Burlington. The next day Lee relieved and got the save and on the third day Willie started Lee and he got the loss. Three straight days of pitching without a rest. I think that may have been the reason Willie got the heave in Winston-Salem, or at least part of the reason. Roland LeBlanc used Lee a little more sparingly.

The first time up against Lee I jumped on a high curveball and got good wood on it. I was a little late on it, but I hit a line drive to the opposite field clearing the fence

Lee Peterson went 19-10 for Winston-Salem and had the second-leading ERA in the Carolina League at 2.22.

(Photo courtesy of Lee Peterson)

by about a foot. Rip Repulski was playing left and I remember seeing him turn and start to run back, but it was over his head. That home run in the second inning tied Zernial's record. All the guys were there to meet me at the plate when I crossed it. When the P.A. man made the announcement over the loudspeaker the fans gave me a good hand.

Shoals Sets HR Record with 42nd

Reidsville	AB	R	H	A
Denson ss	5	0	0	5
Sipek cf	5	0	3	0
Shoals 1b	3	3	3	0
Souter 3b	3	1	1	2
Miller lf	3	0	1	0
Howerton rf	3	0	2	0
Ferrell c	4	0	0	1
Rawlinson 2b	3	0	2	1
Gardner p	1	0	0	2
aMorris	1	0	0	0
Dattero p	2	0	0	2
Totals	39	4	12	14

aFanned for Gardner in 6th

Winston-Salem	AB	R	H	A
DiPrima 2b	4	1	0	3
Lebedz 3b	5	2	3	1
Phillip 1b	4	0	1	0
Neil rf	5	1	2	0
Repulski lf	5	0	3	0
Long cf	3	1	0	0
Frye ss	4	0	0	5
Attaway c	2	1	1	2
Peterson p	2	0	1	2
Totals	34	6	11	13

Reidsville	010	210	000–4
Winston-Salem	112	101	00x–6

E–Denson, Souter, Ferrell. RBI–Neil, Shoals 2, Attaway, Peterson, Howerton, Rawlinson, Repulski 2. HR–Shoals 2. 2B–Lebedz, Repulski, Peterson, Neil, Rawlinson, Miller, Sipek. S–Peterson 2. DP–Frye to DiPrima to Phillip, Denson to Souter to Shoals. BB– Off Gardner 3, Peterson 3, Dattero 2. SO–By Gardner 3, Peterson 5, Dattero 3. H–Off Gardner 6 in 3, Datteron 5 in 5. LOB– Reidsville 12, Winston-Salem 11. PB–Ferrell, Attaway. LP– Gardner. U–Davis, Cofer and Rock. T–2:12.

We were down 4-1 when I came up in the fourth inning. I got a single and was on first base when Andrew Phillips, Winston-Salem's first baseman, said, "Good luck Muscle, as long as you lose." Souter followed with a single and Cart doubled us both home and we moved to within 4-3.

I came up again in the fifth with Lee still pitching. I took a couple of pitches and he threw me a low fastball. It wasn't a good pitch to hit and I should have laid off, but I swung and hit a line drive to right which at first I didn't think was going to get past Al Neil who was playing right field. But the ball seemed to rise and as I got halfway to first I saw Neil turn and look up as the ball cleared the wall.

Today, guys hit home runs and it takes them days to get around the bases. That's showing up the pitcher. I would never do that. Not even on a record-breaking home run. The fans again gave me an ovation and the guys were at the top of the dugout to shake my hand. My only regret was that both home runs were solos and we lost the game 6-4.

> *"The thing about pitching against Reidsville, you'd go down their lineup and when it was time for Muscle to hit, the kids would all go out behind the fence in right field. It was something to be pitching and see all those kids scampering out there waiting for a home run.*
>
> *"Muscle would spot you two strikes and then just dare you to get that third one past him. I had just come down from Rochester. I threw what I called a knuckle drop. I had gotten two strikes on Muscle in one game and I wasted the next pitch and came back with another knuckle drop and struck him out. He started walking out towards the mound and I was thinking, 'What does this big bruiser want?' He said, 'What in the hell was that thing you were throwing kid?'*

"I remember another time he hit one back through the box off me and I never saw the ball, but I could hear it whistling by me. I didn't like pitching against Muscle because he hit the ball so hard.

"I always tried to pitch Muscle outside and hope to keep the ball in the park somewhere. The night he broke Zernial's record, I threw him a changeup the first time and I got it up a little and he hit it nine miles to tie the record. The second time I threw him a fastball down low and he golfed it for the record.

"Muscle was a great hitter. I remember a scout one time telling me that he thought Muscle was the greatest prospect he had ever seen."

– Lee Peterson,
pitcher, Winston-Salem

I had two more at bats in the game in the seventh and ninth innings. I came up with runners in scoring position but I guess Lee had enough. He walked me intentionally both times. There must have been a few fans from Reidsville there in Winston-Salem because I could hear a few scattered boos in the crowd behind our dugout.

"Muscle was a first class player; an outstanding hitter. He was easy to get along with. An all around good fellow. Best hitter I've ever seen and it was because of his quick and strong wrists. The Yankees' Don Mattingly whips the bat the way Muscle used to. And Muscle's size would fool you, but he could field his position at first base. I was playing shortstop the night he broke the record. I remember the second home run

clearing the scoreboard in right. He hit it so hard, the ball landed on the highway beyond right field."

– Walter T. Frye,
shortstop, Winston-Salem

The next day we headed back to Reidsville to play Raleigh. When they announced the lineup, I got a real nice ovation from the fans at Kiker. I really felt good. I know before the game, I was walking along the fence and a guy on the other side says, "Muscle, come here." So I walked over. Didn't know the guy from Adam, but he slips me a $100 bill through the fence. He said, "This is for breaking Zernial's record."

After the game the guy might have wanted his money back as I went 0-for-3, but we did win 4-3. We were heading into the last 30 days of the season and fans were beginning to guess how many home runs I would end up with. I kinda wondered myself.

Chapter 14

When you played minor league baseball back in the 1940s in a small town like Reidsville, it was like you were family. The community invited you into their homes and made you feel like you were one of theirs. It didn't matter if you were from California or West Virginia.

The Luckies management and the fans gave us an Appreciation Night on a real hot, muggy night in August at Kiker Stadium. Winston-Salem was in town and we had just beat them the night before 12-0 and the fans were packed into Kiker. The paper the next morning said there were 3,152 there and I do know they were standing in the aisles and standing around the fences.

Each player was presented with gifts before the game. Helen was carrying Ronnie at the time and she got baby clothes, all blue. I guess if the baby had been a girl we would have had to exchange all the clothes for something in pink.

We all got nice gifts from toasters to can openers to clothes. I mentioned how I was supposed to get that new car, well it was that night that I got the luggage.

Considering the slump I had been in, the luggage seemed appropriate. After I had set the home run record, we won seven of our next eight games, but with little help from me as I was a meager 6-for-27. I did hit my 43rd and 44th home runs and we improved our record to 53-61.

On Appreciation Night I broke the slump. I didn't hit a home run, but I went 4-for-4. We lost the game, though, 7-5. We turned around and lost the next night as well at Durham as Eddie Neville won his 20th game.

Then we got drenched. We got rained out in Durham our last night and it rained us out two straight nights at home against Raleigh.

When everything dried up we came back in style beating Martinsville at English Field 5-0 as Forline threw a dandy one-hitter. Mike went seven innings without giving up a hit, but then in the eighth, with one out, Ted Zak, their center fielder, lined a clean single to left to spoil Forline's gem.

> *"On our bus trips Muscle kept everybody loose. He used to get on there and play the harmonica – with his nose. But he could play you the sweetest tune you ever heard. He was always talking and laughing on the bus. There was never a dull moment.*
>
> *"Boy, could he hit that ball. The way he snapped and twisted his wrists when he hit, it would put a backspin on the ball and sometimes that ball would look like a blue darter going out. The thing about Kiker Stadium, the ball wouldn't carry out of there like other places but Muscle would get it out. We used a 97 Goldsmith ball that year and it was a rabbit ball, but Muscle could have hit any ball out that year, it didn't matter what kind it was.*
>
> *"Of course, along with Muscle, we had George Souter who was hitting home runs too. Muscle hit one out one night and then Souter followed with a home run. Souter was only about 5-foot-8 and Muscle went over to Souter in the dugout and said, 'How does a little squirt like you hit home runs?'*
>
> *– Mike Forline,*
> *pitcher, Reidsville*

We couldn't stand success. The next night we got walloped by Martinsville 18-4 as the Athletics scored 10 runs in the eighth. For a club that finished next to last in the league in hitting, they had a couple of guys who I felt were two of the best in the league – George Staller and their catcher Earle Brucker.

174

Brucker was the son of Earle Brucker, Sr. who was the pitching coach with Connie Mack and the Philadelphia Athletics. Earle Jr. got a lot of bucks to sign with the Athletics in the amount of $30,000 in 1948. Because of the rule which said he had to be on the 25-man roster, he got into a couple of games with the Athletics, but he wasn't ready for the big leagues. In 1949, a new rule was put into place allowing Philadelphia to farm him out for one season. The catch was that the Athletics could not get him back until he went through baseball's regular selection period.

Another bonus signee was Jack Graham of Durham who signed for $17,000 by Detroit. He ended up hitting .251 that season of '49 and led the Carolina League in errors for shortstops with 71. To top it off, he almost got killed at Raleigh when a pitch hit him on the left temple. Luckily, he was out for only a couple of weeks with a concussion. I'm not sure what happened to him after that season, but he never made it up to the major leagues.

He was a little erratic in the field, but I thought he had potential. He was an 18-year-old kid from Brooklyn and I know for a long time the fans there in Durham booed him because he was making so many errors, but he was learning the position as he had always been an outfielder in high school. In spring training Detroit manager Red Rolfe changed him into a shortstop. But Ace stuck with him and finally he won over the fans.

Those bonus rules were crazy. If a boy got more than $6,000 to sign he couldn't be sent out to a minor league club unless the other teams in the league waived on him. If waivers were asked, the team which claimed the player gets him for $10,000.

As for Brucker, he ended up hitting .284 with 19 home runs for Martinsville in 1949, but Earle never made it back to the majors.

"I remember the last series Reidsville
came into Martinsville. We had a pitcher on
the club, Bob Davis, who was a buddy of

Muscle's. Neither of our clubs were going anywhere. We finished last in the league and Reidsville finished just ahead of us. Anyway, we found out later that some fan had told Muscle that if he hit a home run he'd give Muscle $200. Davis was pitching and instead of throwing junk off the plate like he usually did to Muscle, Davis kept coming down the middle with his soft fastball. This was Muscle's final at bat of the game. Muscle fouled two or three off, but he couldn't get one out of the park. I think maybe Davis was making it too easy for Muscle."

– Earle Brucker,
catcher, Martinsville

Bob Davis and I had met earlier that year and we seemed to hit it off. We got to be pretty good friends. Every time our two clubs got together we sought each other out and shot the breeze. But I was in the dugout at Martinsville and somebody slipped me this message that if I hit a home run in my last at bat, I'd get $200. I don't know who the guy was and he probably had some kind of bet going on. Well, one of the guys on our team, and I don't know who, somehow got word over to Bob about the deal. Let me say, I never in my life would ask a pitcher to lollipop a pitch up there with the purpose of letting me hit one out. Never. And I had no idea one of our guys asked Bob if he'd do it.

I'm not really sure Bob actually tried to set me up, but I do know he pitched me differently. He always threw me junk off the plate and in my last at bat I saw nothing but fastballs down the middle. I will admit I was swinging for the home run because $200 was a lot of money. I asked Bob after the game if he was trying to set me up and he just said, "Muscle, do you think I'd do something like that?"

I hadn't hit a home run in over a week, with the rain and all, but I broke that cold spell with a solo shot off Pat

Pasquarella of Greensboro in the eighth inning of a game we won 3-2. That's the best home run you can hit, one that wins a game. I'd rather do that than get $200.

> *"Shucks, Leo just hits them where they ain't and that's why he's the best home run hitter in this league."*
>
> – *Reidsville bat boy Glenn Clark*
> *quoted in Reidsville Review*

A couple of days later we swept a doubleheader from Danville and I hit a pair of home runs and had three hits in the first game. The home runs were my 46th and 47th of the year and both came off Tom Lowe, who was known as Thump.

On August 24th we came back to Reidsville with a 57-66 record, set to take on Burlington in two straight doubleheaders. We split the first twinbill and the next night we were shut out in the first game as Lee Bush scattered seven hits and I went 0-for-3. Ray Hardee also gave up just seven singles, but the Bees scored a run in the second inning when James "Sheepy" Lamb singled home Joe Trotta.

We were asleep in that game, but the alarm clock sounded in the nightcap. We beat the Bees 20-8 and had 20 hits, and I had three home runs and one of those boxscore lines you just like to stare at: 5-6-4-6. The home runs were numbers 48, 49 and 50. James Miller had a home run and three hits, Cart Howerton had four hits and Charlie Ferrell had three hits, including a pair of doubles.

We continued our homestand with Winston-Salem, dropping two games including a 17-inning 5-2 decision. In that one I hit my 51st home run off Lee Peterson.

We were rained out the next night with Durham at Kiker, but it gave us time to reflect. The Luckies still had a shot at .500, but we were 11 games under with 16 to go. More realistically, we wanted to pass Durham in the standings. The Bulls were two and a half games ahead of us and we felt we could overtake them and maybe finish the season in fifth place.

Other than Eddie Neville, Durham was like us and didn't have much pitching. The Bulls didn't have much hitting either, especially in power. As a matter of fact, they had the least number of home runs in '49 in the league with 58. That's compared to the 132 we hit and the 139 with which Martinsville led the league. Almost half of Durham's home runs were hit by Carl Linhart, a 19-year-old who hit 23. In one game Linhart, who would get to the major leagues with Detroit for a cup of coffee in 1952, had eight RBIs against Raleigh. The kid had some talent.

While Durham was a little weak in talent, they had the right man at the helm in even-keel Clarence "Ace" Parker. "Ace" was, and is, a legend in North Carolina. He is one of Duke University's greatest athletes ever. Parker went directly from Duke to the Philadelphia Athletics in 1937 and, in his first at bat, pinch hit a home run. Also, in 1937, he played professional football with Brooklyn and was named All-Pro as a running back.

Parker would play and manage in the minor leagues for a lot of years and, in 1952, took over for the legendary Jack Coombs as the head baseball coach at Duke. But, in 1949, he had a long season in the Carolina League. Some things he had no control over. "Ace" had a problem at third base. He had a good third baseman in Wally Bernat but Bernat broke a finger in June and missed several weeks. Meanwhile, "Ace" put in Claude Swiggett, a Durham boy, but Swiggett saw limited play because he had a job operating a milling machine at a Durham factory working from seven in the morning to three in the afternoon and pretty much was limited to playing home games. "Ace" played third on the road. Such was the life of a minor league manager.

As for the race in the standings, Greensboro was two and a half games behind us at this point and Martinsville was entrenched in last place, trailing us by thirteen and a half games and 33 behind league-leading Danville. We were 20 1/2 games behind the Leafs.

From a personal standpoint, I was leading the Carolina League in hitting with a .368 average with my closest challengers being Willie Duke of Danville at .353, Bill Brown of Danville at .349 and Emo Showfety of Greensboro at .346. I was also leading in home runs and in RBIs with 118. I was looking at the triple crown, if I could keep my batting average up.

Just when I was looking at everything from a positive perspective, we dropped our next two games in which I went 0-for-8 and we headed to Burlington where I hadn't hit a home run all year.

> *"Muscle came into town and it was late in the year and he hadn't hit a home run there all season. The only park in the league where he hadn't hit one out. The players were agitating him. Telling him to go on and lay his bat down that he wasn't going to hit one out. Dick Brockwell was on the mound for us and it was the fifth inning and I was playing third.*
>
> *"Muscle brings the bat around and he hits a line drive which took no time in getting over the right field fence. We barely had time to turn our heads it was out so quick. He circled the bases and when he got to third I remember he had this big old grin over his face.*
>
> *"Muscle was the next thing to Babe Ruth. He reminded you of the Babe just by the way he went up to the plate and the way he circled the bases after hitting a home run and just by the way he played the game having so much fun."*
>
> *– 'Sheepy' Lamb,*
> *third baseman, Burlington*

This is the 1949 Reidsville Luckies and I just can't place all the guys. That's me on the left on the back row and down the line are Dattero, Hardee, Gardner, Rawlinson and Howerton. In front of me is Adams and on the other side of the row is Sipek with Miller next to him. Next to the bat boy on the front row is Downing and down the line is Payne, Ferrell, Hester and Forline.

(Photo courtesy Bob Downing)

I was glad to get that monkey off my back. I remember those guys for Burlington razzing me, but I didn't hear a peep after I hit that home run. I also went 3-for-4 in that game.

I often wondered what it would be like to play in the major leagues, but it seemed no one ever came calling. But it was right after that game that Tom Smothers called me at home one day and said the St. Louis Browns were interested in giving me a look toward the end of the season. But, you know, I really didn't get all excited. For one thing, I wasn't sure it was even going to happen and I didn't want to get my hopes up. And too, at my age, I knew it wouldn't be for the long haul in the majors and I guess I was too old to get too excited about it.

The Browns, too, were a rag-tag bunch on their way to losing 100 games in the American League in 1949. They had some good players like Ned Garver, Roy Seivers, Gerry Priddy and Sherm Lollar, but overall they were a lousy team.

A couple of days later someone in the Browns front office called me and said the club was prepared to bring me up. I told the fellow I'd call him back. I remember Charlie Ferrell asking me if I would go if they called. I told him I really didn't know. Like I said, I was 32 and wasn't going anywhere and after the season I would be back in the minors in 1950. I saw it happen all the time. Plus, it would be for only three or four weeks and I know I would spend most of the time on the bench or as a pinch-hitter and I couldn't have taken that.

I guess now, looking back, it would have been great to tell my kids and grandkids that I once played in the major leagues, but back in 1949 it wasn't that big of a deal. I guess as a fan, people get awestruck but you have to remember I played with and against a lot of great players and they were just like anyone else to me, so I wasn't like some rookie just coming up. Now, if I had been 20 years old again and they asked, you bet I would have jumped at the chance.

For another thing, I couldn't have afforded the move up. That may be hard to understand with the money they make nowadays in the big leagues, but not in 1949. I was making $4,000 playing for Reidsville, not to mention all the passed hats I got when hitting home runs and a lot of the businesses around town gave us discounts. The major league minimum salary was $5,000, but I would have been making considerably less going to the Browns to finish out the season. They did say they would pay my train fare to St. Louis and put me up in a hotel.

I really thought hard about it but I said no, that the cup of coffee wasn't worth it for me to uproot my wife, who was expecting Ronnie on October 21. At that point in my life I was just concerned with making some money and I figured I'd be better off heading home after the Carolina League season ended and going to work.

Just a week later, a fellow from Pittsburgh approached me and asked if I'd like to sign with the Pirates for the remainder of the season. He said a spot on the roster was between me and another guy at Ft. Worth. I guess because I was leading all of organized baseball in home runs they wanted me up to see how I handled the pitching in the majors. I asked him how I could sign with the Pirates when I was property of the Browns. He said the Pirates were prepared to make a deal for me. But, I told the Pirates the same thing I told the Browns.

So, that was my shot at the major leagues. I know some people say I didn't make it because I drank too much. Others said I didn't make it because I offended too many people in high places. Others said I just wasn't good enough for that level. Maybe all those reasons are true, I can't say. I wish I did have the opportunity to give the big leagues a shot when I was younger, but I just never got that chance and I can't say why. I just know that when the time did come and I was offered the chance to play, I was the one who said no.

Frank Spencer of the Winston-Salem Journal quoted a veteran Cardinal player as saying Shoals is the most powerful hitter he has ever seen and has the most powerful wrist action he's ever seen, that Shoals handles a baseball bat like a toothpick. Willie Duke said that while he was manager of the Cardinals they didn't even talk about Shoals, that his pitchers had the answer. His hurlers would merely walk Shoals every time he came to bat.

Dick Herbert of the Raleigh News and Observer says Shoals' home runs are longer than Zernial's, that the Reidsville slugger is built like a ten-ton truck.

But Reidsville fans know that after all "Muscles" is only human. Shoals can be pitched to, but the chuckers had better be careful and make no mistakes.

*– The Reidsville Review,
Friday, June 17, 1949*

Summer was about over now and it was the first of September and we went back to Kiker. We had only five more home games left. The question now was how many home runs could I finish up with over the final 13 games. I had 52 and people were projecting I would hit 60 and I thought that if I got on a good streak, I might be able to crank out eight more, but it would take one heckuva streak.

"I'd have to have two or three hot nights to get 60. But I never make predictions. Predictions have a way of bouncing back in your face and I never like to say something that I might have to take back."

*– Shoals in
The Durham Morning Herald,
August 29, 1949*

Maybe I started thinking too much about hitting home runs because I didn't hit one over the next four games and my batting average dropped as I was only 3-for-15. We swept Danville at Kiker in a two-game set then turned right around and dropped a pair at Raleigh. We came back to Reidsville for our final homestand of the season. We had a doubleheader with Martinsville followed by a single game.

The first game of the twinbill we won 4-3 as Bob Merkle scattered eight hits. I went 3-for-4 with my 53rd home run. Then, in the second game, the Athletics ran into a Mack truck. We won 26-4 as we had 28 hits in the game. I hit my 54th home run which was a long, towering job to left-center. I finished the game going 3-for-4, but I was in a slump compared to some of the other guys. Howerton was 5-for-7, Rawlinson, Sipek and Miller each had four hits each. Even our pitcher, Mike Dattero, had two hits as he went the distance on the mound.

The next night, our final home game, Forline and myself were presented these little gold baseballs for participating in the league's all-star game and then we went out and got drubbed 12-6. However, I bashed my 55th home run and what turned out to be my last home run of the year off Archie Templeton. I went 2-for-5 and over the three-game set with Martinsville I was 8-for-14 with three home runs and seven RBIs and I scored seven runs. I hated for the year to end.

"Muscle was the type of guy once you met him you didn't forget him. When you got on base, Muscle was always talking to you and when he came to bat, he was always chattering about something. He was just being friendly. A majority of the guys didn't talk. One reason was that managers frowned on players from one team fraternizing with players on another team. Even if it was just some friendly conversation during a game. But Muscle was one guy who could do it and

get away with it. I don't know anyone who didn't like Muscle."

– Earle Brucker,
catcher, Martinsville

Most of the guys were ready to go home. It had been a long and frustrating year for a lot of them. Several of the guys were just going through the motions as the season wound down. We dropped two games at Greensboro and then split at Winston-Salem and that's when Souter decided to spend a few days at the beach. The only thing was George didn't ask anybody if he could leave. As a result, the club suspended George for the few remaining games we had. But all was eventually forgiven as George was back in Reidsville in 1950.

> *"One time I was playing shortstop for Winston-Salem against Reidsville. Muscle was a pull hitter and I was playing almost directly behind second base and on the edge of the grass. Muscle hit a shot, on one bounce, that hit me in the chest and bounced away that took me four or five steps to get to. I got the ball and still was able to throw him out. While Muscle could hit the ball a long way, he didn't run well. But it was a wonder that ball didn't kill me. I know I was sore the next day. But you had to think about those things when Muscle came up to bat. I don't know an infielder that didn't take one or two steps back when Muscle came up to bat."*
>
> *– Walter T. Frye,*
> *shortstop, Winston-Salem*

We went to Durham and Neville earned his 25th win against us in the final game of the season by beating Lew Hester, who had 25 wins the year before. If there was one guy I didn't like to face, it was Neville. Eddie was a little left-hander, only about 5-foot-10 with a terrific knuckleball and one dandy pickoff move to first base. Eddie had a lot of guts for a little guy. He'd stand out there and throw that knuckler right where he wanted it to go. As a batter, you never knew where it was going to cross the plate.

Eddie finished 25-10 and I swear I don't know how he ever lost 10. He had an ERA of 2.59 and completed 25 out of 31 starts. See how many guys do that today and let me know. They rave today when a starter goes six innings. They call that a quality start. To me a quality start is when you finish what you start. Eddie had pitched in the Canal Zone League that winter and went 11-3 and in 1948 he was with Tarboro of the Class D Coastal Plain League and went 16-4. Eddie reminded me a whole lot of Whitey Ford when he was with the Yankees just by his appearance on the mound.

I'm convinced that if Eddie had been playing for Danville, he would have won 35 games.

One thing about Eddie, though, he was superstitious. When Eddie wasn't pitching, he would coach third base and when he took his place in the box Eddie would always pick up Ace Parker's glove at third base, spit in the glove and then lay it back down. Eddie, like I said, was pretty good with the stick and he never wanted anyone else to touch his bat. Durham's batboy Don McClintock would always hand the Durham players their bats when it was their time to bat, except for Neville who insisted on picking up his own.

> *"I don't know how many home runs Muscle hit off me, but he hit his share. I remember one in Durham that was a tremendous drive that carried over the smokestack on the building in right-center. Muscle was the most powerful hitter I ever faced.*
> *"It took me more than half the 1949 season to learn how to pitch to Muscle. I learned to never throw him anything, and I*

*mean anything, above his knees because he
would hit it into the next county. I tried to
keep the ball low and to give him tricky stuff,
hard tricky stuff."*

— *Eddie Neville,
pitcher, Durham*

I finished the season in a 4-for-22 slump and lost the batting title to Bill Brown, .361 to .359. Brown had five hits in his last eight at bats in a doubleheader with Greensboro while I went two for six against Durham. I played in 144 games and had 501 at bats to Brown's 136 games and 552 at bats. Bill had 199 hits and I finished with 180. I walked 116 times to Brown's 49. I was second in the league in walks with 116 as Durham's Pat Haggerty led with 128. I also led in RBIs with 137 ahead of Emo Showfety who had 120.

One of the kindest gestures from anybody that year came from Maude Gregory, whom everyone just called 'Ma', and one of Durham's greatest fans. It was toward the end of August and I had just hit my 50th home run and we were in Durham. 'Ma' comes up to me before the game and said, "Muscle, if you hit 60 home runs, I'll bake you a cake when you come to Durham at the end of the year."

I kidded with her and said why don't you make that 55 home runs instead of 60. Several weeks went by and I had forgotten about that because fans were always talking to you and saying things like that. Well, during the last trip to Durham we got rained out of the series. But Ma called down to the park and told someone that she had the cake baked for me. Word of that got to me and I thought if she was nice enough to bake a cake for me, I should accept it graciously. Well, at three o'clock it was obvious we weren't going to play so I had someone in the Durham office call to find out where Ma lived. We got the directions, handed it to our bus driver and told him to stop by Maude's place on our way out of town. We pull up in this big old bus right in front of Ma's house. I got off, went up to the door and when the door

187

opened there was Ma holding that double-layered chocolate cake. She smiles and said, "I should never have let you talk me out of that 60."

> *On the strength of his big home run bat, Muscle has ridden to the heights as the Carolina League's biggest drawing card.*
>
> *"Oh, I just hit 'em as they come up. I'm not aiming for any particular mark," declared Leo (Muscle) Shoals, the Carolina League's home run king."*
>
> *– Greensboro Daily Record,*
> *August 9, 1949*

The 55 home runs, by the way, were the most in all of organized baseball that 1949 season, but barely. Ralph Kiner of the Pittsburgh Pirates hit 54. The Luckies finished in seventh place, 23 games back of Danville. We won 63 and lost 80, but that was better than Martinsville, which was last at 52-92 and 341/2 games out.

I was, and still am, proud of my 55 home runs that year, but there's always somebody who tries to put a damper on things like that. In 1984 I was invited to throw out the first pitch of the Carolina League All-Star Game and the night before we had a banquet. I was sitting on the podium in the dining room of the hotel alongside Mike Cubbage, who at the time was the manager of the Lynchburg Mets. When I was announced as having hit 55 home runs, Cubbage asks me if the ballparks were located in Korea. It shot right through me because that was a putdown and it was the way he said it. But some people are just like that. I think that may have been the only negative comment I ever heard about my hitting the home runs. Anyway, whoever heard of Mike Cubbage?

> *Leo (Muscle) Shoals, who usually hits 'em out of sight over the fences, didn't get a*

188

home run last night but he did hit one out of view – straight up. The ball almost reached the fog over the stadium. It fell near the pitcher's mound and was dropped for an error.

– Greensboro Daily News,
September 8, 1949

If I could relive any season I ever played, it would be that 1949 season. I didn't want it to end. The thing I always hated about ending a season were the guys you knew you probably would never see again. I had some real good friends on the Luckies and other guys in the league as well. On the other hand, I was looking forward to the offseason and being a father for the first time.

"Muscle Shoals was the hero of most of us who played sandlot baseball in Raleigh during 1949. I was only about 13 years old then. In those days Ralph Kiner was busting the ball for Pittsburgh and would finish the season with 54 home runs. But he didn't impress us a great deal, probably because few of our folks had TV sets and we followed his career only in the local paper and through occasional radio broadcasts of Pirates' games.

"But Muscle Shoals was truly a living legend in the Carolina League in 1949 and we could see him play at Devereux Meadow which is now a parking facility for city-owned vehicles. I remember well how we used to collect metal coat hangers and empty pop bottles so we could buy tickets to the games, particularly when Shoals and the Reidsville Luckies came to town.

"Once, when I was short of funds, a security guard caught me climbing the fence.

He was an old man who gave me an especially strong lecture about jumping the fence before giving me 35 cents to buy a ticket. My father, an avid and knowledgeable baseball fan, traveled on business over North and South Carolina during the late 1940s, and he used to tell me great stories about Muscle when he played for Charlotte in 1948.

"The next year, when Shoals began hitting home runs for Reidsville, my dad said, 'Wait until he comes to Raleigh and gets a look at that long right field fence at Devereux Meadow. I doubt he'll hit one out of there. That memorable night when Reidsville played Raleigh, dad took me and a young pal of mine named Jimmy Bowers to the park. Shoals hit a mile-high foul ball about even with the lights and far over the right field wall. He also blasted a line drive over the fence in deep right-center. Bowers and I couldn't have been more excited if we had seen the Babe hit one in Yankee Stadium.

"Dad ate crow that night. After the game, dad asked for an autograph for me from Shoals and Muscle inscribed my program using Jimmy's back as a support. Somewhere I still have that ragged and yellowed old scorecard.

"No player in this league ever hit 'em higher, farther or with more consistency than Muscle Shoals and I thank him for all the thrills and many happy memories."

– William M. Palmer,
Curator of North Carolina Museum of
Natural History in Raleigh

Shoals' Home Runs in 1949

HR No	Date	Opponent	Pitcher	HR No.	Date	Opponent	Pitcher
1	4-20	Martinsville	Neidowicz	29	7-3	At Martinsville	Johnson
2	4-23	At Danville	Lowe	30	7-12	Raleigh	Miller
3	4-24	At Raleigh	Cudd	31	7-19	Win-Salem	Peterson
4	5-7	Danville	Guilliani	32	7-21	At Durham	Bishop
5	5-12	Durham	Neville	33	7-25	At Martinsville	Davis
6	5-13	Durham	Murray	34	7-25	At Martinsville	Melton
7	5-13	Durham	Smith	35	7-28	Greensboro	Zilian
8	5-19	At Danville	Guilliani	36	7-29	At Danville	Angell
9	5-21	Win-Salem	Moford	37	7-30	At Danville	Guilliani
10	5-22	At Durham	Smith	38	8-1	Burlington	Hartley
11	5-30	At Raleigh	Kelly	39	8-3	Durham	James
12	5-31	At Raleigh	Miller	40	8-3	Durham	Sheehan
13	6-1	Greensboro	Zilian	41	8-5	Win-Salem	Peterson
14	6-1	Greensboro	Pereyra	42	8-5	Win-Salem	Peterson
15	6-3	At Martinsville	Hummell	43	8-8	Martinsville	Schoonover
16	6-4	At Martinsville	Templeton	44	8-11	At Greensboro	Zilian
17	6-5	At Raleigh	Cronin	45	8-20	Greensboro	Pasquarella
18	6-7	Durham	Cooke	46	8-23	At Danville	Lowe
19	6-10	At Win-Salem	Grimsley	47	8-23	At Danville	Lowe
20	6-12	At Greensboro	Wargo	48	8-25	Burlington	Jordan
21	6-12	At Greensboro	Wargo	49	8-25	Burlington	Bosser
22	6-12	At Greensboro	Wargo	50	8-25	Burlington	Hancock
23	6-14	Danville	Guilliani	51	8-27	Win-Salem	Peterson
24	6-15	Burlington	Jones	52	8-31	At Burlington	Brockwell
25	6-18	At Durham	Neville	53	9-5	Martinsville	Carpenter
26	6-19	At Win-Salem	Gosselin	54	9-5	Martinsville	Zak
27	6-20	Win-Salem	Curley	55	9-6	Martinsville	Templeton
28	7-3	At Martinsville	Hummell				

191

Chapter 15

About a month after we had been back in Parkersburg, Ronnie was born. Nothing in baseball ever made me as proud as having my first child, or any of my children for that matter. I worked selling electrical appliances, but I learned a lot about taking care of a baby.

I also had to make a decision about baseball. I knew that after the season I had at Reidsville, I'd be offered a job somewhere for the 1950 season. But I was 33 now. The years were rolling along and I had to decide as to whether I got a 9-to-5 job or continued to play baseball. Helen and I talked it over and she knew where my heart was. As long as I was physically able and as long as someone wanted me, I would play baseball.

It was along about the middle of December when the Cincinnati Reds called and said they had drafted me and I was optioned to Columbia, South Carolina of the South Atlantic League. A real good league. I was excited until I got the contract, which was offering me half of what I had made the year before with Reidsville. There was no way I could afford to play for that kind of money no matter how much I wanted to play baseball.

I couldn't begin to support Helen and a baby on that kind of money. I tore the contract up. I never called the Reds or anything and in a week or two I got another contract and I tore that one up too.

A few weeks later Fred Fleig, the Cincinnati farm director, called me at home and wanted to know what the delay was in sending back my contract. Fleig said that if I got off to a good start with Columbia that I'd be certain to move up to the big league club. I told Fleig I wasn't falling for that line. I'd heard it used on too many players to get them to sign. I told Fleig that I was playing for money now, not a promise of a promotion, and that if he wanted me it was going to take more money than what they were offering.

I told Fleig that I got $5,000 for the year at Reidsville and that I wanted $7,000 at Columbia. Fleig said no way his Columbia club, or any club at that level, could pay me that kind of money. He said I must have been getting money under the table at Reidsville, because they just don't pay on that scale.

Fleig finally proposed a deal. The Reds were trying to sign first baseman Earl York to a Tulsa contract. Fleig said he could sign me to a Double A contract at $1,200 a month and when they signed York I would be sent to Columbia for the same money.

I considered the deal, told Fleig I would sign and I reported to Alexandria, Louisiana for spring training in 1950. The Reds still had not signed York as spring training came to an end, so I assumed I would be with Tulsa. Our first real game of the season was an exhibition in Memphis, but I never got to play. Just as we got there, York signed. I knew then my ticket would be for Columbia. Sure enough, I was optioned from Tulsa to Columbia.

I was glad York signed, to be honest. I liked the Carolinas and wanted to go back there to play. It was closer to home, plus I was getting the money I wanted.

Gerald "Gee" Walker, who had played outfield for the Detroit Tigers, was the manager at Columbia. I took to Gee right away. On that club Gee had some bonus players, young guys who the Reds organization saw potential in. Players who the Reds felt would someday down the road help them in Cincinnati. Gee considered me an old vet and, at 33, I was old compared to a bunch of 20 and 21 year old kids.

Gee didn't have anyone on the club to help him coach and he came to me one day and said, "Muscle, you've been around and you know baseball as well as anybody. Any advice you may have to offer or anything you might see to help any of these players, I want you to feel free to jump in and instruct them."

I appreciated that from Gee. It made me feel responsible and I liked the idea of being able to help some of the younger guys. It also made me think that maybe one day I would like to coach. I know that down through my career, veterans didn't go out of their way to help younger players because the vets saw the young guys as a threat to their jobs. But, at this point of my career, I knew I wasn't going to be playing forever and if I could help some young player along the way then I would try my best.

Gee was an easy guy to get along with and he rarely showed his temper. The only time I can really remember him arguing was in a 5-3 loss at Columbus, Georgia. The home plate umpire, a guy named Davidzuk, called two straight balls on pitches thrown by Clarence Zeiser against Joe Penczak of Columbus. Gee went crazy. He charged out to argue and he wouldn't leave. Davidzuk threw Gee out of the game, but Gee kept jawing and fussing. He stood out there a good 20 minutes and finally the club officials had to get a couple of police officers to escort Gee from the park.

There were some good baseball people managing in the league. Dale Alexander was at Jacksonville, Oscar Grimes at Greenville and Rip Sewell at Charleston. Alexander won a batting title in 1932, the year he played for both the Red Sox and Tigers. Grimes was an infielder in the major leagues from 1938 to 1946, mainly with the Indians and Yankees, while Sewell pitched 13 years in the bigs, 12 with the Pirates. He was in his early 40s, but every now and then Rip would go on the mound. Sewell is probably remembered best for the home run he gave up to Ted Williams in the 1946 All-Star game off his famous eephus pitch. It was the only time anyone hit a home run off that pitch until Omer Tolson of Greenville hit one in that 1950 season.

We had a 20-year-old outfielder on the club named Bob Hazle. The same Bob Hazle who picked up the nickname Hurricane later in the majors. Hazle was a bonus baby, signing for $15,000 right out of high school. Hazle finally got up to Cincinnati in1955 with the Reds. He was eventually traded to Milwaukee and went up with them in 1957, the year he got the Hurricane moniker. He hit .403 in the little time he played and helped the Braves get to the World Series. He played one more year in 1958 with the Braves and Tigers before fizzling out.

Bob wasn't that big, but he was big-boned, which made him look bigger than he actually was. Bob had a habit of bailing out on every pitcher, regardless of whether the pitcher was a right-hander or a left-hander. Bob was pulling out and sacrificing his power. I think that was what finally caught up with him in the major leagues. Gee tried to help Bob and even brought in the Columbia groundskeeper to help out. Gee and the groundskeeper built a triangle foot clamp which was made by bolting three short pieces of two-by-fours together in a triangle shape, spiking the triangle down and putting Bob's foot inside the brace, then twisting the clamp so that it was impossible for Bob to bail out. All Bob could do was stay in it and hit by just lifting the foot up and down.

Before Gee came up with the clamp, he would lay on the ground holding Bob's foot during batting practice. I told Gee he was going to get himself killed doing that, but Gee would do anything if it meant helping a young kid learn. Gee, I'm certain, is the reason Bob made it to the major leagues. Bob had the raw talent, but Gee was able to fine tune it.

Before we started the season, the Boston Braves and Cincinnati Reds played an exhibition in Columbia at Capital City Park. The stadium was packed from the $1.15 boxseats to the 90-cent grandstand to the 60-cent bleachers to the 50-cent "colored" section. About the fifth or sixth inning Sam Jethroe, the first black man to play for the Braves, went out to play in left field. It was the first time that a black man ever played with a white team in Columbia. The black section of the ballpark applauded and cheered. Later on in the game, Jethroe got on base, attempted to steal second and was thrown out by Walker Cooper as a big cheer went out from the white section in the stadium.

I struggled in spring training for reasons I can't explain, but that was nothing new as I seemed to always struggle at the start. But I felt ready for the season to begin and we got off in fine fashion with Governor Strom Thurmond throwing out the first pitch. I don't think Strom could have done any worse than I was doing at the plate as I was hitting under .200 through the middle of April. I asked Gee what I was doing wrong and he said I wasn't doing anything wrong so far as he could see. Gee said I was swinging the bat well and just to hang in there and the hits would start falling.

> *"That slow start doesn't bother me. I always start slow. I did last year at Reidsville, when I hit .359. The trouble? Well, my timing is off. It takes a little time every season for me to get it down. I've been experimenting a little since I joined the Reds. I've narrowed my stance and I think that's gonna help. I'll be hitting before long."*
>
> *– Muscle Shoals*
> *quoted in Jake Penland's column*
> *for Columbia's newspaper The State,*
> *April 28, 1950.*

I couldn't hit the ball out of the infield and one of the regular fans kept yelling at me. "Hey, we don't want 55. We just want one." Well, it took a few weeks but I finally caught hold of one and drove it over the center field flag pole my first time up. My second time up, I hit another clear out of the park to right field. I crossed home plate and was going to look for the guy who was doing the hollering but he had left his seat. I never heard another peep out of the fellow.

There was a lady, Mrs. Charles Walker, who rarely missed one of our games and she had picked me as her favorite player. Like I've said, my home runs were coming few and far between. I had hit a couple on the road, but none at home. Mrs. Walker said the next time I hit a home run at Capital Park she was going to pin an orchid on me. Well, I hit my sixth of the year off Fred Woolpert of Macon at home. The next night, before our game, she had the orchid. In a ceremony at the plate, she pinned it on my uniform.

Gee hung with me and he had a way of instilling confidence in you with just a few words. It wasn't long before I started to hit. My first real good game came in a 3-1 win over the Jacksonville Tars as I went 3-for-3 with a double. By the middle of May I had my average to almost .260 and going great. We were playing at Greenville's Meadowbrook Park and in the ninth inning I tied the game with a hit and in the 11th I drove in the winning run. The next day I went 3-for-3 in a 4-3 win over the Spinners.

The fans in Columbia were behind me when I was struggling and they helped my confidence by not getting down on me. We had good fans who, when we weren't at home, followed our games on WCOS radio. Wayne Poucher was the announcer for our home games and on our away games he would stay in the studio and broadcast the games from reports sent to him from whatever team we were playing on the road. People couldn't tell whether he was actually at the game or not. But I would have to say the Columbia fans and I got along well. We even had some good laughs at my own expense.

Muscle Shoals, Columbia's popular first baseman, slipped and fell on his whatchamacallem while trying to field a high fly ball in the Monday night game against Charleston. He couldn't get back up in time but it happened that the ball fell in the vicinity of where he was sprawled out. Muscle was on his back when he caught the ball. The crowd got a big charge out of the play and the spectators roared when the public address man, Tom Daisley, announced that Muscle Shoals and Jackie Price will appear here at 8 o'clock tomorrow night. Price is the baseball trick artist.

I was still swinging the bat good. We swept a doubleheader from Savannah and I hit home runs in both games, including the second-game home run, which went over the brick barrier in right at 350 feet. The ball wound up 425 feet from home plate and they found it next to a car in the lot. A few days later I had a 400-foot home run as I went 2-for-3 and got my average up to .278. In less than a week, I was up to .287.

As a team we were trying to get over the .500 mark, but every club in the Sally League was just above .500 or below with the exception of Macon, which was running away from the pack. Looking back, we actually had a pretty good bunch of ballplayers. After the season started we got Bob Nieman, who played for St. Louis, from Tulsa to play the outfield after Carl Kolosna came down with elbow trouble and went on the voluntary retired list. Then there was Johnny Temple, who had a long career playing second base for the Reds, although he played short with Columbia. We actually ended up leading the league in hitting as Temple led us with a .322 average with Hazle not far behind at .313. Nieman flirted with .300 finishing with a .292. Bill Ford was our third baseman and he gave us a stellar bat hitting .287.

One guy I won't forget was our catcher, Dave Poole. Dave was a solid catcher on and off the field. Dave was in his second season with Columbia when he was invited to participate in a promotion for a new picture being shown at the Palmetto theater called *Kill The Umpire*. Poole, suited in his Columbia uniform, stood beneath the 12-story Liberty Life building in Columbia while on top was Moe Savransky, one of our pitchers. When the signal was given, Moe dropped a baseball from 12 stories up. Dave began weaving back and fourth and caught the ball. The big crowd on the ground ate this up. Moe dropped a second ball and Dave snared this one too. Our backup catcher, Carl Nebel, got a chance to duplicate the feat. Carl dropped the first ball, but did catch the second. After it was over I asked Carl what would have happened if that ball hit him in the head and Carl said: "I guess the club would be looking for a backup catcher."

While talking about this team I have to point out that Savransky was good for more than dropping balls off the roof of buildings. Moe, a fine lefty who had a cup of coffee with the Reds in 1954, would go 15-7 for us that year and lead the league in ERA at 2.25. I'm glad I never had to bat against him.

Moe threw a no-hitter at Savannah against the Indians over seven innings in the first game of a doubleheader. Moe walked three in the game and the other runner to reach was in the third when Charlie Kaiser hit a ball to Temple at short and Johnny gave me a low throw to first which I couldn't come up with. The no-hitter came down to the last batter in the seventh and a 1-2 count on Les Eggers. Eggers fouled one behind me and I got under it and wrapped it in my glove for the final out.

The very next night Moe relieved with the tying run on in the ninth inning with one out. Moe struck out Hargrove Davis and then got George Wright to bounce back to the mound to seal our 5-3 win over the Indians. Moe followed that up with a one-hitter at Jacksonville as Dean Woods beat out a bunt single in the third inning for the only hit.

We had a 19-year-old pitcher, Jerry Blackburn, on the club who had good stuff but he couldn't get it going for us. Jerry was a $35,000 bonus baby and he finished the season with the highest ERA in the Sally at 7.21. But an example of how Jerry could pitch was the time he one-hit Jacksonville in a game we won 1-0. The only hit off Jerry came in the fifth when Tony Ordenana of the Tars hit a ball to Temple and the ball hit a pebble and bounced over Johnny's shoulder for a hit.

One of the greatest guys on the club was Temple. Ronnie was about a year old and he was crazy about Johnny and Johnny loved Ronnie to death. Johnny would come by and pick Ronnie up in his Mercury convertible and Ronnie, as young as he was, loved riding in that car.

Johnny could sing pretty good too. On our bus trips we'd have a quartet and Johnny would sing tenor and believe it or not I sang bass. Now, no one would ever confuse me with Tennessee Ernie Ford, but the other guys got a kick out us singing.

When I first got to Columbia I roomed with Jerry Pless, a pitcher, but he was traded halfway through the season. We were in Charleston, South Carolina and I go to my room and find I have a new roommate. It was a Latin fellow and he was in the corner of the room burning candles. I asked him what in the hell he was doing burning candles in the middle of the day in July. He had all the curtains pulled and the lights off. He mumbled something about a religious ceremony he was conducting.

After the game that night we come back and I go to the bathroom and come back out and he's got the lights off and he's back in the corner again burning those candles and chanting something. I told him to be careful that he didn't burn the place down. He had about six or seven candles on the table burning and I was really afraid he was going to catch the place on fire. I had me a fifth and I stayed up all night drinking that whiskey and waiting for the candles to burn out. I can't even remember the fellow's name now, but he wasn't with us very long before he got released.

On that same road trip to Charleston, we had a lot of our valuables stolen. While the game was in progess, some thieves thought it would be a good opportunity to help themselves to whatever they could find. They took some boards off the outside of our clubhouse and the robbers stole some of our equipment and personal items. Of course those guys couldn't have gotten too much because they were stealing from minor league ballplayers and everybody knows we weren't exactly loaded.

Anyway, we went from Charleston down to Jacksonville and that marked the end of my days with Columbia. We had Thursday and Friday games rained out, so a doubleheader was scheduled for Saturday, but I never made it to the park. During the first day it rained, I met up with some guys and we were seeing how may bars we could hit in Jacksonville. This went on for two days and nights. When Saturday rolled around, I wasn't in any shape to play ball. I may have even slept through the doubleheader. Everyone was wondering where I was. No one could recall having seen me in three days.

Before I go further, I admit this was a pretty immature and irresponsible thing for me to do. Looking back I can't believe I was this stupid. I had a wife and son at home and I was acting like this. But I'm not hiding anything now. I did it and I admit it was stupid. Hopefully, to keep anyone who may be reading this from doing the same thing. My gosh, I was 33 years old and acting like a kid. But until you've been on a team traveling like that you have to understand the temptations that are out there. But I will say this, as God is my witness, I never fooled around with women after marrying Helen. As for drinking, well that was another story.

Anyway, we had a Sunday afternoon game scheduled and by this time the whole Cincinnati organization knew I was AWOL. Well, Sunday I came dragging into the clubhouse. I could feel everyone staring at me like I had some kind of disease. Gee walked over, never asking where I'd been because I think he had a pretty good idea. Gee just told me not to even bother getting dressed. I got my belongings and walked back out of the clubhouse. That was it for me and the Reds' organization, I was given my release. I felt guilty and I was embarrassed, especially for Gee who had put so much trust in me. I let him down big time.

President Bill McCarthy of the Columbia
Reds announced on the eve of the club's

return to its home park for a five-game series with Savannah that first baseman Leo ("Muscles") Shoals has been dropped from the roster for breaking training.

Shoals was a favorite here despite the thin average, mainly because the crowd thought he might put one out of the park every time he stepped to the plate and wiggled that stick.

– The State,
July 10, 1950

I was on shaky ground with Cincinnati before that incident. Earlier that season Dean Wood and I rubbed the brass the wrong way by messing with Blackburn. Dean and I had a lounge we frequented named Mattie's in Charleston, South Carolina where we'd go to have a few drinks and play poker. We went out one night after a game and Jerry tagged along with us. We ordered some drinks, mainly bourbons straight and Jerry, who being just a young kid, had never drank very much, if at all. But we'd have one and then another and about the third drink I could see that Jerry's lights were going to go out and about that time his head hit the table and he didn't move a muscle.

Dean called a cab and we loaded the kid in and hauled him back to our hotel. We didn't want anybody seeing us, so we all crammed into the freight elevator and took him up to his room, put him to bed, locked the door and left. Down in the lobby, Gee and some top official from Cincy were talking.

Meanwhile, Jerry comes to. He gets up and comes down to the lobby and he's wobbling and screaming at the top of his lungs, "Shoals and Wood are the greatest guys ever." Neither Dean nor I were there to see it firsthand, but we got it straight from Gee the next morning when he called us into his office. We told Gee the whole story and Gee just kind of smiled. It was as if he might have been in on one or two of those situations himself at some point.

But Gee had some explaining to do to the brass. After all, they were curious as to why their bonus baby was drunk as a skunk in the lobby of the hotel. At the same time, Gee had been working with Jerry, a hard thrower, on his control. Blackburn never did find his control. He was drafted into the army in 1951, put on some weight and Cincy finally gave up on him. I never did know what happened to him after that. If nothing else, he learned how to drink bourbon straight in Charleston.

I went to the office at Columbia to pick up my paycheck and I ran into Gee and I apologized for my actions. Gee just nodded.

"He's a nice guy with a wife and a young child but I had no alternative. The big guy has been drinking all along and it got to where it was affecting his hitting and his fielding too much. If Shoals had fallen out of line once or twice, I would have overlooked it. He wasn't able to get to the park one day at Jacksonville and there have been other times that he reported to the park showing the after-effects of drinking.

"I feel sorry for Muscles, but I don't think it's fair to keep a fellow who can't give his best. The people who pay their way into the park deserve the best from me and my players. When a player goes too far and can't give his best, you have to get rid of him. Shoals could have been a much better player. He can get by in a league of lower classification, but he can't keep up with Class A pitching and abuse himself as he has been doing. He realizes he is wrong and he told me that he has received every opportunity here.

It's hard not to like Muscles, but there wasn't anything to do but let him go."

– Gee Walker quoted in The State, July 11, 1950

In the end the Reds sold me to the Reidsville Luckies. It was up to me as to whether I wanted to go. What else was I going to do? I went. I hated leaving Columbia. Not that I was having a good year. I left with a .261 batting average and seven home runs in 318 at bats. Quite a comedown from 55 home runs.

But now I was looking forward to renewing old acquaintances at Reidsville. Most of the guys from '49 were gone. Bob Downing, Mike Dattero and Mike Forline were still with the club. Glenn Rawlinson was still there, but soon was sent to Raleigh. George Souter had been with the Luckies for most of the season and then he was sold to Raleigh. But George refused to go and ended up joining the Luckies again the same night I reported back.

The Mighty Man, Leo (Muscles) Shoals, is returning to Reidsville in an effort to bolster the Reidsville batting power and help keep the Luckies in the first division.

The announcement at the Reidsville-Raleigh game last night drew a loud burst of applause from the Reidsville fans at Kiker Stadium.

– The Reidsville Review, July 11, 1950

Who else could make Reidsvillians forget about the Korean War?

– The Reidsville Review, July 12, 1950

Crash Davis had joined the Luckies and so did Tee Frye. With me and Souter on the corners, our infield was the same infield that started the 1949 all-star game against Danville. I mentioned earlier what a great fielding second baseman Crash was, well he set a Carolina League record just about the time I joined the club when he made 13 putouts against Burlington. Crash held the old record of nine in a 16-inning game. Those 13 putouts were quite an accomplishment.

Tee Frye is a guy who never got his due, I don't think. I knew Tee, whose real name was Walter and he was known as "Tee Pot", when I played against him but I got to know him better when we teamed up at Reidsville.

Tee had spent seven years in the St. Louis Cardinals system. He was signed in 1941 before going into service and came back to play with them from 1946 to 1953. He was with Reidsville four of those years. Tee still holds several Carolina League records for most consecutive games played (956), most runs scored (929), most total bases (1,152) and most at bats (3,629). He spent seven years in the Carolina League and was an all-star shortstop six times.

But Tee's athletic life didn't end after pro ball. Tee coached both baseball and basketball at Oak Ridge Military Academy in North Carolina and was also the athletic director. He was at Oak Ridge for 34 years. Tee was a great guy and we had a lot of fun together.

"I remember one time we were in Raleigh and had to spend the night. After our last game, Muscles was the first one on the bus and he'd been to the store and had gotten himself a six-pack of beer. Herb Brett was our manager and he always sat on the front seat of the bus and he went to sleep just like everybody else. Everything would be real quiet and then you'd hear this pssstttt and it'd be Muscle opening another bottle of beer.

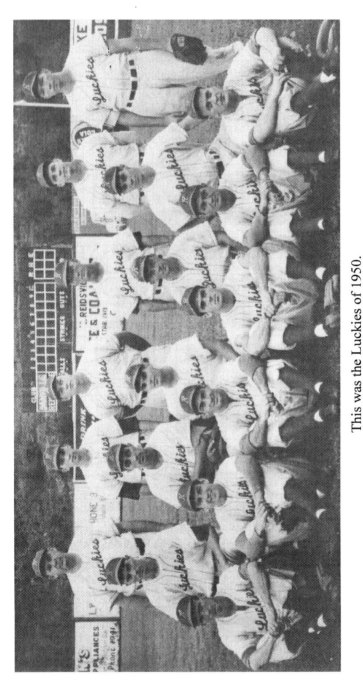

This was the Luckies of 1950.

(Back row, left to right) Manager Herb Brett, Dattero, Shoals, Souter, Nagel and McIntosh. (Middle row, left to right) Pesert, Anthony, Roberts, Miller, Piesek. (Front row, left to right) Tee Frye, Micich, Forline, Charles, Amoriello, Pawlek. (Photo courtesy Sam Amoriello)

Another time Muscle had been hitting the high spirits and we were taking infield. We'd throw the ball to Muscle at first base and he'd hold his glove up like he was going to catch the ball and the ball would go right by his head. Herb noticed it and told Muscle to take an early shower. Muscle was ranting and raving saying he could play. He said the sun was in his eyes."

– Walter T. Frye,
shortstop, Reidsville

Unlike 1949, Reidsville was able to stick with one manager from start to finish as Herb Brett called the shots. I met some new fellows like Andy Piesik, Bill Nagel, a veteran who had been up with the Phillies, Athletics and White Sox as a utility infielder during the war, Ted Pawelek and Elmer Roberts. Also there was Sam Amoriello and Joe Micich, who won 18 games and hit over .300.

My first game back with the Luckies was against Danville and I walked three times and got a hit in a game we won 9-3 and a game in which Danville pitching issued 19 walks. It felt good to be back and it felt even better the next night, in the second game of a doubleheader against Greensboro, when I hit my first home run.

A couple of days later I hit another home run with Souter on base to give us a 3-1 win over Fayetteville. Everything seemed to be going well and then I started having a series of injuries that I just couldn't shake. I was out about three weeks

When I did come back in the middle of August it was in a doubleheader against Durham. In the first game I had the only hit off Bob Cruze and in the second game I went 3-for-3 with a pair of home runs. But then I was back on the bench with injuries again, mainly my ankle which I hurt the first time that took me out so long.

Now, I was mainly just a pinch-hitter and that nearly killed me. I couldn't stand sitting on the bench just watching, but there wasn't much else I could do. The regular season came to an end and the Luckies finally got over that .500 mark with an 82-72 record, we were just a year late in doing it.

Winston-Salem won the title with 106 wins, thanks in part to a dandy little fielding second baseman by the name of Earl Weaver. The same Earl Weaver who would later manage the Baltimore Orioles. Danville was a distant second and 19 games back. Ben Chapman, who managed the Philadelphia Phillies from 1945-48, was the Danville manager. I remember when we played the Leafs toward the end of the season they came out wearing short pants. I couldn't believe it. It was Branch Rickey's idea. Danville was a Brooklyn Dodgers' farm club and they wore these shorts which were referred to as the Hollywood uniforms. Hollywood was a farm club of Brooklyn in the Pacific Coast League and Rickey tried out the shorts on that club and decided to try it with the rest of Brooklyn's farm clubs. I could see me out there wearing shorts. It wasn't bad enough that Danville wore those shorts, but later in the year Raleigh decided to go with the shorts as well. I'm just glad it never caught on.

Anyway, we got into the playoffs losing the first game 1-0 on a six-hitter by Vinegar Bend Mizell. I pinch-hit in that game and walked. The next night at Southside Park in Winston-Salem we lost 8-7, but I pinch-hit a solo home run off Harold Atkinson to tie the game 6-6.

In the third game Micich beat the Cardinals 5-2 and then we tied the series 2-2 as Forline spun a three-hitter. Me and Souter rekindled old times with back-to-back home runs off George Condrick in the third.

Then, in the fifth and deciding game, Mizell threw a seven-hitter against us and we lost 11-2 to Winston-Salem, which ended up winning the title after beating Burlington four out of five. I had a single and a walk against Mizell in that last playoff game, but that was it for me and the Luckies in 1950.

> *The Cardinals gave the big crowd a thrill (3,845 at Winston-Salem) with the Shoals Shift in the eighth inning. Only manager George Kissell at third base was on the left side of the field as Mizell pitched to Shoals. The big first baseman finally worked out a walk.*
>
> *– The Reidsville Review,*
> *September 18, 1950*

I hit five home runs in 116 at bats with a .224 average in my return to Reidsville in 1950. Not much to brag about and certainly a lot less impressive than my stats in 1949. I guess I disappointed a lot of folks who were counting on seeing the Muscle Shoals of '49. But I couldn't do anything about the injuries and nobody was more disappointed in my performance than me.

After the season, Helen, Ronnie and I moved to Kingsport for the winter. Helen was from there and I had played two years there so I liked the town. As it would turn out, I would play there once again.

Chapter 16

Kingsport was like home to me, the people there were so friendly and I loved the area. But I had planned to return to Reidsville in 1951, until W.A. Allen, a millionaire who owned the Kingsport Cherokees in the Appalachian League, kept calling me that he would like to have me play in Kingsport.

The more I thought about it the better it sounded. I mean Kingsport was now my home and I'd be playing right there. I told Mr. Allen I'd love to play for the Cherokees, but that I was still under contract to the Luckies and I wasn't sure I could get out of it. Not bragging, but I was still a big draw for the Luckies.

Allen asked me if I would talk to the Luckies and I said I would. Even before I called Tom Smothers about getting out of my contract, I had my mind made up that if the Luckies didn't let me out of my contract and play at Kingsport, I would just quit. Tom Smothers tried to talk me into coming back to Reidsville, but he understood my situation. Smothers made a deal with Kingsport in which the Cherokees bought me for $1,000. After all the papers were signed, I headed for 12 uneventful days of spring training in St. Augustine, Florida to get in shape for the season. We packed up again and headed north to Kingsport.

Allen was big on promotions in Kingsport. He'd do just about anything to bring fans into the ballpark. He would have greasy pig contests and one time he got this fellow to drive a car through a fire and crash it into some parked cars. The poor fellow had everybody on the edge of their seats, even the players who were watching from the dugouts. He goes through a roaring wall of fire and slams into those cars, making a loud racket. Everybody kept waiting for him to climb out as the flames were shooting up and the smoke was billowing. Emergency crews rushed out and, just as they reached his car, the daredevil climbs out the window, staggers out to where everybody can see him and bows to the crowd. Everybody loved it.

Then there was the time the carnival came to Kingsport and they had this 600-pound fellow who would do different acts. Allen contacted the manager of the carnival and asked if he could get him out to the park. The manager of the carnival agreed, if Allen would pay him $50. At the park, before the game when they were announcing the lineups, the PA guy said, "Playing first base, Muscle Shoals." We had it worked out where I would stay in the dugout and out would walk this 600-pound fellow in a uniform that Allen had made up for him with my number on the back. Everybody got a laugh out of that one.

Jack Crosswhite was the manager at Kingsport and, in my opinion, he was one of the best. Not that he didn't sometimes make bad decisions, every manager does. Such as the decision on Orlando Cepeda. Jack managed Cepeda at Salem in 1955 and actually released Cepeda because Jack didn't think Orlando was making enough progress. Of course, Cepeda went on to play 17 years in the major leagues and retired with a .297 career batting average and 379 home runs.

Our team that year had four veterans, eight with limited service, and the rest were rookies. A veteran was one who had played three years or more, a limited service player had three years and under experience, and a rookie was under 90 days. The Appalachian League then wasn't anything like the Appalachian League is today. The clubs were individually owned, not operated by the major league franchises as is the case with the modern Appy League. While the players today are in their first or second year of pro ball and most right out of high school or college, it wasn't like that then. In the 1950s we had seasoned veterans, some guys who had even been in the major leagues and were on their way back down.

We were a loose bunch on the field and in the dugout. We played with a lot of confidence, but we were always joking with each other. Like the time Paul

211

Musselman was complaining before a game about a sore leg. He said, "Boy, I've got one of the worst charley horses you've ever seen. I couldn't steal a base tonight if a five-year-old was catching." Well, early in the game, Paul got on first with a hit. He proceeded to steal second, then third and then scored on a short fly ball. He came back to the dugout and I said: "Say Paul, what's the name of that charley horse? Citation?"

When August rolled around I was hitting over .400 and I had my home run stroke down. One of my more impressive home runs came at J. Fred in a game against Bluefield. I drove a pitch which hit the flag pole in center field about 50 feet up, a 425-foot poke, and the ball glanced over the hedge. I remember I came back to the dugout and Jack deadpanned it saying, "Muscle, if you knock the flag pole down you're going to have to pay to buy a new one."

Jack may have been the perfect manager for our team that season. A few years later Jack, who lived and worked as an iron worker in North Carolina during the offseason, was on a job in the 1960s and he fell 10 or 15 feet and struck his head. He never regained consciousness and passed away a short time later.

Jack was a character though. I remember one game he and the ump got into it over something. Jack began cussing. The umpire requested that Jack refrain from using the foul language. Well, that got Jack that much madder and he stood nose-to-nose with that umpire and said: "If you think that was cussing, then listen to this you…."

Somebody told me a story one time about Jack when he was managing another club. One of his players was batting with a 3-2 count and the pitcher uncorked a fastball that hit the umpire right behind the ear. Well, the umpire hit the ground with a thud and out rushed Jack to where the umpire was laying flat on his back. Jack bent over and said: "Please ump, before you die, say the pitch was a ball."

When I later managed at Kingsport in 1953, we had an outfielder by the name of Ed Gibson who played for Crosswhite one year in Elizabethton. Gibson told us a story about a catcher on the team who hadn't been in a game for about 40 days and this catcher was pretty put out with the situation by this point. Anyway, Crosswhite and this catcher were sitting on the bench watching the game, which was tied in the ninth inning with two out and the bases loaded and a 3-2 count on the batter. "What'd you call for in a situation like this?" Crosswhite asked the catcher. The catcher spit out a long stream of tobacco juice and snarled, "I'd call for a resin bag to dust the seat of my pants so I wouldn't slide off this damn bench."

Jack told the story of the time that he managed New River in the Appalachian League. The Rebels were in Pulaski one night and getting thumped pretty good. Jack, whose second occupation was to argue with umpires, found reason to start the baiting and eventually got tossed from the game. When a player or manager is thrown out of a game, you have to leave the field and go to the clubhouse. The only problem at Pulaski was that there was no clubhouse to go to, so Jack left the ballpark.

On his way to the bus, Jack noticed a light pole just on the other side of the outfield fence. So Jack climbed up the pole and began giving signals to his team from up there. It wasn't long before someone spotted Jack, called the police and they came and made Jack shimmy down.

Jack had some free time since the game was a couple of innings from being over, so he decided he'd go buy some watermelons to feed the team before heading back home on the bus. After the game, the players boarded the bus and began eating the watermelons. The bus was parked along a city street and the players, with no place to put the watermelon rinds, began tossing them out the window and onto the sidewalk. Where the bus was parked, by the way, was right in front of the police station. An officer came by, saw all the rinds on the ground and made the players get off the bus and clean up the whole mess.

Jack, who never got higher than A ball as a player, seemed content to manage at the Class D level. Jack had a temper sometimes, but he had mellowed by the time I got to know him, from what I understand. He first managed with South Boston, Virginia in 1940 and it wasn't long after that in which he got into a fight with an umpire and it was serious enough that Jack got a one year's suspension. After that, Jack seemed to know where to draw the line when arguing with umpires.

We played the all-star game that year at J.Fred Johnson in front of a crowd of almost 4,500. The Cherokees were leading the league, so we took on the rest of the league's all-stars. We ended up getting beat 2-1 on Dom Commisso's bloop single, which drove in Jim Salinger in the ninth inning. The all-stars had eight hits and four of those were by Commisso, who played shortstop for the Bristol Twins. I didn't help our cause very much by going 0-for-3. As a matter of fact, we only had five hits and two of those were by Hugh Hamil, who we had purchased from Elizabethton over the winter.

Commisso's hit was a fly to center which looked like it was going to be caught by Musselman, but it fell in front of Paul for the hit. Our only run was a home run by Claude (Pappy) Wright off Gary Blaylock's very first pitch in the opening inning. The ball got between left fielder Lantz Blaney and center fielder Elmer Westfall and rolled for the home run.

I might mention here something about J. Fred Johnson Park. Now a lot of parks have their own idiosyncrasies and J. Fred was no different. The oddball thing about J. Fred was that there was no left field fence. Now there was one in right and center, but none in left. I can't tell you why there wasn't a fence in left field, but it was sure a strange setup. We had some very good right-handed power hitters like Bobby Westfall, Hugh Hamil and Jim Watkins. When the right-handed power guys come up, the left fielder is back almost 400 feet. It was an open area back there. Home run balls were being caught and balls that should have been in the gaps for doubles were rolling for home runs.

Of course I had a fence to shoot at in right. I guess the longest home run I hit there must have gone 500 feet. In a game in which we beat Johnson City 14-1, Ned Jilton had his big sweeping curveball working to perfection as he struck out 15 and I had three hits, including the home run which a lot of people said went 500 feet on the fly.

It was a season of odd happenings. Take John Rotche. Rotche was a veteran catcher who started the season with us, but early on developed a sore arm. Allen kept Rotche around, not as a player but as our bus driver.

Well, in early May the Boston Braves fired Norton manager Bob Bowman and named outfielder George Sifft as the interim manager. In the meantime, they had their eye on Rotche to fill the post. It may be the only time in professional baseball that the bus driver of one club was named manager of another.

While we're talking about odd happenings, I'll mention one that happened at J. Fred in a game against Johnson City. In the eighth inning Jilton hit a ball that cleared the center field fence by about five feet. The umpire raced from his infield position into center field as soon as the ball was hit and signaled that it was a home run.

Like something out of a Keystone Cops movie, all the Johnson City outfielders went out to center field and jumped into the bushes looking for the ball. If they came up with a ball that meant Jilton's hit wasn't a home run, but a double. Enter Johnson City manager Ben Catchings. Ben comes running out of the dugout with both his hands stuck in his back pockets. Ben gets out there and jumps in the bushes himself. Like a magician pulling a rabbit out of a hat, Ben pulls a ball out of the bushes.

The umpires smelled something fishy at that point. After talking for a few minutes, the umpires upheld the home run ruling on Jilton's hit. Ben starts jumping up and down and yelling at the umpires while holding the ball up as proof that the hit was a double, not a home run. One of the umpires took the ball and threw it from center field to the Kingsport dugout and walked away with Ben following, jawing all the way.

We ended up winning the pennant by 18 games and I found my stroke again winning the triple crown with a .383 batting average, 30 home runs and 129 RBIs.

Bluefield's Lantz Blaney was second in hitting with a .364 average. However, I really do think I would have had more competition there in the batting race if Elizabethton's John Davenport hadn't been sent up to manage Wilmington in the Phillies organization. Davenport had a nice stroke. When Davenport left in mid-June he had 55 hits to my 52. But that's the way minor league baseball is, you move around and around.

We breezed into the playoffs and then we proceeded to sweep the Elizabethton series two games to none and followed by beating Bluefield in the best of five 3-2. We did it without our best pitcher – Jessee James. James, a right-hander who played fullback three years for Emory & Henry College in Virginia, had a phenomenal year going 23-5 with a league-leading 1.91 ERA. He started 27 games and completed 23, striking out 206 in 231 innings.

The thing about Jessee, who stood about 5-feet-8 and weighed 190 pounds, is that he loved to play baseball – a little too much.

It seemed that while we had a day off a week or two before the playoffs were to start, Jessee was pitching in the semipro Burley Belt League for Abingdon, Virginia. He thought he could get by with it as he went by his real name of George and not Jessee, but somebody recognized him and before long word was out. George Trautman, president of the minors, suspended James for the playoffs and then slapped a $200 fine on him. To beat it all, James lost the game for Abingdon 2-1 against Saltville.

But, we still had enough to win it all despite not having James. After beating Elizabethton, we opened the second round losing to Bluefield 6-5 in a game that was called after seven innings because we ran out of baseballs. It

CHAMPIONS
APPALACHIAN LEAGUE
1951

I was proud to be a member of the 1951 Appalachian League champions in Kingsport. Some of the names escape me but here's who I know.

(Front row, left to right) Paul Musselman, Bobby Westfall, Gene Reynolds, Newt Johnson, George Howard. (Second row, left to right) Don Russell, Hugh Hamil, Jessee James, Claude Wright, Jack Crosswhite, Muscle Shoals. (Back row, left to right) Johnny Spriggs, unknown, George Wright, unknown, Powell King, Jim Watkins, unknown, Ned Jilton. (Photo courtesy Powell King).

had been raining the entire night in Kingsport and the balls kept getting wet and waterlogged. Finally, we just ran out of dry baseballs. There were no more balls left in the clubhouse and we even tried to use some of the batting practice balls, but they were in no shape to use either. The umpires did all they could do and that was to call it at that point with Bluefield leading.

We had taken a 5-0 lead in that game. I had a two-run home run, but things fell apart when Ned Jilton left in the sixth inning with a sore arm. Bluefield scored all six runs in that inning.

The next night we come back and we were tied 3-3 after 14 innings. But it was all for nothing because there was an 11 o'clock curfew mandating that an inning could not start after 11 p.m. We had to start all over the next night and play that game from the very beginning.

Buster Brown came through for us with a four-hit shutout as we won 4-0, scoring all four runs in the first inning. We won the next night 12-9 as I went 3-for-4 with a home run. We now had a 2-1 advantage in the series and if we won the next night we'd take the title. However, if we lost we would have to play a second game that night.

The fourth game was a dandy. Hugh Hamil had a two-run double, which tied us with Bluefield in the third 2-2. We went up 3-2 in the fifth and 4-2 in the eighth as I hit a solo home run. But Bluefield exploded for four runs in the bottom of the eighth at Bowen Field to take a 6-4 lead.

Well, we took the lead back with three runs in the ninth to go up 7-6. However, Bluefield scored twice in the bottom of the ninth on George Owen's two-run home run.

That made it necessary to play the fifth and deciding game that night. I helped get us started with a two-run home run in our three-run second inning. Bluefield battled back to tie us at 3-3 in the second and then took a 5-3 lead in the fifth.

Our backs were against the wall. But, we still had a lot of life left in us. In the sixth we scored four runs as Jim Watkins hit a two-run double and George Wright had a two-run single. We took a 7-5 lead and hung on for the win and the championship.

I want to tell you right now that there's nothing like winning a championship. I'd give up any batting titles or home run titles any time to be able to say we are the best team in the league. I must say that winning that championship is one of my fondest memories.

You start thinking that maybe there would be no more titles to be won. I was getting older and tomorrow might be the end of my career. As it turned out, however, there were still a few good years remaining.

Chapter 17

I thought I might be back with Kingsport in 1952 and, at the age of 35, I was ready to put down permanent stakes and no place had been better to me than Kingsport. But the Cherokees were in bad need of cash and they got a call from Rock Hill, South Carolina of the Tri-State League about acquiring some players. Apparently Rock Hill wanted some veterans to mix in with some kids and I certainly would be considered a veteran. Helen and I discussed the move to Rock Hill and I told Helen that with the money being decent and as long as I could do a respectable job and as long as I can play within the Carolina and Tennessee area, I wouldn't mind going to South Carolina.

I would be joined in Rock Hill by Cherokee teammates lefty Ned Jilton and second baseman George Wright. Going with guys you knew made it a lot easier trying to break into a new city. It's tough joining a club where you really don't know anybody, although it usually didn't take me long to make friends.

Of course, Ned and I had known each other for a long time and I had gotten to know George Wright pretty well. George was a fine gloveman at second and he wasn't too bad with the bat either. The one thing I remember about George was that he used a Charlie Gehringer model bat, which had a thick handle. I called it a banjo bat. When George would make an out I'd tell him, "George, you better tighten up those strings on the banjo."

George told me a story one time when he was playing for Clinton, North Carolina of the Tobacco State League in 1950. The team bus broke down on some country backroad, so George and another player volunteered to go get help. They start walking and a few minutes later they see a farmhouse, so they cut across the field. They hadn't bit more got into the field when they saw this bull standing near a tree giving them the eye. George and the other guy began walking a little faster and about that time the bull began running after them. George and the other fellow ran through a cornfield before running up on the porch and into this farmhouse. George said, "The people were listening to the radio when we ran in and must have thought we were crazy or trying to rob them. The bull had run through a barbed-wire fence and right up on the porch after us."

I was looking forward to making the rounds in the Tri-State League once again. I had been away from the Tri-State League for about four years, since playing for Charlotte in 1948. Eddie Allen, a real good sportswriter for the Charlotte Observer, wrote a welcome back column, which was one of the best I ever had written about me. I think it's worth repeating here. Eddie had one thing wrong in the column, however. I went from Columbia to Reidsville in 1950, not vice versa as he states.

Welcome Back, Muscle Shoals;
Please Forget Bees Sold You!

While it is still safe to express such sentiments in Charlotte, let us welcome Leo C. Shoals back into the Tri-State League. For although he now fills out the enemy grays of Rock Hill and coyly concedes he is 30-umph years of age, ol' Muscles is sure to contribute a bonus undertone of excitement to tonight's Griffith Park opener.

Hornet fans whose allegiance dates back to 1948 will understand this. They loved him here that year. Like no Charlotte slugger since Bobby Estalella (the Bobby of 1938, not 1951) broad-backed Leo of the mighty wrists brought in the crowds. And while he faded in the season's Indian summer he finished with 21 home runs, including eight of the longest balls ever howitzered out of the spacious local

221

yard. Both figures stand as Hornet records for Tri-State play.

It was also no coincidence that with an otherwise drab, fifth-place club that season, Charlotte drew 10,000 more spectators than it did while winning the pennant by 15 games last year. Economics, television, etc., admittedly figure in the paradoxical comparison, too. But a big factor was Shoals' constant appeal to homer-happy customers. Almost no amount of speed and fielding finesse can equal that kind of attraction. The singles that helped build his .287 average are overlooked.

In a way it was a shame that Muscles was a minor league version of Babe Ruth off the field as well as on it. His unorthodox theories on training kept him at odds with manager Joe Bowman. One night in Anderson their differences in viewpoint almost resulted in open civil war. As men they were not truly dissimilar, but Shoals was a player and Bowman the manager and Joe wanted that distinction remembered. Forgetting which was technically in the right (or wrong), it is a fact that by the following year neither was employed here and Shoals, without a doubt, was missed more.

Five-Five Embarrassing Homers

The Hornets' decision to continue the travels of the journeyman Shoals was understandable. He didn't fit in with plans for the care, feeding and training of young players. But I've heard General Manager Phil Howser admit he was sorry he sold Muscles to Reidsville that winter of 1948 for a price that could almost be figured by the pound.

When the deal was made it was thought probable that Leo, who had finished his Hornet race in a shuffling walk, was nearing the end of the line. That idea was upheld when he was reported to have become involved in some extracurricular unpleasantness on his very first day in Reidsville.

But as the 1949 season wore on, with the Hornets languishing from lack of power, the news from the Carolina League (also Class B) became more and more embarrassing. Shoals, it seems, had spied a new and friendlier right field fence and had instantly "reformed." All he did for Reidsville was to blast (count 'em) 55 home runs, more than anyone else in all of baseball that year; hit .359, missing the league batting title by two points; and accumulate 137 RBIs, 131 runs scored, 365 total bases and 116 walks!

Still, upheld was the precedent that with the exception of Kingsport, Tenn. (where he could easily be elected mayor), Muscles never stays with the same club for two consecutive full seasons. When Columbia of the Sally League bought him in 1950, he was hitting a meek .228 for Reidsville. In Class A, his average slipped to .261 and his homer production to seven. So, last season, he was probably content (certainly Kingsport was) to return to Tennessee and lead the Class D Appalachian League with .383 and 30 home runs. Likewise he didn't mind ambling down to Rock Hill this spring for another try in the Tri-State. It could be he still considers

Griffith Park's distant barriers a true challenge for his strength.

A Few Couldn't 'Pitch To Him'

Most of Muscles' opponents claim that he "can be pitched to." Give him the curve, they say. Change up on him. Stay away from his power and you'll get him out. Now this may be true, but that constitutes a lot to remember and put into use when you're actually out there facing the big guy. And the dog-eared record books disclose that since he broke in with Monessen of the Pennsylvania State League in 1937 he has hit over .300 eight seasons (not counting four out for the war).

Along the way he has collected a total of 250 or more home runs. So quite a few rivals obviously weren't able to "pitch to him."

That's in the Class B minors and below. In higher classification, where the pitching is sharper, Shoals has been no sensation in brief stays. He was batting just .222 when Chattanooga of the Class AA Southern Association sent him down to Charlotte in '48.

Neither is he a Hal Chase or even a reasonable facsimile in playing first base. What ground he covers he covers professionally – what ground he covers. Like Zeke Bonura he may lead the league in fielding percentages (as he did in the '48 Tri-State), but nobody will ever accuse him of being a dancing master around the bag.

Yet all in all, what difference does that make to minor league crowds? They pay their money to see men like Muscles deposit 400-foot line drives beyond their sight. They wait to see him come to bat – for this might be the time he poles one.

So welcome back, Mr. Shoals. We're looking forward to seeing you work again. But in Charlotte tonight – gently, boy, gently.

I may not have been a gazelle at first base, but I wasn't that bad. I don't think.

Anyway, when we got to Rock Hill we didn't know if we were going to have a club to play on or not. Rock Hill had been affiliated with the Chicago Cubs, but right before the season the Cubs pulled out. That put Rock Hill in a bind and the club announced toward the end of March that it didn't have enough capital to operate the season on. But never fear. Like any good business you have to have a good business manager and H.S. Buck, an appropriate last name, came up with the idea on how to fund the club. All the club had to do was sell 103 shares of stock at $110 a whack.

Apparently the stock wasn't selling all that good and, by the middle of May, the buck stopped with Buck. Old H.S. decided to give it up and quit the club. Club president Earl Sherer went searching for a replacement for Buck and that's when he came up with Calvin McCaw, the baseball coach at Rock Hill High School. I don't know how much McCaw knew about business, but Sherer figured McCaw, who was a popular figure around town, might be able to drum up some much-needed cash.

I think Calvin was able to sell some more stock, but it wasn't near enough to keep the club afloat. About the middle of June the Rock Hill board of directors sent letters to all the stockholders asking for $10 donations to keep the club from folding, which wasn't a bad idea. If you're a stockholder wouldn't you part with $10? If the club folded, your stock wouldn't be worth a red cent. A few stockholders felt that way, but after about a week or two the response wasn't too good. So, Sherer went pleading to the fans. He could get a

$10,000 loan, enough to float the club, if he could get 100 fans to underwrite that loan. Not too many put their John Henry on the dotted line on that proposal. But, there were a few businesses around town which came to the rescue. Sherer got the loan and the club kept its head above water.

I posed in my stance for photographers at Rock Hill.
(Photo courtesy of Sholes family)

It was a tough time for the club, which encountered some bad weather for the first month and attendance was averaging just a little over 900 a game. They actually needed to average a couple thousand to keep operating. But one reason our attendance was so bad, aside from the weather, was that the economy in Rock Hill was on a downslide. There were 15 textile mills and factories in Rock Hill, which employed close to 9,000 people, but a lot of those factories were only operating three days a week and a lot of folks couldn't afford to come to our games. Admission was 65 cents, which doesn't sound like a lot of money now, but in 1952 that was quite a bit of money, especially if you were only working three days a week and you were taking your family along.

There may not have been a lot of people coming out to our games, but it wasn't for the lack of not knowing when our games were going to be played. At the Andrew Jackson Hotel downtown, there was a big sign posted out front promoting all our home games. Then there was the taxi cab company which carried an announcement of each home game on the spare tire which was right on the back bumper of each cab. So, if you were driving around town and pulled up behind a taxi, you couldn't help but know when our next home game was to be played. But the best was Mack McMurray, a local radio and television dealer. He had a panel truck and he put loud speakers in the bed of the truck. Mack would drive the truck through the streets of Rock Hill blasting away to advertise our games.

Rock Hill was a city of about 25,000 then and I think they all came out on opening night. They were packed in like sardines at Municipal Stadium, a concrete structure which seated 5,000 and served double duty as the high school football stadium. I don't think you could have squeezed another two people in that place that night.

And those fans got a real good show to watch as Jilton pitched the game against Charlotte and beat the Hornets 4-3. He really did beat them too. Not only on the mound, but he had a ninth-inning game-winning single. I had tied the game 3-3 in the eighth with a two-run home run off of Zeke Zeisz into the right field bleachers, which they measured at 400 feet. I started off batting cleanup, but then later on was moved to third in the order, which was fine by me. I'd just as soon hit third because you're sure of getting a time at bat in the first inning and you have a good chance of coming up five times in a game.

It was a good start for the Chiefs and our manager Harry Land. Like a lot of managers in the minor leagues, Harry wore two hats. He was the manager, but he was also our starting catcher. At least he was our catcher for about the first week before he broke his hand one night in Charlotte when a pitch came in and he couldn't get out of the way. Popped him right on the wrist. Harry said he never even saw the pitch, blaming a white beer sign on top of the center field fence at Griffith Park, which he said the ball blended in with. We had to come up with a catcher quick and we signed my old buddy Mike Garbark. Mike wasn't playing anywhere and was out of baseball after managing Greenwood in 1951. Mike was 35 and he was really out of shape. After struggling behind the plate and hitting only .220, the Chiefs released Mike after a couple of weeks.

While Harry was mending, we managed to put some people behind the plate to catch after Mike was let go. As a club we struggled, but I got off to a great start. I had a nine or 10-game hitting streak, which paled in comparison to Jim Thomas who hit in about 15 straight. Jim, who was from Concord, N.C., would change hats when he got on base. Somewhere along the line Jim had been hit in the head and after that he would wear what was a forerunner of batting helmets. It was a special skullcap which had two thick chunks of leather shaped in semicircles covering his temples.

We hit the ball as a team, but we couldn't get any pitching except for Jim Patton who won three of his first four games. Jim was a strange sort. After he won his first three games he asked the club for a $25 raise and got it, but then he left the club for several days and nobody knew where he was. He came back and pitched well, but then he left the club again. Harry had no choice but to suspend Patton, which was too bad because he had a lot of potential, I thought.

Too bad the photographer didn't catch me hitting a home run instead of checking my swing while playing for Rock Hill.
(Photo courtesy Sholes family)

229

Bob McNeil finished with a 5-9 record, but he had one of the lowest ERAs in the league at the end of the season at 2.93. One week our pitching staff gave up 12 home runs and four of those were off McNeil. Bob had a quick wit and said, "It ain't flying saucers these people are seeing. It's Bob McNeil's pitching." Al Costa, a right-hander from Chicago, was our winningest pitcher and he finished 12-14 with a 4.05 ERA. Al was a battler and he was actually a pretty good pitcher. He had three shutouts that season, including a one-hitter over the Spartanburg Spinners. Al started his career in 1945 as an outfielder with Elizabethton, but along the way Paul Dean, Dizzy's brother, was coaching somewhere and turned Al into a pitcher. Al was an ironman. He started 23 games for us and finished 20. I look at guys today who start and they get all kinds of praise and the big money because they start a game and go six innings. Al missed a week to go back home for the birth of his daughter and the day he got back he pitched both ends of a doubleheader, winning one and losing the other.

We had a guy named Alex Zych, a right-hander and a pretty hard thrower, who everybody thought had a chance to set the world on fire. Alex, who would be in the dugout doing situps before every game, had gone 22-7 for Kinston in 1951. But he couldn't get untracked in '52. Alex lost his first six games of the year and was finally sold to Gastonia where his record sank to 3-12. Alex could never find his control. He ended up walking 95 in 149 innings.

Jilton had flashes of brilliance like he did in the opener. About the middle of July Ned shut out Knoxville 5-0 to run his record to 6-7. The next day Ned went to the front office and asked for his release. After the Knoxville game Ned and I were in the clubhouse changing and he showed me his elbow which had swollen to twice its size. We went out after the game to a place we liked on the Charlotte Highway called Porter's Grill, which had some of the best barbecue around. We were sitting there eating and Ned said, "Muscle, I can't go on. This elbow's killing me. Anyway, I got a business offer from a firm in West Virginia. I'll be studying and training to be a chemical engineer. I have my future to think about and I'm convinced my future isn't in baseball."

I hated to see Ned leave but I understood what he was going through. He had to make a tough choice.

Ned was a serious sort of fellow, not like Luther Mathews. Luther was a left-hander who won 10 games for us. Now pitchers are renowned bad hitters and Luther fit that bill as well as anybody. He was 0-for-33 before he got his first hit, a single. He ended up scoring a run and came back to the dugout and, as serious as he could be, Luther said, "It's always good to have a good-hitting pitcher in the lineup."

Luther, we called him Buster, had a good sense of humor. He kept the other guys loose and he could take a joke. Buster had gotten knocked out of the box in one game and the next day he was in the outfield running. Zych was standing there when Buster ran by and said: "One thing about you Bus, you work harder than any pitcher I know just to go two or three innings."

Buster didn't drink or smoke, but one night he was coaching first base and one of the guys talked him into chewing some Bull of the Woods. He stuck a wad in his mouth and it wasn't long before he had that stuff dripping all over his uniform. About the second inning he was out there and somebody hit a ball down in the corner and Buster got excited and was waving the runner to second and swallowed his cud. He never made it back to the dugout. Right there in front of a thousand people Buster began throwing up. We got him on the bench and put some cold towels on his head. After he recovered Buster said: "I got sick smoking a cigarette when I was a kid and I haven't had a cigarette since. As far as I'm concerned my drinking career never started and my chewing career ended tonight."

Harry had a tough job managing that outfit. We really had a terrible ballclub. Guys coming and going. We couldn't field the ball. George Wright started the season at second base but just wasn't hitting. Harry decided to try and find a second baseman who could hit so he bought Bill Ballinger, who had played with Greensboro in '51, from Roanoke. Ballinger lasted about a week. He made four errors in one game and the next day he was off to play for Reidsville, and Wright, a 20-year-old kid from Bridgeport, Connecticut, was back in. George was OK defensively, but he couldn't hit worth a lick and he admitted it. I remember him saying one time that he was the only player who could go 1-for-4 and raise his average.

Injuries played a big part in our poor start. Guys were missing games here and there, but the big blow was when we lost third baseman Herb May for about a month. Poor old Herb. During the winter, he fell off a ladder and broke his elbow and wrist. He got over that and along about the middle of June he was sliding into home plate at Greenville and ended up with a couple of broken ribs. Herb was a tough cookie. He was a veteran of World War II and Korea and was coaching baseball at Fort Benning when he was signed by Rock Hill.

Right after he broke his ribs Herb said: "I've got war wounds all over my body. I got my head laid open by a German bullet, I got hit in my back by shrapnel, I got hit in the arm by a bullet and I had a German woman, who hated Americans, run a pitchfork through my right leg. I come home and then have to go to Korea. But, you know, I didn't get a scratch in Korea. I come home and fall off the ladder and now I'm laid up with these ribs." Herb was a good hitter. He ended up hitting over .300 for us. Hal Ivey, the only guy on the club who was with Rock Hill in 1951, had to fill in for Herb.

While talking about Herb, I remember a story he told one time. Herb was playing for Rocky Mount of the Coastal Plain League in 1946 in a game against Tarboro. Herb hit a home run over the left field scoreboard and just as he was rounding third the umpire called him out for failing to touch first base. The Rocky Mount manager protested and the game was played from the protested inning about four weeks later. Herb came to bat again and hit another home run against the same pitcher in the same spot. Guess what? He

Robert Wainwright

Ralph Brawer

Jim Thomas

Leo Spools.

Rock Hill Chiefs

233

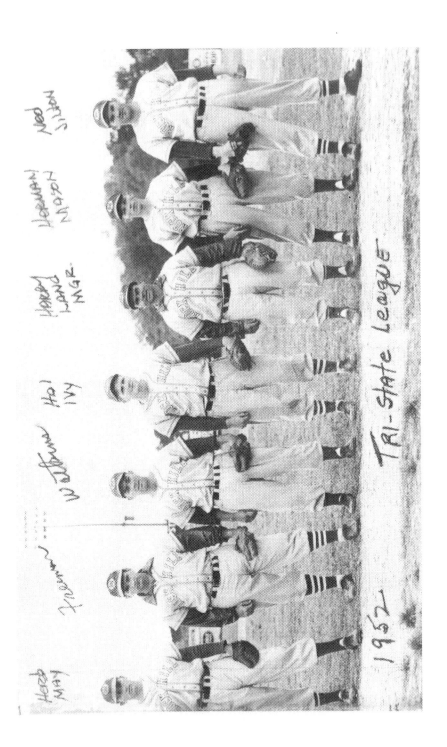

HERB
MAY

TRUMAN .....

WILLIAMS

HAL
IVY

HAROLD
LAND
MGR.

HERMAN
MASON

NED
SILTON

TRI-STATE LEAGUE

1952

was called out for failing to touch first base again. Herb said he got so upset with the umpire that he got thrown out of the game and was fined $10. This is the same Herb May who found an injured squirrel near the park one day and adopted it as a pet. He kept that squirrel in the clubhouse in a cage until it got better and then turned it loose.

Meanwhile, we kept losing. Harry was on the bench, nursing his own injury, and watching us get blown out. I was sitting next to him and said, "Harry, we ain't got too much do we?" Harry had been taking heat for our losing and he shook his head, "When a club loses, it's always the manager's fault. But, it's just like a carpenter trying to build a house without tools. It can't be done. Winning can't be done without the players to do it with." The most baffling thing was that we were playing great at home, where we were 18-11, but on the road we had won seven games and lost 26.

Harry finally got over his injury and got back in the lineup, but May was still out and we still needed a third baseman, so the club signed 33-year-old Leon Culbertson. Leon had played some third and the outfield for the Boston Red Sox from 1943-48. Leon was managing Middlesboro of the Mountain States League and was hitting .345 at the time he joined us. In 1951 he had hit .319 in 103 games with 14 home runs and 80 RBIs for Rome, Georgia of the Class D Georgia-Florida League and he was also the manager. When Leon joined the club, Harry told me he had a feeling his days were numbered. I said, "Harry, they ain't going to let you go." Two days later they let Harry go and named Leon our manager. I think one reason the club got Leon was because since our attendance was down they wanted to get somebody with a name and Leon had played in the majors so the front office thought his name might be worth a few folks at the turnstiles.

Right before he got released, Harry was talking about the situation our club was in mentally: "You know, ballplayers are human the same as anyone else. They get discouraged when they try hard and still lose. We have about the worst park in the league and have the worst uniforms. People make fun of our uniforms, how worn and dirty they were, when we were on the road. They laughed at us cause we were losing and called us a bunch of tramps. Those things eat away at a man. Jibes like those hurt."

I liked Leon OK. He was always telling stories, especially when we were sitting in the dugout waiting out rain delays. Leon liked telling about the time he got four hits off Allie Reynolds of the Yankees with President Harry S. Truman watching the game in 1948 and he told a story about Jim Bagby Jr., a teammate and pitcher on the Red Sox. Bagby was afraid of flying and somebody told Bagby that if it wasn't his time to die he wouldn't. Bagby shot back, "It might not be my time, but it might be the pilot's time to go."

On the day Leon took over we swept a doubleheader from Spartanburg. But things weren't much different for Leon than for Harry. Leon didn't want to play anymore, he just wanted to manage. Leon played a couple of games at third before signing Jim Watkins, who I had played with the year before in Kingsport. Jim was rusty coming to Rock Hill because he hadn't been playing anywhere all year and, after five or six games, he was released. Leon went back in for one game and decided to put in Don Phipps, who had been with us all year but hadn't played much. In Don's first game at third he was sliding into home against Asheville and broke his ankle. Leon was back at third once again. By July 1, we had used seven third basemen.

I liked Rock Hill. There were some good fans like Lee Deese. Lee was always at the ballpark. He sat right behind home plate. First thing when you came to bat Lee would holler at you. "Come on Muscle, knock one out of here." Lee told me one time that he had missed only two games since 1947. One time he went to a funeral and the other time he went fishing with his preacher and the preacher kept him out too late to get back in time for the ball game.

The one thing I didn't like about Rock Hill was the ballpark. It had to be one of the worst in the league. The stadium was used by, besides us, two high school teams in the spring, a junior legion team and a black team in the summer. They played high school football there and had other things going on like horse shows.

One of our outfielders, Ralph Brawner, said one time he didn't know when he went to catch a line drive if the ball would land in his glove or go over his head because the outfield was so uneven. Ralph was a good outfielder as he set a Tri-State record for putouts with 401, but Ralph also led the league in errors that year with 16. May said he was afraid to get down on the ball at third because it might end up in his teeth and Greenville third baseman Johnny DiFresco hurt his hand taking infield one day when the ball hit a pebble and caught him on the wrist. Greenville manager Ralph DuLuilo said the best thing to do at Rock Hill would be to drop an atomic bomb on Municipal Stadium. I led the league's first basemen in errors with 18 and several of those were on ground balls that took funny hops. It was frustrating, especially for our pitchers.

Then again, it was just as bad for the other teams that came in. So, I guess I can't put all the blame for our mediocrity on the stadium.

I'm going to stop talking about baseball for a minute or two because I have a confession to make. I got arrested once in Rock Hill. Don't jump to conclusions just yet though. I may have been a bad boy along the way, but I had mellowed a great deal by this point. Anyway, 1952 was the year of the centennial celebration in Rock Hill in which the men grew beards or else face the prospect of being "arrested" and put into the "stockade." The women dressed in clothes their great-grandmothers would have worn. From every business in town hung a red, white and blue flag with a centercrest proclaiming "1852-1952: 100 Years of Progress."
There were beauty pageants, a huge birthday cake and fireworks during the celebration.

No, I didn't grow a beard but that's not why I got arrested. I was arrested for what they called "abusing a horsehide." Rock Hill had a day of activities and I was paraded through town tied up in chains on a flatbed truck.

I could swing the bat, but I wasn't too bad with the glove either.

(Photo courtesy Sholes family)

They had this overweight bearded fellow guarding me with a whip as we made our way to the ballpark where my "trial" was held. My crime was cruelty to animals and my defense was that I'd never been cruel to an animal in my life. I wouldn't hurt a fly. I loved animals. They had these two guys acting like lawyers complete with a judge and jury. This one guy gets up, acting like a prosecutor, and says, "So, Mr. Shoals, you say you've never abused an animal? Well I have evidence that for several years now that you are guilty of abusing a horsehide. But as long as you abuse those horsehides for Rock Hill, we'll let you off." There was a big crowd at the park and they loved it.

I really was abusing the horsehide early in the season. While they were using our field for the celebration, we went over to York to play our games. Ned was pitching again and he beat the Anderson Rebels 9-5 and I helped him out with three hits, including a home run.

> *Carl Powis played center for Anderson and he was talking after that game with Anderson broadcaster Raleigh Powell. Powell said, "Muscle could hit 30 home runs a season out of our park. He could get home runs on pop flies over that 296-foot right field wall of ours." Powis shot back, "Yeah, but Muscle doesn't hit pop flies. He lines them out."*
>
> *– Rock Hill Evening Sun,*
> *August 1, 1952*

I ended up with 17 home runs that season, but it should have been 18. I hit one at home that landed near the press box in the center field bleachers. But, we got rained out and I lost it. It wasn't just home runs that year, I was hitting the ball for a good average. I ended up at .320, but I think at one point I was up around .340. We were at Gastonia one time and their manager, Harold Van Pelt, decided he was going to stop me one way or the other so he came up with the Shoals Shift. The third baseman would play at short, the shortstop would play near the left side of second base and the second baseman would position himself between first and second. The first baseman would be almost on top of the bag at first. The first time up I hit a double to left and my next two times up I had singles between the first and second basemen. After my third hit I rounded first and came back to the bag and saw Van Pelt throwing his cap on the ground and stomping it. That was the last time I saw the Shoals Shift.

One of my favorite places to play in that league was Knoxville at Caswell Park, which is where they played before Bill Meyer Stadium was built. We were there one night and it was Country Night. If you were a paying customer you might be lucky enough to leave the park with a chicken, a duck or a turkey. They were actually giving away farm animals. That might be one of the most unusual promotions I ever saw. I remember there were chickens getting away and coming on the field pecking at the ground and ducks squawking and turkeys gobbling.

Anyway, early in the season I hit a home run at Caswell that cleared the right-center field fence, it was over 400 feet. The fans began to jeer me in a nice sort of way as I rounded the bases and I doffed my cap to them. We went back there in June and every time my name was announced, the fans would start yelling at me.

> *"Leo (Muscle) Shoals, giant right-handed first sacker who has been the target of clean razzing by some Smokey fans during the series, made the Knoxville partisans sorry with his bat last night.*
>
> *In the eighth inning, Shoals belted one of the longest home runs witnessed at Caswell Park in many a day to break a tie and give the Chiefs a 5-4 lead. Muscle's blow was a line drive that cleared the center field fence, estimated to be around 425 feet. The home run was off Paul (Lefty) Harrison."*
>
> *– Knoxville News-Sentinel,*
> *June 26, 1952*

240

Just like it is today at ballgames, the fans get into it. They yell and scream and have a good time. Every now and then one or two will get out of hand like the time at Rock Hill when we were playing Greenville. A fellow in the boxseats was getting on the umpire whose last name was Thomas. The guy was yelling, "Thomas you're a stinker. You cost us a run tonight and you've cost us a lot of games this year." This went on and on. Finally, Thomas called time and told the guy to shut up or he'd have him thrown out of the park. This didn't deter the loudmouth who kept up his tirade. After the end of the next inning, Thomas ordered policemen to evict the guy from the park. As the police were about to escort the fellow from his seat, a couple of the Rock Hill stockholders met with the umpire and they discussed the situation. The umpire agreed to let the guy stay to watch the game, but that he would have to sit in the pressbox where he couldn't be heard. That loudmouth, by the way, was Bob Foster, president of the Greenville team.

It wouldn't be minor league baseball if there wasn't some kind of tempers flaring like that. Our own president, Earl Sherer, fueled the flames with our rivals over in Charlotte. The Hornets were at Municipal Stadium for a June contest and we had about 2,000 people in the stands. It was drizzling about game time, but not enough to postpone. We were ready to play when Charlotte manager Ivan Kuester announced he wasn't going to put his young players on the field and risk getting anyone hurt. Sherer wasn't concerned about injuries, he was concerned about losing that 2,000 gate.

Sherer wrote a letter to the paper and he let it all fly. Sherer referred to the Charlotte players as the "little darlings." Sherer went on to say that the next time the Hornets came to town that "The stadium concession stand will have the bottle warmer ready so the little Charlotte darlings can have their nice, hot milk between innings." Needless to say the fans got into the games every time we played Charlotte for the remainder of the season.

The kind of season I was having I was heading to the all-star game, which was going to be at Sims Legion Park in Gastonia as the stars would play the league-leading Rockets. But a few days before the game, I was hitting against Charlotte's Bob Danielson and a fastball got me on the wrist and the wrist swelled up like a balloon. I was replaced on the all-star team by Greenville's Bob Suba. I went to the all-star game, but sat in the pressbox and watched Gastonia win the game 3-2.

One of the guys in that all-star game was Asheville catcher Dick (Yogi) Elkind. Yogi was one tough character. He caught the all-star game with a broken index finger on his throwing hand. He wore a steel splint and may have been one of the first catchers I ever saw who put his hand behind his back when the pitch was on its way. Back then catchers wore the bulky chest protectors and when the weather got real hot Yogi would discard it and catch the game without a protector.

One time that year in a game, and it wasn't against us but against Spartanburg, Yogi was catching a pitcher on his club who had a hard time seeing the signals. So Yogi carried a pencil-length pocket flashlight under his chest protector and would signal the pitcher with the flashlight. It's guys like Yogi Elkind who made minor league baseball such a wonderful game.

Everybody in the game today is so stiff. It's like they're cardboard cutouts, they're all the same. You'd never see a manager today come out like Charlotte manager Ivan Kuester did at the all-star game. Kuester was introduced and the fans began booing. Kuester doffed his cap, smiled a toothy grin and made several sweeping bows while waving his cap.

It's just like a story that our shortstop, Herman Mason, was telling one time. Herm, who we called "Henneybird", played for Harry Land in '51 at New Bern and before a game Herm took the stuffing from a seat on the team bus and he put some under his cap and some more under his armpits. Herm was batting and the umpire called a

242

bad pitch. Herman threw his hat down and began pulling that stuffing, which looked like hair, from his head. He then reached under his armpits and pulled more of that stuff while pretending to go into an uncontrollable fit. The umpire ran over to the dugout where Harry was and said, "Harry, that kid's pulling his hair out. You've got to stop him." Harry shot back, "It's your fault the kid's cracking up." By this time everybody was laughing except the umpire who caught on and proceeded to toss Harry and Herm out of the game.

Harry had a sense of humor. Harry went to the plate one time wearing these huge glasses attached to a big nose, the Groucho Marx look. The umpire didn't see the humor and Harry got the thumb again. Harry was a lot of fun.

As for me, people look at my final home run total of 17 and figure I didn't have a good power year. But it took me a while to get over that hand injury completely and then, on August 19, I hurt my knee on a play at first base. My knee swelled up like a basketball and I had to go on crutches. I didn't play the rest of the year.

As a team, we didn't do squat. We finished dead last, 39 games behind Gastonia. We didn't have much talent, but there were other clubs which had guys who could play. Guys who later went to the majors like Bruce Barmes, who was only about 5-foot-7, 160-pounds and a slap-hitter, but he led the league in hitting with a .360 average. Jose Zardon, Dean Stone, Jim Constable, Rocco Colavito and Ryne Duren also made it to the bigs. Colavito was a 19-year-old from the Bronx and everyone compared his actions to Joe DiMaggio. He had a lot of power, but the one thing I noticed right away was his arm in right field. It didn't take a lot for me not to run on outfielders in trying to take an extra base, but the guys on our team with speed were careful with Colavito.

Zardon was a guy who knew how to handle the bat. Zardon, a slim Cuban, had played for the Senators in 1945 and hit .290, but he never made it back up. He went back to Cuba and played there for five years before returning to the States. He hit .329 for Charlotte in 1952, but the thing I remember about Zardon was that he was a smart ballplayer.

243

There was one time we were playing the Hornets in Rock Hill. Culbertson, our manager, figured out the signs that their catcher Orlando Echevarria was giving. Culbertson would then relay to our hitters what was coming. This went on for an inning or two. Well, Zardon was playing left field and he called time and came running all the way from left field to the mound to tell Echevarria that we were stealing the signs.

Duren pitched for Anderson that year and in 71 innings he struck out 100 batters, but he walked 73. But boy, could he throw that ball. I would have to say he's one of, if not the, hardest thrower I ever faced during my career. Of course when he went up to the majors they eventually made a relief pitcher out of him and I could see why. He was a starter with Anderson, but after two or three innings he didn't have anything left on his fastball.

I know one game I was fouling pitches off him one right after another and I was thinking I have got to adjust to this guy. He was still pitching in the sixth inning, so when I came up I choked up just a hair. There were a couple of men on base and I hit a shot off Duren that rattled off the fence and we ended up winning the game. Duren was sawing that bat off in my hands and I don't like that so I had my mind made up that I was going to beat him someway, somehow.

Anderson manager George Hausmann, who was one of those players in the big leagues who jumped to the Mexican League with Sal Maglie and Vern Stephens back in '46, saw me after the game and said, "You didn't do bad for an old man."

Another guy that year who gave me trouble was Dean Stone of Charlotte. He threw a sharp-breaking curve that rolled right off the table and it came in about as hard as his fastball. All I could do with his pitches was top them in front of the plate. That pitch would come up to the plate and the bottom would drop out before it reached the plate. I thought to myself, he's not going to get away with that. I'm hitting his pitch and he's winning all the battles.

We were in Charlotte one night at Griffith Park. I liked hitting there because it was just 320 down the right field line. I liked hitting there unless Stone was pitching and he's pitching this one game and the count is 3-2 with men on first and second. I backed out of the box and I told the ump that I was going to lay off the next pitch because I knew that he was going to throw that breaking pitch. I told the ump to pay special attention because I wasn't swinging and when that pitch broke it was going to be a ball.

Well, sure enough Stone throws that thing, I lay off and it breaks right in front of the plate and drops about six inches. The ump yelled "STRIKE THREE! YOU'RE OUT!" Well, I let it all go. I seldom got on the umpires because they have a tough job and they're going to miss one every now and then. But I turned around and faced this umpire and I said, "I can't believe you did what you did. You called that a strike and after I told you what was coming." I guess a good pitcher can fool a hitter and an umpire.

I know another fellow I had trouble with was big Jim Constable. I got to know Jim better later on when we both played in the Burley Belt semipro league, but when he was with Knoxville I couldn't touch that guy. I knew that he would pitch in the majors one day and he did with the Giants. He had a real good fastball which would run into left-handed batters and away from right-handers.

Another guy was Zeke Zeisz of Charlotte, whose given name was Francis. He had great control and every now and then he would throw a knucklecurve and it was impossible to get wood on it. It would come in knee-high and just roll over. I couldn't see it, so I know the umpires couldn't. Then there was Ralph Groves of Charlotte, a right-hander. He gave you that big motion which made him seem faster than he was. The Hornets had the best pitching in the league, without a question. Bob Danielson and Mike Kvasnak threw as hard as anybody and Danielson ended up leading the league in ERA at 2.62.

The one player everybody was talking about was 19-year-old Billy Joe Davidson of Spartanburg. As a matter of fact, this kid was the talk of baseball even when he was a sophomore in high school. He was from Marion, North

Carolina and had pitched at Oak Ridge Military Academy in North Carolina. The Cleveland Indians, who had their farm club in Spartanburg, made him the highest bonus player up to that time by giving him around $150,000. That kind of money was just unbelievable. I didn't make that much money for all the years I played.

Davidson had a pretty good season going 16-8 with a 3.91 ERA. But it just goes to show you how scouting young kids and projecting them several years down the road is not an exact science. The Indians invested a lot of money in Davidson at that time and he never made it to the major leagues.

Of course there were a lot of guys who should have played in the major leagues but never did. Before Jackie Robinson came up with Brooklyn in 1947 a lot of African-Americans got left behind. Robinson broke in with the Montreal Royals in 1946 in the International League. But, seven years later, there were still no blacks playing in the Tri-State League. Word was spreading like wildfire that blacks would be coming into the league in 1952 to start the season. A lot of people were worried that our little circle was going to be broken.

> *Negro players may make their debut in the Tri-State League this season. At least there is talk of some young colored major league prospects being used.*

> *Red Miller, sports editor of the Asheville Citizen, passes out the following information: 'There were rumors around yesterday that the Tourists might bring some Negro prospects back with them. But the reports are unfounded since manager Bill Hart was to have no idea who his players would be until the assignments were made to all the Dodger Class B clubs. Should this be true, it would*

mean that Asheville would be the first club in the Tri-State League to use Negro players.

– Bob Wilson,
Knoxville Journal,
April 13, 1952

Well, it didn't come about. Nobody had the guts to put a black guy in their lineup because they knew what the reaction would be. It finally came about, but not before the season was almost over. I guess it happened that late because whatever heat was coming wouldn't last too long and by breaking in a black player at that time would make it easier in 1953. Everybody knew it was inevitable, but a lot of people wanted to make it a white man's game in the Tri-State League for as long as they could.

But like I said, the first black in the Tri-State League played for us. He was David Mobley, an outfielder, who made his debut on August 26 against the Smokies at the stadium. The Ku Klux Klan in Knoxville must have been getting worried because they began writing Knoxville general manager Jack Aragon asking him not to use black players on his club. Aragon shot back in a letter himself: "I take this position. I'll use any ballplayers that the New York Giants send me. There may be some Negro players among them in the future. If there are and they have the ability to make our club, we'll use them."

Mobley, who was from nearby Lancaster, was 5-foot-8 and weighed 175 pounds. He had been playing for the Birmingham Barons of the Negro American League and was hitting .318 when he left the club to return home to be with his mother who was ill. Mobley was 22 and had played with a Pacific Coast all-star service team and played in service in France while in the Army. Leon called a team meeting one day and said it looked like we were going to sign a Negro. "Look you guys," Leon said. "If you are going to play baseball for a living and if you expect to advance higher in minor league baseball, the chances are you will have to play with Negroes." Leon took a vote and I don't remember anyone saying they wouldn't play with Mobley. As for the Knoxville club, manager Fred Gerkin made it clear before the game that he had no objections and neither did his players.

Asheville and Charlotte both gave Negro players trials earlier in the season, but never signed them. I recall Mobley being a really nice fellow. He hustled during his workouts with us and he seemed to have a good bat.

There was a big commotion made over Mobley. You have to remember this was in 1952. Blacks could not eat in some of the restaurants, which had signs in the windows "No Colored." It was a time when department stores had restrooms and water fountains with "White" hanging over one and "Colored" hanging over the other. This was before desegregation. You didn't have black children going to school with white children.

It was expected that Mobley would be in the starting lineup in left field, but there were a lot of behind-the-scenes talks going on between Tri-State president Bobby Hipps and Sherer. I'm not sure what was said, but Mobley wasn't in the starting lineup. Hipps said that there was nothing in the league rules or bylaws to prevent Mobley from playing, but that several of the league directors expressed to him their sentiment that a Negro should not be allowed because they felt it would lead to the breakup of the league.

As fans were lining up to buy tickets to the game, they were told that Mobley would not be playing and a lot of fans just turned away and went home. But during the early part of the game the Rock Hill directors met and decided that Mobley should and would be given a chance to play.

Mobley had already taken off his uniform, but when told he might be put in the game he rushed back to the clubhouse and dressed. At the start of the sixth inning, Leon sent Mobley to left field. As the fans noticed him running to his position, a small ripple of applause could be heard and then it seemed the whole stadium was clapping. I personally did not hear any negatives like booing or jeering or name calling. We had about 780 people in the park and the bigger part of the crowd were those sitting in the seats in the outfield set aside for the Negro fans.

Mobley got his first at bat when he led off the sixth with a drag bunt down the first base line, but was thrown out. Then, in the eighth, he hit a single to center. After the game Mobley was asked if he was nervous: "No, I wasn't nervous. I just wanted a chance. I was happy to get that hit. I think if I had gotten another at bat, I would have gotten another hit."

Leon was already pencilling in Mobley in left field for the next night but, when game time came around, Mobley was not in the lineup. Hipps, getting pressure from the other team owners, asked Sherer to keep Mobley out of the lineup. Leon had no choice but to comply.

Spartanburg was apparently the real culprit behind the coup. Spartanburg told Hipps they would pull out of the league if Mobley played. I'm not sure what all the other clubs felt. I know Greenville's players took a vote and were in favor of Mobley playing, while the front office wasn't in favor, and Charlotte general manager Phil Howser made his position clear.

"If Greenville and Spartanburg don't approve of Negroes playing, they better get out of the league because we expect to have one next year in Charlotte. He's coming down from our Class C club in Drummondsville, Quebec. I'm surprised that there is any doubt in anyone's mind about my position on that. This is America and I see no reason why we can't play Negroes if they're good enough. Baseball is entertainment and we don't object to applauding other Negro entertainers, so why should baseball be any different."

I can recall one night, before a game in Charlotte, the Ku Klux Klan was trying to make a statement when a few of those hooded nuts came riding through the gate on horses, paraded around and then left.

But that was it for Mobley. He never got into another game. He went back home to Lancaster and played in a semipro league. As it turned out, our paths would cross again in 1953. I would be with Kingsport of the Mountain States

249

League and Mobley would be with Knoxville of the same league. He played in only 22 games and was hitting close to .270 when he decided to go back home. From what I understand, Mobley went back to playing semipro ball and did so for many years.

I really think Mobley could have been a very good player if he had been given a legitimate opportunity. I look back on that and it's really sad that our country couldn't give a fellow an equal opportunity just because his skin color was black instead of white. But, that was life back then.

On the lighter side, I can't close out my year in Rock Hill without telling you a funny story. Helen and I lived in a small housing complex in Rock Hill and Helen's mother and father were coming to stay a night. They were real religious people. Lots of times I would visit the liquor store across the street from the ballpark and a few days before Helen's parents were to visit I stopped and got a half-pint of Old Hickory bourbon. I came home and Helen said I shouldn't have that bourbon there with her parents coming. She took the bottle and hid it, but I found it and drank the contents. So Helen wouldn't suspect anything, I filled it back up with vinegar and put it back in the closet where she had hid it. At the end of the season as we were packing, Helen suggested we celebrate with a drink from that bottle she had hid several months ago. I had actually forgotten about putting the vinegar in the bottle, but as she poured it I suddenly remembered. It was the same color as the bourbon. She poured us both a glass and proposed a toast of another fine year. We clinked our glasses and down the hatch. I didn't drink it but watched Helen and she began spitting and sputtering. I was laughing my head off. She said what is that stuff and I told her. She wasn't too happy at first, but she got over it and had a big laugh too. Helen's got a wonderful sense of humor. If she didn't, I don't think we would have stayed married.

Yvonne was born in August of 1952 and I was thinking hard about what to do in 1953. Jim Thomas, an outfielder on the Rock Hill club, was going to form a mill baseball semipro team. He asked me if I was interested. But Helen and I wanted to get back to Kingsport. We returned and I got a job with Mason-Dixon Trucking Company working on the freight docks. I later became athletic director of the company's recreation program and I had pretty much decided to give up pro ball.

Several semipro teams contacted me about playing. Up in Saltville, Virginia there was a semipro team that played twice a week – the Alkalies. Jim Mooney, a former left-hander with the St. Louis Cardinals, was on that team and I was thinking about joining up playing on Saturdays and Sundays at 50 bucks a game. I was also contacted by some teams as far away as Minnesota and Hamilton, Ontario. But the cold winters didn't appeal to me. I liked the warm South.

But I would have some other options as it turned out.

Chapter 18

As the spring of 1953 was approaching, I had convinced myself that playing baseball was over. I had given it a lot of thought and I really felt like it was time to quit. I was 36 years old. It was time to get on with my life and find something to do other than swing a piece of lumber during the summer.

But, not so fast. Now if it meant going back to Rock Hill, I probably would have hung it up. Don't get me wrong, I loved Rock Hill. It's just that I wanted to be home. I had a family and I wanted to be close to them. I couldn't expect Helen to keep moving around.

Then I got a call from Mack Ray, a Tennessee State Senator who, along with Sam Bray, a Kingsport insurance broker, owned the Kingsport Cherokees in the Mountain States League. Mack asked me if I would be interested in playing with the Cherokees. Helen and I thought about it and it seemed like a good opportunity. I could keep on doing something I loved and get paid for it and still be close to home. Even the travel part of it wouldn't be bad because every city was in close proximity.

However, there was one slight problem, I was still the property of Rock Hill. I called Earl Sherer, Rock Hill's club president. I told him straight out how I felt. I liked Rock Hill, but I wanted to plant my feet a little more solidly and closer to home. Earl said he understood but, at the same time, I was a drawing card there and it would mean a big loss. Earl said to have Sam call him up and he'd talk it over. A few days went by and Sam called me and said the deal had been completed and that I was now a member of the Kingsport Cherokees.

I don't know exactly what transpired, but I do know Sam had to fork over a few dollars to get me out of my Rock Hill contract. Of course, Earl understood that if he didn't let me out of my contract that I was going to quit anyway. But, it all worked out, I think, to everyone's satisfaction.

It was good to get back to Kingsport. I was excited and it seemed like the town was happy to have me back. I was happy to be wearing the Cherokees' uniform again. Little did I realize that I would be wearing two uniforms in Kingsport.

Tommy O'Connell was the Kingsport manager but, along about the middle of April, O'Connell resigned as his wife was not doing well after giving birth. So Tommy went home and the club didn't have a manager. Mack and Sam asked me if I would consider being the manager. I kind of always thought of what it would be like to be a manager and felt it might be a challenge I could handle. I thought about it for about five minutes and said I'd do it.

After it was announced that I would be the manager somebody became a poet by putting the following in the Kingsport Times-News:

Oh, the fans file in and they look about
And what do they see to make them shout?
A round first baseman with locks receding.
And a bat that responds to home run pleading.

Shoals is his last name, he's the new skipper.
Off the field he's a lamb, at bat he's a ripper.
He's gained loads of fame with his home run bat.
But he's the same likeable guy – size seven hat.

The Mountain States League dated back to 1911 when it was originally formed and was called the Mountain State League. But, after two years, it was disbanded before returning in 1937 and lasting until 1942 at which time it folded again. It then came back a third time in 1948 before finally closing its doors for good after the 1954 season.

The Mountain States League was a Class D classification and, in 1953, was made up of Big Stone Gap, Virginia; Harlan, Kentucky; Knoxville, Tennessee;

Maryville-Alcoa, Tennessee; Morristown, Tennessee; and Norton, Virginia. Norton was a small town of 4,318 people in the coal mining region of Southwest Virginia. Now you wouldn't think that a small town like that would draw fans, but they would draw in over 21,000 that season. But, as small as Norton was, it wasn't the smallest town to field a minor league team. That distinction went to Graceville, Florida, a town of about 1500, in the Alabama-Florida League.

Then you had a big city thrown in the mix like Knoxville, which drew well in 1953 with over 36,000 fans. However, there were a lot of dissatisfied people around Knoxville. Knoxville had been in the Southern Association but, in 1953, a new stadium was being built over at the old stadium site of Caswell Park. So, for 1953, Knoxville dropped out of the Southern Association and joined the Mountain States League.

A group of five young businessmen got together and put up $2500 to run the team. But they got into financial trouble early. Right off the bat they had to fork over about $8,000 for lights and it was downhill after that. Knoxville was playing its games about 15 miles away in Sevier County and because they didn't have a real home in which to play, the franchise was losing money. It was nearly $21,000 in debt at one point. As a matter of fact, Knoxville was hosting Morristown in a game and along about the seventh inning they ran out of baseballs and had to forfeit the game. Knoxville had been purchasing just enough balls to get by and the skimping caught up with them. The next day, so they wouldn't have to forfeit, they asked youngsters who had retrieved foul balls to please return them. But Knoxville was able to get some more investors involved and the club finished the season.

There was some talk early that the Knoxville franchise might move to Hazard, Kentucky. A group of Hazard businessmen united and offered the club $1,000 a game to play one game a week the last three months of the season in Kentucky. But, it never came down to that. A group headed by Knoxville's Dr. Edgar Grubb bought the team and was able to get it back on stable footing.

Since this was Kingsport's first year in the MSL after being in the Appalachian League, we had to really hustle to put a club together. We were an independent team so we contacted organizations for optional players. Cleveland wanted to send us a black player, but we didn't know how the people would react having a black in Kingsport. We had some Cubans on the team, but no blacks. I was all for getting anybody for our team who could help us out. I didn't care if they were black, blue or purple.

Bray, who always wore a bowtie and had a cigar in his mouth, asked me how I felt about having a Negro player on the team. Sam was feeling me out and I told him what I thought. Sam said he was glad I felt that way because he was bringing in a black player.

It was time to end the black-white situation and put that stuff behind us. The Maryville club had three blacks under contract as did Knoxville, including David Mobley, who was the center of attention in the Tri-State League the year before. Norton had two or three blacks. I remembered a few years before when Bristol had a chance to get a black for the first time. The Bristol Twins were a farm club of the New York Giants at the time and word spread that there was a kid who could do it all – hit, run, hit with power. Then the Bristol officials were told the kid was black. They closed the door real quick when they heard that. Oh, by the way, the kid's name was Willie Mays.

Louis Caperton Knight, a 23-year-old rookie from Richmond, Virginia, became the first black to ever play professional baseball in Kingsport. Knight had played ball a couple of years at Tennessee State in Nashville and was probably better at basketball. As a matter of fact, the Harlem Globetrotters extended him an invitation to try out at the end of our season, but I don't know if he ever did.

Knight's first game was on the road in Morristown and I put him in defensively in left field in the eighth inning just to break the ice. I didn't want a big deal made out of it.

If there were ever any doubts as to how the fans in Kingsport were going to treat Knight the answer came when he entered our home opener as a pinch-hitter and the crowd there at J. Fred Johnson gave him a real nice hand. I didn't hear one thing derogatory. We were trailing Harlan in this game by 14-13 and we had the tying run on third base with two out. Moe Garbedian, one of the more popular players on our team, was due up, but I thought this was a good spot for Knight. I knew I'd be second-guessed if Knight struck out or popped up. Instead, Knight lined a single to left that tied the game and we eventually won.

After the game Knight told reporters: "It really surprised me when I got that big hand from the crowd. I wanted to get a hit bad and my knees were knocking. The pitcher came in with a dinky curve and I hit it. And, man, was I glad to get that single. It was one of my biggest thrills."

Knight played in 14 games and had 19 at bats with nine hits and only struck out three times. I thought we had us a player here. And Louis could play anywhere, which was the problem. He went in to catch one night and took a pitch on the finger. We were at the point where we had to get our roster down and we had to cut two players and Louis was one of the two. I don't know if Louis ever came back to baseball or not because that was the last I ever heard of him.

The big news in the league was down in Knoxville, which had two black pitchers who were brothers – Leander and Jim Tugerson. They both had been with Hot Springs in the Cotton States League during spring training in a league which had always been lily white. The league's board voted to oust Hot Springs from their little circle if the Tugersons weren't dropped from the team, and league president Al Haraway backed up the directors. Hot Springs wouldn't go along with what the directors wanted. The team kept the Tugersons and, as a result, the league kicked Hot Springs out. But minor league president George Trautman intervened and put Hot Springs back in the league because Trautman said that the Cotton States League acted illegally. Despite

Trautman's ruling, the league's directors were going to pack up their teams and call it quits if the Tugersons stayed. They weren't about to be integrated. Both the Tugerson brothers decided it wasn't worth all the trouble, so they asked to be sent to another league where integration was in place, thus they found a new home in Knoxville.

Well, that wasn't the end of the Tugersons in Hot Springs that season. Hot Springs had no pitching and they were looking for help about a month into the season, so they brought Jim Tugerson back in the fold. Tugerson's first assignment was to be a start against the Jackson Senators. But, before one pitch was thrown, Haraway forfeited the game to Jackson. The forfeit was later overturned by Trautman, but that was the end of Jim Tugerson in Hot Springs as he was sent back to Knoxville for the rest of the season.

Jim didn't take it lying down. He later filed a $50,000 racial discrimination suit against the Cotton States League claiming his Constitutional Rights had been violated. However, United States District Judge John Miller ruled that Tugerson's rights were not violated because the Constitution protects individuals from government conduct and not from corporations such as the Cotton States League.

On his return to Knoxville in early June they had a Jim Tugerson Night at Chapman Park. The club admitted all blacks in the park for free and they made up half of the 1,100 fans there that night. Tugerson ended up pitching a one-hitter over Maryville-Alcoa.

Jim's brother Leander never did too much that year finishing with a 3-5 record. Jim, on the other hand, was one good pitcher who threw very hard. Jim finished the year at 29-11 with a 3.71 ERA. He started 37 games and completed 35 and ended up pitching 330 innings. He was a workhorse and he was the first player in organized ball that season to win 20 games. He also won four games in the playoffs as the Smokies won the league pennant.

But, like all pitchers, Jim had his moments when he wasn't on top of his game. He was pitching against us one night and gave up 20 hits. Raul Llaneras, a 140-pound left-handed hitter, had the game winning hit in the 13th inning and we won 6-5. The next night Tugerson came in to relieve against us to start the ninth inning and got three outs on five pitches.

Leander never pitched much after that but Jim went on to pitch a few more years in the Southwest League with Dallas and Amarillo before getting out of baseball. I really believed Jim had a chance to pitch in the major leagues, but never made it. I wondered how he would have done if he didn't have to worry with all that racial stuff. I understand that both the Tugerson brothers passed away. They were pioneers of their era and they fought for what they believed. I admired them both for that.

One of the most talented black players in the league was Willie Kirkland with Maryville-Alcoa. Big strong kid who later went up with the San Francisco Giants in 1958 and spent nine years in the major leagues. He was one of those who threw right-handed but hit left-handed. Willie had some awesome numbers in 1953. He finished up hitting .326 with 35 home runs and 164 RBIs. I know people talked about me and how they would back up at first base when I came to bat. Let me tell you, they backed up on Kirkland, myself included.

I know one night I had backed up about three steps further than I usually did against left-handers, but Willie hit a line drive at me that I backhanded and I still feel that hand stinging. There was one game against Norton that Willie hit three home runs with 10 RBIs. Now that's a night.

One of the more unusual situations that year was at Morristown where the small town became the league's Cuban connection. Atlanta of the Southern Association optioned14 Cuban players to Morristown, including manager Nap Reyes, who had played for the New York Giants. I got to know Nap pretty well and I thought he was a swell guy, but the players feared him. He would tell them, "If you don't produce, you're going back to Cuba and cut sugar cane."

And Nap was a man of his word. If a guy didn't put out, then he'd send him back to Cuba and bring in another one.

I usually cut my sleeves. Not to show off, but it gave me more freedom of movement.

(Photo courtesy Sholes family)

I liked Nap. As a matter of fact, the managers voted for the North-South All-Star game and right before the all-star game when our two clubs were playing we met at home plate in our pre-game conference. Nap said, "Muscle, I fixed you up. I picked you on my list for the South at first base." I said, "Nap, you haven't got a thing on me because I put you on my choice at first base too."

Nap once was accused of spitting on an umpire, but he denied ever doing it. Morristown was hosting

Middlesboro and Charlie (Monk) Anderson was umpiring. Anderson, in his first year as a professional umpire, made an unpopular decision and claimed he "almost got killed by the fans in Morristown." Anderson also claimed Reyes cussed and then spit on him, which Nap and Morristown owner Dr. Hobart Ford, a dentist in nearby Newport, said never happened. Of course this is the same umpire who accused Middlesboro fans of carrying guns and was quoted as saying: "We feel that one of them nuts will take a shot at us." I don't know whatever happened to Anderson. I guess he went back to his old job in New Haven, Connecticut where he was a school custodian. Then again, you couldn't blame the umps for getting frustrated lots of the time. They were only getting $250 a month, plus five cents a mile for expenses.

As for the Cubans, one was Pedro Ramos, who later became a pretty good pitcher with Cleveland and the Yankees and who played some outfield for Morristown. He was a right-hander with a decent fastball, but he also threw a little forkball which dropped straight down. One day I struck out against him on three straight pitches, the first time I ever faced him. I stood there in front of the plate and I said, "What in the hell was that you're throwing." He just stood out on the mound smiling.

But I remember one time we were playing Morristown in Kingsport and in the 13th inning I hit one over the lights against Ramos. It was me that was smiling then.

> *"Muscle Shoals was one nice guy and a good, strong hitter. He was just a great guy and a very good manager. He was the friendly type, the type you like to play for. I remember I got here from Cuba and they put me on a bus in Miami and said I was going to Texas but I wake up in Morristown, Tennessee. I was a blue-eyed, Cuban, not very dark, so I did not experience a lot of racism. I was accepted and never had problems. When I came I had three pitches – fastball, fastball*

and fastball. I had no breaking pitch. I could speak no English. I go to the Rainbow Café in Morristown and first time I pointed at pork chops and rest of season that's what I had to eat. I loved pork chops. I didn't understand English and I said yes to just about everything. I later went from playing at Morristown to playing for Muscle in Kingsport. One time in Kingsport a bunch of the guys picked me up and carried me to home plate like a king. I asked another of my Spanish speaking buddies what was going on. He said, 'They're celebrating your birthday.' I said, 'My birthday? It's not my birthday.' Since I said yes to everything, somehow they thought it was my birthday. I used to go to the movies to learn English and with Muscle we had some hand signs and he learned a little Spanish, enough to communicate."

– Pedro Ramos,
pitcher, Morristown and Kingsport

One Latin on that Morristown club, who you will hear a lot about later on, was Aldo Salvent. Salvent would later play for me in Kingsport in 1954, but he didn't get to Morristown in 1953 until early June. The first game he got in he collected a pair of hits but Salvent, who was a very good fielder, also got a nickname because of his lack of fielding.

On his first fielding attempt at third, he was rushing in on a popup and was yelling, "I've got it, I've got it." Salvent overran the ball and it fell behind him for a hit. After that he was known as "I've Got It" Salvent.

The fans in Morristown took to the Latin connection. Bill Barron, the PA guy there at Sherwood Park, would sometimes give the hits, runs and errors after the half inning in Spanish.

I even had three or four Latins on my club, which presented a very interesting situation seeing as how the Latins spoke no English and I spoke no Spanish. However, there was one exception, a kid named Jesus Gonzales who had gone to the University of Havana and who we picked up from Morristown. Gonzales was bilingual and he taught me a few words of Spanish, enough so that I could halfway communicate.

We had a Latin left fielder, Hooks Badia, who was a pretty good player. One night he lined a single past the third baseman and in the paper the next day he wasn't credited with a hit. Well, before the game the next night Hooks went to the pressbox and in his broken English was trying to communicate with the official scorer. Hooks asked: "Why did I not get hit in the paper?" The official scorer replied: "It must have been a typographical error." Hooks raised his voice in anger: "What do you mean. The third baseman didn't even touch the ball."

I had a lot of new experiences that year. As a player you don't really understand all the duties of a manager. There's a lot of pressure in the job. When you're playing all you have to worry about is one person and that's you. As a manager you have a bunch of guys and they're all different and you have to try and understand that.

I know one lesson I learned and that was never to let a player know he's being watched by scouts. An example was Jesus Gonzales who, in addition to being my interpreter, was also my third baseman who owned one of the best throwing arms I ever saw on an infielder. He could fly on the bases, too, and he was hitting the ball very well at the time. Sam and I thought maybe we could peddle Jesus for some much needed dough. I contacted several scouts and told them about Jesus.

We had a Sunday doubleheader and Jimmy Grudinck of Cleveland, the scout who found Eddie Mathews, came down as did Mace Brown of the Red Sox, Syd Thrift of Pittsburgh and a couple more. I really didn't want word to get out to Jesus that he was being scouted but Jesus found

262

out. Jesus tried to play with one eye on the ball and the other eye on the scouts. He didn't pull the ball all day and he dogged it running to first base after flying out his first at bat. Brown offered us $3500 for Gonzales on delivery to Louisville, but then he stuck around a couple more days and changed his mind. Grudinck didn't want him but suggested we make a pitcher out of Jesus. Jesus never regained the same enthusiasm he had before and he began loafing and that was something I couldn't take. He wouldn't run on popups and, after striking out, he'd just drop the bat on the plate. Even in infield, instead of firing the ball over to first, he'd send it over on a couple of hops.

It seemed as if Jesus just didn't care anymore. We began to think that maybe he was hurting, so we had him checked out by a doctor and Jesus got a clean bill of health. After one game in which he went after a routine ground ball and let it get by him, I pulled him aside and told him he couldn't play with that kind of attitude. The next day it was the same and I blew up when he didn't run out a fly ball. I sent him to the showers and told him to start packing.

I guess one thing that was getting me upset, and it was totally selfish on my part, was a clause I had in my contract. I had it written that if we finished in first place I would get an $800 bonus, $700 for second and $600 for third. At the start of the season I thought I had a chance to get that $800. As it turned out, we finished third, one game behind second-place Knoxville, and I have to believe that Gonzales cost me that spot in the standings.

We didn't release Gonzales, but we sold him to St. Petersburg. I found out sometime later that Jesus was released and went back to Cuba. It was situations like that which drove me crazy as a manager. As for Jesus, he would be back next year.

Sometimes you never know what you're getting in a player at that level. Along about the middle of May we signed a 19-year-old kid from Kingsport named Bucky Collette. Bucky had pitched for Dobyns-Bennett High School in Kingsport and went 12-1 the previous season. In

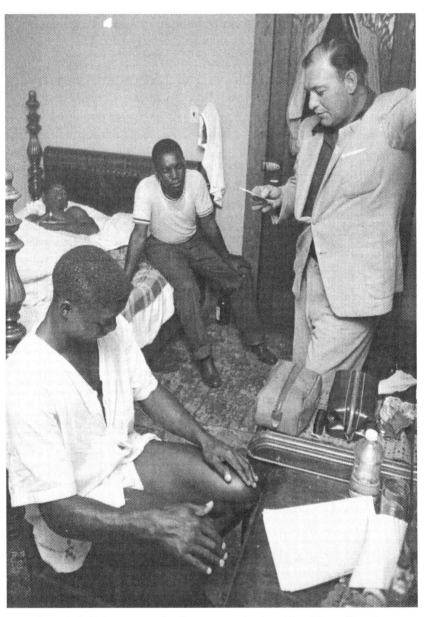

The Latin ballplayers were, for the most part, hard working fellows. Here I am talking to three of the Latinos in the hotel room.

(Photo courtesy Sholes family)

the semifinals of the state tournament Bucky hurled a no-hitter against DuPont of Old Hickory retiring 20 straight batters, but then walked the 21st man on a 3-2 count – the only runner to get on.

Bucky had scholarship offers from everywhere, including the University of Tennessee. The major league scouts were after Bucky too but Bucky signed with Tennessee. Bucky never played an inning because he never graduated from high school. We were lucky enough to pick him up and Bucky went 15-8 for us with 19 complete games in 22 starts.

As a player, though, I was doing OK. I hit .427 that season, which was the highest average of my career, and I had 30 home runs and drove in 142, which was the most I ever had. I thought I had a chance at winning the Silver Bat, which goes to the minor leaguer with the highest batting average, but Russ Snyder of McAlester in the Sooner State League got a couple of hits on the last day and finished with a .432 average. The talent in the league wasn't that great, so I'm sure that accounted for a lot of my success but I also believe that my good numbers had something to do with me being manager. I was more serious. I even used to challenge the players. I'd bet them that if they would outhit me for certain games, I'd buy them a steak. Luckily, I didn't have to buy too many.

"If that guy had taken the game seriously when he started out, he could have been one of the greatest."

Billy Meyer, former Pittsburgh manager and present Pirate scout was watching the big guy with No. 22 on the back of his jersey during batting practice at J. Fred Johnson Park last week.

"Look at that swing and that wrist action. Man, I wish I could sign a few rookies with a swing as faultless and effortless as that. They

still talk about the guy in the major league dressing rooms."

– Kingsport Times-News,
August 8, 1953

That from Bill Meyer came out of a column by sportswriter Jack Kiser. Toward the end of his column Kiser wrote:

As a player Leo has few equals in the minors. As a manager he has one fault – he's too good hearted for his own good.

He's not bitter over not making his rightful place in the majors. "It's my own fault," Leo states. "I wish I had things to do over again. They would be different. But I'm not mad at anyone."

His ambition now is seeing his young son, Ronnie, make a name for himself in the baseball world. Ronnie's only three years old, but it's nothing unusual to see him swinging a bat a la Leo Shoals and throwing from the port side.

His other child, Yvonne, was two years old yesterday. No future baseball plans have been made for her. She'll probably be content to keep Ronnie's scrapbook for him. And Leo's too, if they come up with some rule saying you don't have to run to first base. For, like John Mize, the big guy will probably be able to hit the ball a country mile as long as he can walk up to the plate.

I can tell you truthfully I never got tired of hitting home runs and in this season I felt like I could hit them forever. I mentioned the home run I hit off Ramos in the 13th and I remember another I hit off Pedro that cleared the right field fence at J. Fred Johnson Stadium, went across the highway and ended up in a field. Somebody estimated the ball went 480 feet.

It's funny how some of those home runs stick in your mind. It's like some movies you have seen as a kid and some of the scenes you never forget. I recall we were playing Big Stone Gap on the road. Normally, we played at Big Stone but this time they were having a district fair and we moved over to St. Paul for the game. Anyway, I hit a two-run home run off Bill Halstead to win the game 10-9. Halstead actually played outfield and, because he had a pretty good arm, got to pitch some. Later, Halstead would become president of the Appalachian League, a position he held for 12 years.

A special home run came in the all-star game, which I managed, at Maryville at Hunt Field. I pinch-hit a two-run home run in the eighth inning to tie the game and Ed Gibson of Kingsport hit a three-run home run in the 11th to win the game. From the opposing dugout was a fellow who knew something about home runs. Jim Poole was managing the Maryville-Alcoa team. Poole was an active player for 35 years, from 1912 to 1946, including 1925-27 with the Philadelphia Athletics. In 1930, Poole hit 50 home runs and drove in 167 runs for Nashville.

Then there was the night where I hit a couple of home runs against Norton, drove in five runs and we won 6-5 and in the postseason playoffs I hit a couple of home runs in the opening game, which we lost. But it's not only the home runs I hit that I remember, it's the home runs which made an impact on our team by the opposition that I remember too.

Home runs can be like a knife in the back. That was the case in the second game of the playoffs when Kirkland hit a two-out, 3-2 pitch over the right field fence in the fifth inning off Ned Jilton to give Maryville a 6-5 win to knock us out of the playoffs. Yeah, the same Ned Jilton who gave up baseball the previous year at Rock Hill. Ned was like me, he couldn't give the game up and he finished with a great

267

season going 19-3 with a 3.11 ERA. So much for his bad elbow.

I have to mention the time I got thrown out of a game because the ump gave the home run sign on a ball I saw bounce over the fence. We were playing Big Stone Gap at Kingsport in the second game of a doubleheader. Like I've said before, I didn't argue that much with umpires. But I was playing first base and Robert Benintendi led off the game with a solid smash that I thought was going over the fence. I saw Ed Gibson in right field racing back for the ball but he never got to it. Then I see the ball hit a few feet in front of the fence and bounce over right at the 308-foot mark. I never saw the umpire give the signal, but then I see Benintendi rounding second and going to third in a slow trot and then he rounds third and heads for home.

I was confused. I walked to home and asked plate umpire Ed Castellano what the heck was going on. I said that ball bounced over the fence. It's a double, not a home run. Castellano, a big guy from Brooklyn, wasn't about to change his mind of course. But I was convinced it was a double and I was mad. I told him he was blind as a bat and those were the magic words as he thumbed me from the game. I said, "OK, Mr. Ump. Before I leave I want to call my right fielder into this little conversation and get his opinion." So I turned and waved in Gibson from right field. I asked Ed, "Did that ball go over the fence or did it bounce over?" Ed kinda looked at me like I was crazy. "That ball went over by about 20 feet Skip." I just turned around and walked to the dugout. I sat down on the bench and Castellano came over and said, "Sorry, Leo. You can't stay there. You have to leave and sit in the stands." I did him one better than that. I left the dugout and then I left the ballpark and went downtown to The Strand Theatre to watch Jane Russell and Marilyn Monroe in *Gentlemen Prefer Blondes.*

At least I didn't do what Norton manager Walt Dixon did in a game he got thrown out against us one night. I don't remember what it was over, but he argued a call and the umpire threw him out. Dixon went to the dugout and a few seconds later he comes out waving a bat with a white flag tied on top. At J. Fred the dressing rooms were under the football stands and it was a long walk from the first base dugout. Dixon walked across the diamond with that white flag held high and waved it back and forth all the way to the dressing room. All the way there the fans were yelling, some jeering, some cheering.

When the fans came out to J. Fred they never knew what was going to happen. We led the league in attendance that year with 46,717. To some that might not sound like a lot of people, but in the towns our size that was great. Morristown was second in the league with a little over 39,000. There was usually something for the fans and our club had some good promotions. There was Men's Night where the men would get into the park free and receive a complimentary cigar when accompanied by a female. There was Cash to Carry Night where $1,200 in coins were poured onto a canvas at home plate. A lucky fan was given a shovel and a large canvas sack and was given a certain amount of time to shovel up as much of that money as he could and then put it into the sack.

And there was the ever popular Greased Pig Night. Any fan who could catch the pig would receive $50. That poor old pig would be running all over that field with people falling down trying to catch it. Virgil Q. Wacks, president of the MSL, did our games over WKIN radio but he would get on the PA and do the play-by-play of fans going after that pig.

As this season entered the month of August, I was holding up pretty good for an old man. I must say I was pretty proud to be hitting as well as I was. You might say there were some inflated batting averages. I finished with a .427 average and Dixon was second with a .415. But after that the averages began dipping. Oscar Rodriguez of Middlesboro was third in the league at .384 and Nap Reyes ended up at .370. Dixon and I were neck-and-neck for the longest time. Usually August is the hottest month and it can drain the strength out of you, but during the first week of

August I was on a streak where I was hitting just about everything they threw up to the plate.

> *Maestro Leo Shoals wielded the big baton in Kingsport's basehit symphony at J. Fred Johnson Park Wednesday night as the Cherokees waltzed by Norton to the tune of 11-4.*
>
> *Shoals collected his 27th home run and added two singles and as many walks to boost his league leading average up to .426.*
>
> *– Kingsport Times-News, August 6, 1953*

That's another thing too, I led the league in walks with 110 and my official at bats totaled 396. So about a fourth of my at bats were free passes. I was also proud of the fact that I only struck out 30 times. That was a far cry from Willie Kirkland who led the league with 142 strikeouts.

I had gotten my average up to .430, but then I fractured my left thumb and was out for 10 days. We had another all-star game pitting the northern teams against the southern teams at J. Fred. I went 0-for-3 in a 9-8 north win.

When I came back, we only had about 10 days left in the regular season, but the injury didn't seem to slow me down at the plate. I was able to maintain my average. The highlight of the season came on the last day when Kingsport held a Leo Shoals Night at the park. I got a truckload of gifts and the fans took up a collection in the stands and gave me $90.01. The fans were always digging in their pockets for money like the time Bob Pratt, our catcher, got spiked early in the season. Well, Bob was told to go home and the fans passed the hat and collected $51.11 to help pay Bob's expenses back home to Illinois. And the fans did the same for Dick Miller, our second baseman, who in early August was sliding into second and broke his shoulder.

I wished we could have repaid those fans with a better year, but we finished 69-56 and were third, nine and a half games behind Maryville-Alcoa and just one game behind Knoxville in second place. We wouldn't have finished that good if we hadn't really put on a great streak in late June where we won 14 out of 16 games and actually were within two and a half games of Maryville. But we started having some costly injuries and we just didn't play well late in the year.

Our pitching let us down some, but one guy who didn't was my old buddy Ned. Like I said before, Ned finished 19-3 that year and had a shot at 20, but he might have lost that chance when he got thumbed out of a game in July. Ned was pitching pretty decent against Morristown, but in this game he wasn't getting any calls and he was getting frustrated. It might have been about the fourth or fifth inning, I really don't recall, but the umpire behind the plate, Matthew Ryan, was missing the calls on Ned's breaking balls.

Ned was getting it across the plate, at least from my view, but wasn't getting the calls. Ned walked a batter on a pitch he thought was a strike and threw his glove in the air as high as he could while beefing with the ump. The umpire said, "If that glove comes down, you're out of here Jilton." The thing about it, after Ned was thumbed I looked over at the base umpire, Robert Cook, and he was grinning and making a motion to me to indicate that Ned's pitches were breaking over the plate.

The last several weeks of the season were tough all around. We had a chance at making the playoffs and did, but we just couldn't get untracked in the postseason.

Oh, well, there was always next season. Unfortunately we would go through again in 1954 what we went through in 1952 at Rock Hill with David Mobley and that would take some of the fun out of the game.

Chapter 19

When the 1954 season rolled around, I was back in Kingsport. I don't guess there was ever any question about my coming back. I lived in Kingsport and, after the 1953 season, Sam Bray said see you next spring and I said OK. So much for binding and complicated contracts.

But everyone in the Mountain States League wondered how long they would have a job. The league wasn't on stable ground financially. As a matter of fact, the team in Newport, Tennessee – the Canners – dropped out of the league on the first day of the season. That left us with seven teams and nobody wanted that setup because it was too hard to schedule games. But league president Virgil Q. Wacks said the league would continue and it would continue with seven teams.

The snowball began to roll at this point. Morristown pulled out of the league just a few days later because Morristown president W.E. Hodge didn't like the seven-team league setup and just for the reason I've already mentioned. Trying to run a club in that situation actually can cost a team more money because you end up with more traveling between towns.

We were down to six teams now, but a much better situation. The day after Morristown exited, the Cincinnati Reds, which operated Maryville-Alcoa, threatened to quit the league when only 68 fans turned out for a game in mid-May. So, here we go again. But Wacks met with Cincinnati officials and was able to convince the Reds to stay.

While all this was going on we were actually trying to play baseball. If one good thing came out of these clubs shutting down was that when Morristown folded, we ended up getting seven Cubans off that team. Bray signed outfielders Dagaberto Lopez and Orlando Leroux, infielders Aldo Salvent and Nap Reyes, who was also the Morristown manager, and pitchers Jorge Lopez, Lorenzo Onate and Pedro Ramos.

Ramos was a tough pitcher and when we got him I was real happy. The first game that Ramos pitched for us, he went the distance and pitched a seven-hitter in a win over Harlan.

However, when we signed the seven Cubans we had to release seven fellows on the Cherokees and one was my old friend Ned Jilton, which I hated to do. Jilton had gone 19-3 in 1953, but was struggling early in 1954. A few weeks later Ned signed with Johnson City in the Appalachian League, but would pitch in only four games.

I have to tell a story about Ned before I go on. Ned was pitching in the Southern Association and was pitching the first game of a July 4 doubleheader, there were close to 7,000 people in the stands according to Ned. Somewhere along about the fourth or fifth inning Ned wound up but got his foot caught on the rubber. As he threw the pitch he went every which way, but his foot didn't move and he ended up with a broken leg. Ned used to say that the broken leg didn't hurt half as much as the roar of laughter from the crowd.

Another fellow we got was Salvent, who was leading the league in hitting at the time with a .429 average. Salvent had a potent bat and I'll have a lot to say about Salvent a little later. Salvent turned out to be the center of some ugly racism.

I felt like I had a good rapport with the players, even though I didn't communicate that well with the Latins. We got along great and I think that may have surprised a few folks in Kingsport who wasn't in favor of having Latin players on the club.

I never thought of myself as being prejudiced. Maybe I was in some ways. Then again, most folks from the South back then had some prejudice in them, mainly from not understanding blacks and for not being around them.

I never played in a league with black players until the last four or five years of my career. In those days the blacks couldn't even go in the restaurants where the white players

273

went in to eat. They had to stay on the bus and have food, usually sandwiches, brought to them. The Cubans couldn't understand that. I know when we made the trip to Knoxville, I made arrangements with old man Regas, who had the best restaurant in Knoxville, about serving our black players and Cubans. He had two dining rooms, which he generally only opened on weekends when he had his biggest crowds. During the week, I would use the dining room that was idle and feed the blacks in real fashion. I tried to treat them as nice as I could and I believe they appreciated that.

I remember during the off season I got a package from Cuba and it had some Cuban cigars and brandy in it and a note from a couple of the players thanking me for what I did to help them. While segregation was part of the South in those days, Kingsport seemed different from other towns we played in. It seemed as if most people accepted the black players, but I know it wasn't easy for those guys.

For now, though, we were shuffling players in and out of Kingsport at a record rate. On May 21, we had three players – myself, second baseman Jesus Gonzales (yeah, the same Gonzales who turned his attitude around) and pitcher Buck Collette – who had been on the roster at the start of the season. We had gone through close to 40 players during that time.

We were playing pretty decent baseball, but we were having trouble putting people in the seats. Sam tried all kinds of promotions like Ladies Night, where each lady coming to the park would get a pair of nylon hose. In another promotion Sam gave away to one fan a picture of Grover Cleveland Alexander. I don't think they were standing in line to get into the park that night. One fan volunteered his services to boost attendance. He told Bray that he would astound the crowd by drinking a bottle of pop while standing on his head at home plate. Sam wasn't about to turn anybody down. He didn't think much of the idea, but he figured if that fellow would bring a couple of his friends to the park to watch this feat then that would be two more fans then he would have otherwise. What the fans really liked was the

South of the Border singing group. Several of the Latin players, including Ramos and Salvent, would get together before a game and sing for the fans. No one knew how to play a guitar, so they got Ernie Clark, one of our pitchers, to accompany them.

Nothing seemed to generate interest in the Cherokees and the people continued to stay away from the park. Bray got so frustrated that in early June he offered to give away the Cherokees "lock, stock and barrel", plus $3,000 in cash, to anyone who thought they could run the team. Not sell the club, but give it away. The only condition to that was the buyer had to finish the season in Kingsport. The offer included uniforms, the team bus, concession stock and players' contracts. Bray dared anyone who felt they could run the $40,000 a year operation.

Sam got all kinds of offers from all over the country after the story got out. He received calls and letters from Chicago, New York, Pittsburgh, Atlanta, West Palm Beach and other places. He even had a letter from a fellow from out in California who wanted Sam to pay his expenses to come look the situation over. Sam declined.

He got a letter from a 60-year-old bowling pin setter from Chicago who pointed out that he was a good checker player. Don't know what that had to do with running a baseball team though. Then there was another letter from a man in Chicago who described himself as elderly. He said that he couldn't come to Kingsport to actually run the club, but that he would give advice for $50 a week. There was some youthful interest too, such as the 17-year-old young man from Pinehurst, N.C. who said he would cut expenses from the start by managing the club himself. And there were lots of other inquiries, but Sam wanted someone local to take him up on the offer and no one ever did.

Meanwhile, we began to play poorly and some fans thought I might be the problem. But Sam backed me up. He was quoted in the paper: "Some have suggested I fire Shoals because we are in the league cellar. Leo has, of course, made mistakes, but his first decision has to be the one he stands on.

Maybe some of the second-guessers will take the team. I hope they do. But as long as I'm running the club and Leo continues to do as well as he is right now, he's going to remain as the manager." I appreciated that vote of confidence from Sam.

Sam had a lot on him at that time. We were losing and he was losing money at the gate and a lot of people were blaming Sam. But, if it wasn't for Sam, Kingsport might not have had baseball for the last few years. Going back to 1951, a group of five Kingsport businessmen bought the Cherokees, who were in the Appalachian League. The team that season won the league title and, in the process, drew the second largest home attendance among Class D teams in the entire nation, but the team lost money.

The next year W.A. Allen bought the team and in 1953, after losing money, sold to J. Mack Ray and Bray. The team left the Appalachian League and joined the Mountain States League. Both Ray and Bray split a loss of more than $3,000. Then, in 1954, Bray went alone with the Cherokees hoping that a move up into Class C would spur interest. It just didn't happen.

We were set to take on Maryville-Alcoa at Kingsport, this was in the middle of June, and we got word that the Maryville-Alcoa franchise had folded. The owner had even sold the team bus to try and pay off some bills. At the time, Maryville was tied for the league lead with Lexington. But Bill McKechnie, the director of the Cincinnati Reds farm system, ordered the players to go to Kingsport for the game anyway. So, without a team bus to travel on, the players all piled into their own cars, drove to Kingsport and we beat those weary guys 7-4. It was just a few days later that Maryville-Alcoa made the switch to Morristown. To make sure that the club had good leadership in the front office, Warren Giles Jr., son of the National League president, took over as business manager. The position was filled when Giles Sr. was in nearby Knoxville to dedicate the new $600,000 stadium, which became known as Bill Meyer Stadium.

Meanwhile, down in Oak Ridge, that franchise was on the brink of collapsing. This was on June 24 and club president Ross Charles said the club needed $10,000 by July 4 to keep going. He came up with the idea of selling 1,000 shares of stock at $10 a share to the residents of Oak Ridge. I don't know how much stock they sold, but Oak Ridge managed to stay afloat.

As for the Cherokees, we actually began to play good baseball. We were riding an eight-game win streak as we were set to make a trip to Harlan, Kentucky. Harlan, now that was some place to go play ball. Harlan was a rough place back in the 1950s. It was a coal town deep in the coal belt. People back then in Harlan knew only one thing and that was working in the mines. It was a generation of coal miners who came from several generations of coal miners.

I can't say for sure, but I doubt there was a black person living in Harlan at that time. Like I said before, we had quite a few Latins on our Kingsport club and they were mostly black Latins. We had been promoted pretty heavily for a Saturday night game in Harlan and when we got to the park it was half full and by game time it was packed.

The situation didn't get off to a good start that night because one of our Latins was warming up near the bleachers before the game and some fan in the stands threw a rock and hit him in the head. I ran out there and he was bleeding. I couldn't find any police and even if I had they couldn't have done anything. Couldn't or wouldn't. My guy wasn't hurt that badly, but we were a little worried the situation at the park could get worse before the night was through.

Well, Harlan jumped out to a lead early in the game and was still leading as we came to bat in the top of the ninth. We scored a couple of runs to tie and then I hit a home run to put us ahead and that turned out to be the eventual winning run. We took the field in the bottom of the ninth and when I came out to take my position at first base, the fans got on me calling me everything you could think of. At least it took the heat off the Latin players. The fans had been calling them every name in the book as well from the moment they stepped onto the field. I told them before the game what to expect and that they had to keep their cool and just not pay any attention.

Anyway, we had two out and the last Harlan batter popped up to me at first base on a ball that glanced off a creosote pole that stuck out too close to the field. But the ball was in play and I wrapped my glove around it for the final out. I had a habit of tossing the ball in the stands and I did with that creosote ball. I ran on into the dugout and was helping the bat boys load up the bats and I grabbed the ball bag. I was starting around the dugout and just about the time I did a crowd of people were coming down the grandstand steps and before I knew it they had formed a circle around me.

They were about four deep and cussing and calling me an SOB. I could smell the moonshine as they took turns getting in my face. There was a woman, I didn't know her name but she and her husband ran the local motel in Harlan, and she was yelling: "I ought to beat your brains out." I was trying to look over them hoping to find the batboys so that maybe I could grab a fungo bat and make a break.

As the crowd was calling me a "nigger lover" because of the Latins on my club, I was afraid of getting knocked down and getting the devil kicked out of me. I also was hoping the Latins had already boarded the bus to keep clear of this mob because we would have had a scene then. I was about as scared as when the Japanese had us surrounded during the war.

I kept thinking that surely someone had called the police and they were on the way. Then again, who in Harlan would call the police to come to my rescue?

About this time, a half-witted boy who we took along with us sometimes on road trips, came up to me. He was the type of kid who, after he got to the park, would yell for us to get beat. We all got a kick out of the kid and felt sorry for him at the same time. But this boy somehow made his way through the mob and got right up in my face. He started

278

cussing me like the rest of them, but he was grinning all the time. I took advantage of him, using him as a shield and started backing out of the ring. I saw some daylight and I made like Red Grange making a dash for the bus.

I look back and there's the mob coming behind me. A few minutes later the Harlan police arrived and sent the mob home.

Just as I was getting on the bus George, one of our fans who made the trip, came up to me and he was as drunk as a sailor on leave. He said, "Muscle, you weren't afraid of those people were you? I wouldn't have let nothing happen to you." That's when he pulled a .38 revolver out from under his belt. I began to get more nervous over George and that gun than I did the mob. As drunk as George was, he could have pulled the trigger and shot me.

We were scheduled to play a Sunday afternoon game the next day and I contacted league president Virgil Q. Wacks and told him what had happened and I threatened to take my team home if we didn't get some protection. He assured me things would be taken care of. We arrived at the park and all was quiet as plenty of security officers had been called in. Some of our blacks were a little leery after what happened the night before. There were a few troublemakers lined up along the fence, but we had no more problems. Except George was there again and all through the game I kept one eye on him. I knew he had that gun.

Things like that happened not only in Harlan. I remember a first base umpire being hit with a large cinder right under the ear and he dropped like he'd been shot one time in Welch, West Virginia in the Appalachian League. And more than once we had our tires slashed on our bus.

I recalled back in 1946, Bob Bowman, who was pitching for New River, told me a story about the time he was pitching for Jenkins, Kentucky at nearby Lynch. Bob, who pitched in the majors with the Cardinals, Giants and Cubs, said the stands were full of miners who were placing bets on their home teams and they were taking this game serious. Bob said he was as nervous as he had ever been, before or after, and that he hit the first Lynch batter. The crowd was getting unsettled and the second batter Bob plunked right in the side. About that time fights started breaking out all over the ballpark and a couple of fans came after Bob.

Bob said one of the miners even pulled out a six-shooter and it just so happened that one of Bob's teammates was standing right there with a bat and knocked the gun from the fellow's hand. Bob said it wasn't too long that state troopers came and escorted him and the rest of the team out of town to safety.

The Mountain States League was divided into two halves and the first half wasn't smooth sailing as far as franchise stability. First, Morristown had played only 14 games before it dropped out of the league on May 15. But baseball returned to Morristown on June 19 when the Maryville-Alcoa franchise shifted to Hamblen County. But, that moved failed too on July 2.

We needed some offensive help, so we picked up Bob Shaulis, a 24-year-old limited service man, to play outfield. Bob was hitting .290 with Morristown and the first time up for us he hit a 10th-inning home run to beat Lexington in the first game of a doubleheader and in the second game he hit another home run. Ramos won his 12th game in the opener and the next day Pedro picked up win No. 13 over the Colts in front of 1,200 fans at J. Fred.

We had a 40-minute delay in that game when home plate umpire Norman Leip ejected Colts' manager Zeke Bonura and two of his players. Zeke wouldn't leave the field. He just stood there at home plate jawing with Leip. After about 30 minutes, the Cherokees were all sitting down and some even went to the dugout. Zeke told Leip that he wasn't leaving the field. Finally, Kingsport police chief Bill Fletcher and officer Jim Owens escorted Bonura off the field and the game resumed. We won 16-4.

Word was spreading quickly that Lexington was on the bubble. Club officials were trying to raise $10,000 to keep the club afloat. They were in such bad shape that they sold the team bus to some church group in Kingsport while they were here playing us. The Colts, after their series, had to travel back to Middlesboro for two games, but they had no bus. Virgil Q. Wacks and a couple of Kingsport people lined up transportation by way of several cars. As a matter of fact, while the players were in Kingsport word got out how bad things were that the Kingsport fans passed the hat and collected $118 so the Lexington club could eat.

As the league was trembling, Wacks' words were that the Mountain States League was "as steady as a rock." On July 7 Lexington folded and we were down to only four teams – Middlesboro, Kingsport, Harlan and Oak Ridge, Tennessee.

The league went ahead with its midseason all-star game despite all the turmoil. Middlesboro had won the first half of the season by two games over Harlan, so Middlesboro hosted the all-star game. It was Middlesboro against all-stars from the three remaining teams in the league. It wasn't much of an all-star game, but Wacks felt it best to try and play it. I'm glad we did because we beat Middlesboro 18-2 and I had two home runs, two sacrifice flies and drove in seven runs.

Right after the all-star game I took over the batting lead from Salvent – .361 to .357. Ramos won his 15th, I hit my 18th home run in a 10-9 win over Oak Ridge and Ramos came back in his next start to notch his 16th win. We had just started the second half, played only six games, when Harlan fell out. Dr. Willard Buttermore, who was the president of Harlan, said financially he just couldn't keep the club going due to the lack of fan support. We were supposed to play Harlan in Kingsport, but the night of the game they didn't show. Turned out, the Harlan players had been paid only $30 for the past 19 days. So, Harlan manager Bill Steinecke and several of his players just packed their bags and left town. We were there at the stadium and we had some paying fans in the park. We managed to contact the Kingsport Merchants, a semipro team out of the Lonesome Pine League, and we played them winning 6-1. The next day, on July 20, the Mountain States League was no more. We all hated to see it happen, but we saw it coming. I hated it for personal reasons because I was hitting .351 and leading the league in home runs with 18.

I really thought this was it for me in baseball. But I got a call from Ossie Bluege, the farm director for the Washington Senators, who asked if I'd manage and play for Hagerstown of the Piedmont League. He said I was exactly what that team was looking for. They had some pretty good hitters and, with my bat in the middle of the lineup, he felt Hagerstown could win it all. They signed Ramos to a contract and he ended up 4-2 for them after winning 16 games for Kingsport.

I wouldn't have minded the job, but like I told Ossie, I had promised Helen that I was through traveling all over the country and that in fact I had considered giving up baseball a couple of years before because of that reason. Ossie was persistent. He kept after me, pleading with me. I kept saying no and finally he saw that I was serious and gave up on me. If I had been a few years younger, I might have gone.

Ossie asked me if I knew of anyone who would be right for the job and the first name that popped into my head was Zeke Bonura, who had been managing at Lexington. We had been up there playing just before it folded and I asked Zeke what he had planned to do and he said he guessed that he'd just go back home to New Orleans. Ossie called Zeke and Zeke got the job.

I saw Ossie sometime later and I asked him how Zeke was working out. Ossie said Zeke was a heck of a manager, just like I had said he would be, but that he was a little extravagant. Zeke would use new balls for batting practice and he tripled the meal money. Despite that, Ossie thanked me for suggesting Zeke.

I got Zeke a job, but I was still unemployed. Then I got a call from Ira McCollister, general manager at Knoxville in the Class B Tri-State League. He asked if I would come to Knoxville to play and manage. Lew Davis had been the manager but he broke an ankle and was going to be out a while. Ken Polivka, who had pitched some for the Reds and was still active with the Smokies, had taken over as manager, but he didn't want the job.

Knoxville was an independent franchise with a lot of veterans on the roster. I figured that since Knoxville was so close to Kingsport it might not be all that bad, so I told Ira OK, I'd come down. Knoxville bought my contract from Kingsport and also that of Aldo Salvent. Aldo was a black third baseman who was a native of Cuba. He was a heck of a fielder and he could hit with some power. I knew he could play at Knoxville.

Aldo, who led us in Kingsport with a .358 average and led the league with 36 stolen bases, wasn't going to go at first because of the fact he would be the only black on the team. I told him to at least give it a try. I told him to look at Jackie Robinson, he was the only black in major league baseball in 1947 and he made it.

Aldo and I drove down to Knoxville together and the Smokies had been playing pretty good baseball under Polivka. I signed a contract at $900 a month. McCollister was going to give me an extra $100 to manage, but I told him since the club was winning why not try and keep Ken as manager, that is if he could talk him into it. All I'd do was play first base. So Polivka remained as manager, which was fine with me.

The first game Aldo and I played in was against Greenville, South Carolina. I went 0-for-3, but Aldo picked up a couple of hits in the first game of a doubleheader at Municipal Stadium. In the second game I got three hits and Salvent had a single to drive in Max Davidson with the winning run in the ninth. I got off to a pretty good start, hitting in nine straight, and Aldo was batting .280. Aldo wasn't playing in every game, although he should have been starting every game. He couldn't because he was black.

It's hard to understand now, but back in 1954 and seven years after Jackie Robinson broke the color barrier in the major leagues, there were a couple of towns in the league which had an ordinance against blacks and whites mixing on the baseball field. One of those towns was Anderson, South Carolina and another was Spartanburg, South Carolina.

We made a trip to Anderson and Salvent sat out three games, but then we came back home to Knoxville with Spartanburg coming in for a series. Spartanburg was managed by Jimmy Bloodworth, a former infielder with Cincinnati. Bloodworth didn't have a prejudiced bone in his body, I'm convinced, but he was told by Spartanburg owner R.E. Littlejohn to bring the team back home to South Carolina if Knoxville put Salvent in the game.

Apparently there was some agreement between the Knoxville front office and Littlejohn that Salvent would be held out. But in the first game of the series Salvent played third base and shortstop in a game we won 5-1. Bloodworth, after the game, told McCollister his orders were that if Salvent played he had to go back to Spartanburg. McCollister called Littlejohn and pleaded with him and said that Salvent wouldn't play the next day. But Jim Burke, a co-owner of the Smokies along with Dr. Edgar Grubb, told Polivka to start Salvent. The Peaches didn't wait around. They boarded the bus and went home to South Carolina. Not only did Littlejohn pull his players home, but he notified Tri-State president Bobby Hipps that he was withdrawing from the league. There was some talk that Littlejohn was in financial trouble and was looking for an excuse to get out and Salvent was that excuse.

Littlejohn issued a statement on the situation: "I promised the Spartanburg City Parks Board that I would not allow my team to play against teams using Negro players. I stuck to my word by bringing the team home Sunday and I intend to remain firm in my convictions."

Nevertheless, the league was in trouble because of this. It appeared as if the league might fold. Hipps was pondering four alternatives to solve the matter. One was to disband the league, which I'm sure was the last alternative. Another was to let Spartanburg stay in the league but cancel the series between the Peaches and the Smokies for the remainder of the year. Another alternative was to operate with five teams and yet another option was to move the franchise to another city.

Meanwhile, in Cleveland, which was the parent organization of the Spartanburg franchise, the Indians front office was voicing disapproval of Spartanburg's actions. Hank Greenberg, Cleveland's GM, tried to talk to Littlejohn but Greenberg summed it up when he was quoted in the paper saying: "We have no jurisdiction over Spartanburg. We're disappointed in their action but, having no financial interest in the team, all we can do is protect our own players."

I don't know whether something like this had ever happened before or not. I guess everyone before abided by the ordinances these towns had against playing with or against blacks. I know on a road trip to Anderson, South Carolina earlier, Salvent was held out when the Anderson club officials asked McCollister not to play Aldo.

On August 2, the third day of this controversy, Sam Bray in Kingsport was raising $3,000 to field the Spartanburg franchise and move it to Kingsport for the final few weeks of the season. He was serious about it and I think Hipps might had been considering the move when, on August 3, the league directors met in Asheville and the next thing we know Salvent was sold to Hagerstown in the Piedmont League.

Apparently, Littlejohn said that if Salvent was gone, he'd come back into the league. I think it became a financial thing for Knoxville. If the league went under, it would be a huge monetary loss for a lot of people. I do know that Burke was furious because he liked Salvent and wanted to keep him.

At first, Aldo didn't want to go to Hagerstown. You have to understand that here's a guy from Cuba who starts the season in Kingsport, Tennessee. The league folds and he moves to Knoxville, Tennessee. A big fuss is made because he's black and now he's headed for Hagerstown, Maryland. Aldo was getting homesick and tired of all the moving around. I told Aldo, "You'll be getting a lot more money if you go to Hagerstown." Aldo said, "Yeah, I know, but I'll be paying a lot more taxes. I think I'm going back to Cuba." I told Burke about Aldo's concerns and Burke talked with the owners up in Hagerstown and they said that if Aldo would come, they would pay his taxes. Aldo liked that and he went. If anything at all good came out of this whole sorry mess it was that Aldo went to Hagerstown and tore the league apart, hitting .354 in 32 games

While he couldn't do anything about losing Salvent, Dr. Grubb let his feelings be known: "We brought (Salvent) to Knoxville because we felt he was a good ballplayer and could help us. He did help us. We thought it was best for the fans. However, if I am in baseball next season I will not be a party to any discrimination to any player regardless of color, race, creed or religion. There are between 15,000 and 20,000 Negroes in Knoxville and I believe they are entitled to see players of their own race. I believe that we should be able to improve our club any time we can do so. We did that with Salvent, a fine ballplayer."

Apparently Aldo Salvent was a victim of circumstances. From outward appearances he was the tool the Knoxville Smokies chose to use to force an issue upon the people of five other Tri-State League cities. Perhaps the Smokies' management did not realize how bomb-like the signing of the Negro third baseman could be. At any rate, the move almost cost us a baseball league.

Was it worth it? Is Salvent that good a third baseman? I can name at least three keystone men in the league who are better ball players than Salvent appeared to be in the four games he played here. There is Tom Marino of the Greenville Spinners, Mel Kerestes of the Rock Hill Chiefs and Jack Whitehead of our Tourists.

We are lucky the incident turned out as it did. There were indications of the league falling apart at the seams after Spartanburg refused to continue the series in Knoxville Sunday and announced its withdrawal from the league. It must have taken quite an oration from Bobby Hipps to patch up his league at the Tuesday meeting.

– Bob Terrell,
Asheville Times, 1954

Salvent was that good of a third baseman. Had Aldo been in the league from the start, instead of coming in the middle of July, he could have shown something. Aldo ended up hitting .280 getting eight hits in 25 at bats. Aldo could have been a great player in the Tri-State League if he had been given the chance. By the way, the Jack Whitehead mentioned hit .221 and led the Tri-State League in errors with 31.

There were some repercussions after that. I know at Rock Hill, some of the blacks picketed the park when Spartanburg came there later in the season.

As for the Tri-State League and all those fine owners, well the league came back in 1955 with only four teams – Asheville, Greenville, Rock Hill and Spartanburg. After 1955, the Tri-State League folded. I would like to think the owners' bigotry was its undoing.

Despite the fiasco with Aldo, the season went on. We were in Rock Hill one night and Jim Smiley, our pitcher, plunked Chiefs' outfielder Omer Tolson. We had a bench-clearing brawl but nobody got hurt. Then the next night at Rock Hill Polivka was pitching and beaned Ronnie George knocking him unconscious. That started another brawl. An eye-for-an-eye I guess.

The season was winding down. Ken had done a good job taking the club to a 29-13 record after he took over and we finished the season in second place, but 13 games behind ·

Asheville. We made the playoffs and eventually won the title over Asheville. But once the regular season was over, I was gone. I was tired, just like I'm sure Aldo was tired, of everything we had to put up with that season. I didn't exactly tear up the league with Knoxville, although I was respectable with a .297 average, six home runs and 27 RBIs in 42 games.

Like most places, Knoxville had an Appreciation Night for the players. We got all kinds of gifts, including a box of bananas. I remember our last home game Wild Red Berry, a professional wrestler who was putting on an exhibition at Chilhowee Park, asked to umpire and they let him do an inning on the bases. We finished the season in Asheville and lost 4-0 in the most embarrassing way. Bud Shaney, a former Asheville star who was now the groundskeeper, asked the club if he could pitch and they said why not. Well, Bud, who was 53-years-old, four-hit the Smokies over the first five innings. Ray Hathaway, the Tourists manager, came on to finish up and retired 12 of the last 14 batters he faced. I can say I wasn't a part of that debacle as I wasn't in the lineup.

I had asked for, and got, my release as soon as the regular season was over. Helen was pregnant with Tim, but that wasn't the reason I didn't go back because she wasn't due until March. There wasn't any extra money for being in the playoffs and the playoffs lasted almost two weeks and I was ready to go back home. The whole incident with Aldo just soured me. Anyway, the Smokies won without me.

Chapter 20

I liked Knoxville and it was a good baseball town. But Kingsport was getting back into the Appalachian League and I knew I had a job there if I wanted it. I felt that 1955 would be my last year. My service-connected disability of feet and legs began bothering me, making the game a burden instead of a pleasure.

But, I wanted to give it one more shot in 1955. I liked playing for Sam Bray and I was going to manage again. The hardest part about managing isn't on the field. It's those times when you have to go up to a kid or a veteran and tell him he's off the club. In the Appalachian League we had a 21-player limit the first month of the season, but after that first month the roster had to be trimmed down to 16 players. Sometimes the choice of who to cut was easy, sometimes it wasn't. But it was never easy having to go up to a guy and tell him he was the one.

Leo (Muscles) Shoals will be back in Johnson City today at Cardinal Park with his 1955 edition of the Kingsport Cherokees.

(Muscles) is perhaps the best known man in the minor league player ranks.

Almost legendary in these parts, (Muscles) has become a part of the professional baseball scenery in the Appalachian area.

Ask anybody who's familiar with baseball, and they'll tell you that (Muscles) swings a baseball bat like a toothpick.

– Jimmy Smyth, sports editor,
Johnson City Press-Chronicle,
May 8, 1955

It was a crazy season in '55. I knew right off the bat we didn't have a great ballclub. We had no pitching, but boy we sure could hit. Bluefield found that out early in the year when we beat the Blue-Grays 34-2 at Bowen Field in Bluefield. I had a couple of our 24 hits as we scored 13 runs on 10 hits in the eighth inning, sending 17 batters to the plate.

One of our better hitters was Waldo Gonzalez, who could also handle the glove at third base. I can't recall ever having seen an unassisted triple play in all my playing days, until Waldo pulled one off early in the year against Welch, West Virginia. We were tied in a game at Welch 7-7 and had the bases loaded in the ninth inning with nobody out. Al DePhillips was on first, Jack McDevitt on second and Art Oody on third. Welch manager Herb Mancini sent up Stan Olszewski to pinch-hit and Olszewski hit a ground ball to Waldo at third.

Oody, at the crack of the bat, took off from third and headed home but, at the last second, changed his mind and tried to get back to third. Waldo tagged Oody for the first out and stepped on third to force McDevitt coming down from second base. For some reason DePhillips, who was on first, was watching the whole thing unfold over at third and decided he'd go to second base. I don't know where our second baseman was and why Waldo didn't throw the ball to him, but Waldo began running to second and just beat DePhillips to the bag and tagged him for the unassisted triple play.

The whole thing would have been more memorable if we had won the game. Instead, in the 10th inning, Joe Kostelac of the Miners hit a three-run home run and we lost 10-7.

But things like that kept plaguing us all season. Like the time we lost a game to Bluefield at J. Fred Johnson Stadium when they scored three runs on one sacrifice fly. It happened, believe it or not. It was in the first inning and the Blue-Grays had the bases loaded. John Liprando hit a long fly ball to deep center field. Johnny Charles, who was a brother of the boxer Ezzard Charles, kept backing up and backing up, tracking the ball and he pulled it down. Except just as he did, he fell backward into the hedges that bordered J. Fred Johnson. By the time Johnny got out of the bushes and on his feet, all three Bluefield runners had scored.

Those hedges were always causing problems it seemed. Balls, and outfielders, were always getting lost in those bushes. They looked pretty, but they were trouble. I know one time that season I got thrown out of a game because of those hedges. Chuck Sedor of Salem hit a ball in the hedges that the umpire called fair but I saw it landing foul. I argued too much and got thrown out. Which, in the end, may have been a good thing. In that game Carmon Dugger was pitching no-hit ball in what was a first game of a doubleheader. We weren't getting anything off Carmon who, by the way, operated the Elizabethton Twins in the Appalachian League for a number of years. Anyway, after I got thrown out, Bob Wyzykowski went in to play first base for me. As it turned out, Bob had the only hit of the game for us. A double right into those hedges, where else?

I must have been plenty mad over that first game because I came back in the second game and hit my 27th home run of the year in the eighth inning driving in two runs in a 5-2 win for us.

Getting back to Waldo Gonzalez. He was a puzzle and I don't think all the pieces were there. Oh, he was a very good hitter and a fine fielder, but you never knew what he was going to do next. He was very emotional. We had Bluefield in for a doubleheader about the middle of July and Waldo was hitting the cover off the ball. As a matter of fact, he and I were the only ones hitting over .300 for the Cherokees. But in the first game, in the sixth inning, Waldo grounded out and, instead of coming back into the dugout, he just walked right out of the ballpark. I sent one of the other guys after him and he found Waldo in the parking lot ripping his uniform off. Bray fined Waldo $60 and suspended him indefinitely.

After the game I tried to find Waldo to talk with him and try to get him to come back, but I never did find him.

I'm trying to give catcher Robert Pratt a few words of advice.
(Photo courtesy Sholes family)

Somebody said he caught the first bus out of town. He was without question one of the brightest prospects we had on that team and I don't know if he ever came back to play somewhere else or not. I often wondered. Maybe that's where that kid's book "Where's Waldo" originated.

At the midway point of the season I was having a pretty good year and was picked as the starting first baseman on the all-star team, which would be played in Salem against the Rebels.

If there was anybody in the league who should have been playing in that all-star game, it was Grady Chavis of Johnson City. Chavis, an outfielder, never made it to Salem, however. Chavis, who would end up leading the Appalachian League in hitting with a .377 average, was suspended five days and fined $30 by Appy president Chauncey DeVault. It seemed that Grady and an umpire by the name of Tom Simon just couldn't hit it off. Johnson City was playing in Wytheville on a Sunday and Grady got into an argument with Simon and spit on the arbiter. Well, on Monday, Johnson City was at Bristol and Simon was calling behind the plate. Grady got into it again with Simon and Simon got all wet again. It would have been bad enough for Simon to get spat on except that Grady mixed his saliva with tobacco juice.

Chavis, who was from Laurinburg, N.C., was a very good hitter. He was with Johnson City in 1953 and hit .285 with 124 walks and 120 runs scored and was hitting .320 in 1954 with Lynchburg in the Class B Piedmont League before he hurt his throwing arm. Chavis came back to Johnson City late in the year and finished hitting .379.

Despite not having Grady's bat in the lineup, we still beat Salem 15-8 at Municipal Stadium. I had a single, double and a grand slam and drove in six runs to aid the cause of the all-stars against the Rebels.

Zeke Lavelliere of Wytheville wielded the biggest home run bat, slamming two roundtrippers. Ray Vescovi and Muscles Shoals also poled four-baggers. Shoals was the hitting star of the game and the bases-loaded homer he hit cleared the fence at the 400 foot marker. It probably traveled about

500 feet and drew gasps of admiration from
even the home-standing Rebel rooters.

- Jimmy Smyth,
Johnson City Press-Chronicle,
July 21, 1955

The biggest concern that season in the Appalachian League wasn't batting averages or who would win the pennant. It was whether or not Kingsport could keep its head above water financially to remain in the league. But Kingsport wasn't the only team having problems. It seems we've heard this story before, just a different year. The Pulaski directors had voted in early July to drop out of the eight-team league. Pulaski was apparently losing money, so team president Leonard Shavian asked the Philadelphia Phillies, which was the parent club of the Pulaski franchise, to help keep the team afloat. Philadelphia initially refused any financial help and it appeared as if Pulaski would fold. Well, Philadelphia gave it more thought and eventually came to the rescue to bail Pulaski out of trouble.

About that same time Kingsport and Wytheville, which had no major league affiliation to call on for help, were both crying they were in financial trouble. Kingsport was over $3,000 in the hole and Sam Bray came out and said that if the club didn't raise $3,000 in five days to pay the bills, he would have to fold the Cherokees. Being an independent was a risky business during that time of minor league baseball. If you were an independent owner, you had to pay the bills. The Cherokees had been averaging about 300 people a game and Bray indicated that it would take an average of 500 to meet expenses. He pointed out that it took about $250 a day to operate the club.

We, the players, didn't know what was going to happen. The club put on a drive to raise money by asking fans and businesses to contribute if they wanted baseball to remain in Kingsport. Apparently not a lot of people cared.

By the end of that five-day span in a drive to raise $3,000, a total of $255 had come into the coffers.

Welch was the first team in the league to actually fold. Welch just couldn't hack it. Nobody was coming to their games and the front office couldn't make ends meet. The Miners had a debt of $13,550 and still were in debt for $4,500 from the year before. Welch, which had been in the league ten years, was a farm club of the Kansas City Athletics and the people in KC listened to an offer from some businessmen in Marion, Virginia.

While I'm on the subject of Welch, there was the time the Welch business manager – Jack Paris – and the Wytheville manager – Frank (Bull) Hamons – each swore out a warrant on the other. It seemed that Hamons was arrested and charged with assault on Paris in a pregame argument in the Welch dressing room. Paris charged that Hamons entered the dressing room, accused him of heckling him at the game the night before and then struck him.

Later, Paris was arrested on a warrant sworn out by Hamons, charging Paris with brandishing a deadly weapon – a bucket of money and a broom. I think the charges were eventually dropped.

Anyway, the move to Marion was approved and the switch was made in the middle of July. The Miners were supposed to have had a game in Welch, but it was cancelled so the players could have the day off and travel to Marion and get settled in their new home.

Bray saw what happened with Welch and he figured he could do the same and move the Cherokees from Kingsport to Morristown. There were some people in Morristown who wanted baseball back, but the Appalachian League board of directors voted the move down. I guess it was because Morristown had baseball before and couldn't support it.

Bray kept pushing for the move to Morristown and he finally got the league to OK a plan for the Cherokees to play a couple of home games in Morristown against Bluefield. If the fan support was good, then the league said it might consider a permanent move. Well, we played two games there in bad weather and drew over 1,700 fans. It looked like Morristown was ready for baseball again and it looked like Kingsport was going to lose a team.

However, somewhere along the way Bray had a change of heart. When we got back to Kingsport he said: "I've decided to keep the Cherokees in Kingsport. I feel I'd be letting down the 200-or-so fans in Kingsport who have been supporting the team all season if I moved it to Morristown."

I, for one, was happy about that. I didn't want to have to move to Morristown for the final month of the season. I celebrated by hitting my third home run in two days with my 31st coming against Wytheville and tying Wytheville's Mike Coppola for the league lead. Back in 1947 I had hit 32 home runs, which stood as the Appalachian League's all-time mark for home runs. But, on August 25, Coppola hit his 33rd. I came back the next day and hit my 33rd. As it turned out, neither one of us hit a home run the rest of the season and we finished tied for the league lead with 33 home runs.

Nobody had heard of Coppola before. He was a 22-year-old from Stamford, Connecticut who had spent the previous two years in the army. He was 6-feet-1 and weighed close to 210 pounds, a right-hander who took advantage of the short left field fence at Withers Field in Wytheville. Coppola's only previous stint in pro ball came in 1952 when, as a farmhand of the Boston Braves, he hit 10 home runs for Danville of the Mississippi-Ohio Valley League.

I never really got to know Coppola that well, but we made the home run race exciting that season.

As a team we didn't have a good year. We finished 64-62, 22 games behind Salem, which was 84-38. Jack Crosswhite had a pretty darn good ballclub in Salem and it was an independent club.

Somebody asked Jack what was the key to handling the team and he said, "I teach them sound baseball, tell them what the score is and treat 'em right and play no favorites." He left out the part about the sandpaper.

Salem was playing a game at Bluefield and their pitcher, whose name I don't recall, was scuffing up the ball with sandpaper. The pitcher had two kinds of sandpaper in his pocket – one white and one red. Late in the game the white sandpaper was worn down, so the pitcher switched to using the red sandpaper. Well, one of the Bluefield batters hit a foul ball into the Bluefield dugout and somebody noticed red on the ball and showed it to Leonard Okrie, the Bluefield manager. Leonard went rushing out to the umpire holding up the ball. When they went out to the mound the umpire found the red sandpaper in the pitcher's pocket and he was thrown out of the game.

The thing about Salem that season was that their pitchers didn't have to resort to sandpaper to win ballgames. With Paul Johnston winning 20 and with guys like Dugger and Ben Swaringen, the Rebels had a darn good staff.

We made the postseason Shaughnessy playoffs, but the bad news was we had to play Salem. We played the first game at Municipal Park in Salem and got beat 5-3, but I still think we got robbed out of at least one run and maybe more.

In the very first inning Johnny Charles scored, or at least I thought he scored, on my sacrifice fly. I hit a long fly to right field that Salem's Charley Weatherspoon caught. He made the long throw into the plate to catcher Frank Jessee just as Charles slid across. After I saw the ball was going to be caught, I hustled back to home plate to see the play. From my angle, Jessee never made the tag. If he had, then Charles would have been out. But umpire Jerry Zuzzio saw it otherwise and called Johnny out. I went crazy and so did Johnny. Several of the other guys came running up to Zuzzio arguing and we had him surrounded. Zuzzio gave us a warning and said if we didn't back off, he was going to start throwing people out. I knew we couldn't afford that, so we all backed off. But you should have seen Zuzzio's blue jacket, it had dusty hand marks all over the back of it. Salem was by far the better team though and it was probably only a matter of time that we got knocked out. The next day Carmon Dugger went the distance and beat us 3-2.

Johnson City had defeated Bristol, whose players were wearing the uniforms of the 1953 world champion New York Yankees, in the other playoff and it was to have been Salem and JC for the championship. But, that never came off as bad weather set in and they could never get the games played. So, Salem and JC were declared co-champions. Johnson City had a good ballclub, but there no way Salem would have lost.

I ended my career with the type of season I could be proud of. I hit .362 and tied the Appalachian League record for home runs with 33 and led in RBIs with 134. After a season like that, I could walk away with a good feeling. Everything has to come to an end sometime. Oh, I might have come back to Kingsport in 1956, but that issue was settled when the Appalachian League's Class D status was ended and the league became a rookie league, just like it is today. There was no place for veterans like me in the Appy anymore. My career had been exciting. I enjoyed playing baseball and, looking back, I would have liked to have a least had a cup of coffee in the big leagues, just to say I was there.

But, when I had the opportunity, there were things more important in my life. I'm just thankful that I could play as well as I did after returning from the war. I'm always asked if I would have stayed in the lower minors as long as I did if I had it to do all over again and my answer is a definite yes. The experience was worth a million dollars to me. The solid friendships I made with people in baseball have lasted a lifetime. You develop a closeness in the minor leagues that never goes away. I guess it could be because of all those long bus rides you take.

In the winter of 1955 I got a call from Jack Diggs in Saltville, Virginia, who wanted to know if I would be interested in coming up there to work for the Olin Mathieson Chemical Company and to play on and manage the semipro club in Saltville – the Alkalies.

Helen and I had moved back to Parkersburg and I was working for Electromat, a division of Union Carbide, when Diggs called. I talked to Helen about moving to

Saltville and she was thrilled because we would be back closer to Kingsport. Olin made a deal with me where they paid to move our furniture and put me up in a hotel until I found a house. Helen and the kids stayed with her parents in Kingsport until I got things settled.

That's my grandson Derek up at bat in a Little League game. Notice he's a left-hander just like his granddad.

(Photo courtesy Sholes family)

Just when I thought baseball was over in my life, here I was playing again. I began to think if I ever would give up the game. I had a good time playing with the Alkalies. Our league would play two games a week, which isn't enough to keep your timing sharp. You have to play baseball every day to keep on top of your hitting, but it was fun.

There were a lot of guys on that team like Chub Arnold and Willis Oakes who were pretty good ballplayers and maybe could have played professionally. They just never got the break.

I played for the next three or four years, mostly just pinch-hitting, but I worked for Olin for 15 years. Olin eventually liquidated its operations in Saltville due to an environmental condition. I found a job not far away in Glade Spring, Virginia at the Casket Hardware Company. They made the metal parts that went on caskets. I worked there for eight years before retiring in 1980.

I mentioned Ronnie and Yvonne and Tim, who was born in 1955. Helen and I were blessed with two more children – Greg was born in 1956 and Gary in 1957. While baseball has been my life, my family has been the most important part of my life. They've been with me through thick and thin.

I tried to stay active after retiring, but I have had my share of ups and downs. I injured my right hip on a hill with a mountain bike and arthritis set in. The doctor said I had a degenerative arthritic hip and there was nothing to do but have a new hip put in.

That's me and Helen with Yvonne and Ronnie in the back and Tim and Greg in the front. The year was 1961.

(Photo courtesy Sholes family)

I entered the veterans hospital in Johnson City and had a steel cap placed on the femur bone head as the cartilage was all dried up. The hip had to be ground out and a plastic cup with the steel cap inside making a perfect fit for the mobility of the joint. The new hip isn't as good as the old one, but I'm thankful that I can walk at all.

I used to go to the old timer's game they had all around the area, but I've slowed that down a bit. Cart Howerton, when he ran the Winston-Salem club, would put on a game every year and I'd go over on his invitation. He'd have Enos Slaughter, Bobby Richardson, Smoky Burgess and Vinegar Bend Mizell among others. But, as the years went on, it got tougher for me to go to those old timer's games.

I remember the first time I went to Howerton's old timer's game, in the late 1960s, I took three of my children, who were all small at the time. Mizell was a North Carolina congressman then and he was the starting pitcher in this game. Mizell really hadn't been out of baseball that long and he was being a little cute on the mound. He pitched the first inning and he was firing the ball up there. I never got ready on any one of his pitches. I took all three pitches for strikes without lifting the bat off my shoulder. As I walked back to the dugout, a couple of guys said, "Muscle, we wanted to see you swing. We've heard of you and how long you used to hit them home runs."

It was rather embarrassing for me, but I played the whole game and got a couple of hits off guys lobbing the ball up to the plate. I got invited back the next year and wouldn't you know it, Mizell is pitching again. When I went up to hit the kids told Gary, who was the youngest there at the game, to close his eyes because daddy can't hit Mizell. The first pitch I sent on a shot to right-center, ringing like a bell off the wall. The kids were up jumping and clapping and shouting, "Gary, open your eyes, daddy can hit Mizell."

There was another time we had an old timer's game in Bristol and Gail Harris, who is from nearby Abingdon originally and played in the major leagues, was there. Gail

301

and I were first basemen by trade. I was put down as the starting first baseman and I said no to the manager. I told him I'd play the outfield and let Gail play first because he had been in the major leagues and the people around there wanted to see him play. But Gail insisted that I play first and he'd go to the outfield. I was a little older so maybe he felt sorry for me. Anyway, there was a high fly ball to Gail in right and I turned and shouted to Gail, "Plenty of room Gail, plenty of room." He finally caught the ball up against the fence. He came back in and said, "Muscle, I thought you said I had plenty of room. Did you see where I ended up catching that ball?" I said, "Gail, I must have misjudged that one just a little."

That's the family a few years later in 1986.
(Photo courtesy Sholes family)

The old timer's games are supposed to be fun, but the competitive fires never burn out completely. You can joke about a strikeout, but inside it kills you. I remember one year we had Lefty Gomez pitching and an error or two were made behind him while he was on the mound. He was peeved as could be when he came into the dugout after the inning and a couple of runs scored off him. He was blasting the guys who had made the errors and he wasn't joking either.

No matter how old you are or how long you've been out of the game, you still have that drive inside you that was there when you played the game as a young man. I don't guess I'll ever lose that fire and I don't guess I'll ever lose the love that I have for the game of baseball. I hope I never do.

It seems just like yesterday when I was a small boy in West Virginia at Camden on Gauley. I can close my eyes and I can still hear the sound of those metal cleats on the wooden boardwalk outside our house. I can still taste that lemonade they used to serve on the hill. I can still smell the new leather on that catcher's glove my daddy gave me.

I'm just glad I had the chance to play baseball. My years of playing baseball were gone a long time ago and generations keep coming and going. But, in a way, I can still play baseball. Because I can close my eyes and I can see that pitch coming and I'm swinging the bat and the ball is heading over that right field fence. What a feeling.

Chapter 21

Muscle Shoals played with, and against, literally thousands of ballplayers over his minor league career. Following are some remembrances of those former players, as well as some memories from umpires and fans.

*

"I didn't have a lot of trouble with Muscle. He never hit one off me in the Tri-State League, but he did in semipro when he was at Saltville and I was with Greeneville. You had to be careful with Muscle. He was strong and could handle that bat like a toothpick. He was very quick with the bat. I remember one time he hit a home run off lefty Paul Harrison that beat us late in the game. It went out of that Knoxville ballpark like a rocket."

JIM CONSTABLE

Pitcher for Knoxville of the Tri-State League in 1952. Also pitched in major leagues for New York Giants (1956-57), San Francisco Giants (1958, 1963), Cleveland Indians (1958), Washington Senators (1958), Milwaukee Braves (1962).

*

"Muscle was a guy with great power. There wasn't a ballpark that he couldn't hit one out of. He was the leader of his team. He never self-proclaimed himself as the leader, but he was the leader just by his presense and by example."

TOM GIORDANO

Third baseman for Augusta in the South Atlantic League in 1950. Served 12 years as farm director for the Baltimore Orioles and currently serving as major league scout for Cleveland Indians.

"I recall Muscle. He was big and strong and had his shirt cut off at the shoulders and arms to show those huge muscles. He scared all the 18-year-old kids. Just watching him take batting practice told you to pitch him inside hard. That way we could make our stuff look better then when we threw him down and away. He could cripple your mistakes. Before I ever saw him, I had heard about his mountainous home runs."

BILL MONBOUQUETTE

Pitcher for Bluefield in the Appalachian League in 1955. Also pitched in major leagues for Boston Red Sox (1958-65), Detroit Tigers (1966-67), New York Yankees (1967-68), San Francisco Giants (1968).

Ron Necciai is the only pitcher to ever strike out 27 batters in a professional baseball game. I never faced him but got to know Ron from old timer reunions.

(Photo courtesy Sholes family)

"It was a joy to watch Muscle play ball for two reasons. One was the beautiful home run trot; the way he pranced around the bases. Secondly, the way he played first base. He would receive the throw and gently, with his left foot, he would touch the bag. I played for Muscle one year at Kingsport and he knew how to handle players. We were in Bluefield and I had batted twice and both times I hit into double plays. I was disgusted. My third time came around and Muscle said, 'You're up Bill.' I said, 'Put somebody else in for me.' He said, 'Get on up there and hit the ball.' Well, I went up to the plate and hit the ball off the wall with a man on. If Muscle believed in you, you had his confidence. Another thing I remember about Muscle was when we were traveling on the bus, he loved to sing. He had some toothpaste jingle he would sing. Muscle was just a lot of fun to be around."

BILL HALSTEAD

Pitcher-outfielder for nine years in minor leagues, mainly in the Mountain States League and the Appalachian League. Also was president of Appalachian League 1982-95.

*

"When Muscle came to bat and I was playing first base, I would get as far back as I could. Now, you have to remember he must have been in his 40s by this time, but he could still kill the ball. He would swing a bat like a toothpick. He would get down to first base and he was always talking. He never knew a stranger."

BOYCE COX

First baseman for Bristol in the semipro Burley Belt League. Also played two years for Bristol Twins in Appalachian League.

"My grandfather was a barber in Johnson City and when I was in high school I would meet him at the barber shop after closing and we'd go down to Cardinal Park and watch Muscle when he was with Kingsport. I've seen Muscle hit home runs out of that park over top of lights, half way into the football stadium beyond the outfield fence. In my opinion, he could have played in the major leagues."

JOE MCCLAIN

Former pitcher for the Washington Senators (1961-62).

*

"Muscle was such a good hitter. Every player had his own bat. Muscle had his too but he didn't care what bat he used. If someone batting in front of him got a hit, Muscle would say, 'I think I'll use that bat.' It didn't matter the length or the weight of that bat. The thing about Muscle was that he had great power, but he hit for average too."

PAUL MUSSELMAN

Center fielder for Kingsport Cherokees in 1951

*

"Muscle had more control with the bat than any other player I ever saw, bar none. He would get that bat going around at full speed and would stop it on a dime. That's how strong his wrists were. I recall one game I was playing the outfield for Bristol in 1947 and we had a left-hander on the mound – Deon Lampros. The first time up Muscle popped the ball up and he got so mad and he yelled out to Lampros 'I'll get you the next time' Well, the next time up Muscle hit one about 500 feet. He was something else."

RANCE PLESS

Also played against Shoals as member of Jacksonville Tars in 1950. Played in major leagues with Kansas City Athletics (1954).

"Muscle was a tremendous player. We played together at Kingsport, then I played against him in 1953 in the Mountain States League when he was with Kingsport and I was with Maryville-Alcoa. I remember at Kingsport he would clear that right field fence with ease. The only other player I ever played with or against who could equal Muscle's power was Willie Kirkland, but Willie struck out a lot more."

HUGH HAMIL

Outfielder on the 1951 Appalachian League champion Kingsport Cherokees

Johnny Vander Meer, who pitched back-to-back no hitters, and I sign autographs at Durham in 1993.

(Photo courtesy Sholes family)

"As a kid I would stay outside J. Fred Johnson Stadium to try and get a home run ball that Muscle hit. The only thing was you never knew where to stand. I've seen him hit the ball across the four-lane highway behind right field and then across the sidewalk and into the field. Later, when I owned the clothing store I would have Muscle come in to sign autographs. I would stand outside and make popcorn and hot dogs."

NORM SOBEL

Owner of Sobel's Clothing Store in Kingsport

*

"Muscle came to Columbia with a great reputation as a home run hitter because the year before he hit the 55 at Reidsville. I can remember a home run he hit in Savannah one time. Savannah played their games in an old football stadium and there was a big tree behind the high wall in right-center. Well, Muscle got hold of one and knocked it over that tree. It must have been a 500-foot drive. We all just marveled at his power."

CARLTON NEBEL

Catcher for the Columbia Reds in 1950

*

"I was basically a fastball pitcher with a little curve. When pitching to Muscle I tried to get the fastball by him. I don't remember him hitting any home runs off me, although he may have. If he didn't hit many, then I must have pitched him pretty good."

CHARLIE HUMMEL

Former running back for Penn State who pitched for Martinsville in 1949

*

"I never knew Muscle personally, but I can remember all the buzz going on that year about his home run hitting. Everybody was talking about Muscle Shoals. I can remember that old park in Winston-Salem, it was up on a hill, and Muscle would hit home runs there and when he did the ball would disappear like a pea. I played third base, so I didn't

309

worry about too many of his line drives coming at me as he was strictly a pull hitter to right."

GEORGE LEBEDZ

Third baseman for Winston-Salem in 1949

*

"The name Muscle fit his personality. I can remember those big, bulging muscles coming out of those sleeves of his uniform. I can remember a brick building beyond right field at Durham and Muscle hit one on top of that building for a home run. You had to tie yourself down when Muscle hit the ball."

CARL LINHART

Outfielder for Durham in 1949. Played in major leagues with Detroit Tigers (1952)

*

"Muscle loved for me to throw batting practice to him. There was a group of kids that gathered on the top of the bank at Kiker Stadium. I'd throw Muscle 10 pitches and he'd hit eight of them onto the bank."

DEAN FRYE

Infielder for Reidsville in 1949

*

"My recollection of Muscle Shoals is that he hit a lot of home runs the year I played against him, which would have been 1951 when he was with Kingsport and I was playing for Bluefield. They would pass the hat after a home run and I know that he made a lot of money that season."

BOBBY MALKMUS

Infielder for Bluefield in 1951. Played in major leagues with Milwaukee Braves (1957), Washington Senators (1958-59), Philadelphia Phillies (1960-62).

"Muscle looked better striking out than a lot of people did hitting home runs. He had a beautiful swing. He had a great eye at the plate. But, Muscle also liked the alcohol. Not often, but sometimes he would come up to the plate and he'd say, 'Bernie, let me know when this game is over with.' Sometimes he would just say it kidding of course, but sometimes he would have a little buzz. Muscle was full of life."

BERNIE WEBB

Umpire in the Appalachian League and Mountain States League

Enos Slaughter and I are having a good time at Greensboro's old timer's game in 1986.
(Photo courtesy Sholes family)

"I was just a young kid at the time and Muscle was a veteran ballplayer by then. We didn't converse a great deal. I just remember him hitting some gigantic home runs like I'd never seen before."

JOHN GORYL

Infielder for Bluefield in Appalachian League in 1951. Played in major leagues with Chicago Cubs (1957-59),

*Minnesota Twins (1962-64). Also managed in major leagues
with Minnesota Twins (1980-81).*

*

"They didn't make many better hitters than Muscle
Shoals. I can remember Hobe Brummette throwing batting
practice and Muscle would hit the ball out of the park just
about every time. Hobe said, 'Muscle, I'm going to take you
to the World's Fair because with me pitching and you hitting
we'll put on one heck-u-va show.' He was something."

RAYMOND JOHNSTON

*Outfielder for Kingsport Cherokees in Appalachian
League in 1946*

*

"You tell people who never saw Muscle about the
way he hit the ball and they don't believe you. He was on par
with Babe Ruth. I was at all the games. I remember he and
his wife Helen had an apartment over the Tiny Tim Market
in Kingsport. One thing about Muscle, he was modest. Just
like his experiences in World War II. He never told a lot of
people but we'd get to talking as friends and he would open
up. One time they were on an island and came to a cliff and
the only way up was by climbing it. Muscle went up first and
he looked over and saw a Japanese camp. He dropped a rope
over the edge and began pulling other guys up. They set up
machine guns and got the Japanese before they knew what
hit them. Another time, he had a buddy who was shot dead
and Muscle was pulling him back when the same Japanese
soldier shot him again. Muscle got mad and went after the
Japanese soldier and literally beat him to death with his
fists."

KIM KOFFMAN

A Kingsport Cherokee fan and friend of Shoals

"Muscle had lots of power. He was a tremendous low ball hitter. One of the best I'd ever seen. I'd tell our pitchers to keep the ball up. Sometimes it worked, but he still got his share of home runs.

IVAN KUESTER

Manager of Charlotte Hornets of Tri-State League in 1952

*

"I used to shine the players' shoes and I would use the liquid polish on all the players' shoes except for Muscle. Muscle wanted me to use the paste type polish. It was harder doing the shoes the way he wanted but Muscle always gave me a big tip."

JOHNNY SPRIGGS

Batboy for Kingsport in 1951

*

"I used to help out the regular batboy and I remember one time Muscle had gone to the lockerroom. It was Muscle's time to bat and he was supposed to be in the on-deck circle and he wasn't anywhere to be found. Anyway, the manager told me to go to the lockerroom and to see what had happened. I went in there and he was drinking a beer. I told Muscle it was his time to bat and he said he was coming. Well, he finally came out and sauntered up to the plate. Dick McNabb was umpiring and he was fuming. Leo took his time swinging six bats and loosening up. Finally he stepped into the batter's box but then stepped out again to tie his shoe. Muscle swung at the first pitch and corkscrewed himself into the ground. On the second pitch he swung and sent a drive to the big left field. Well, he fell down going to second. He got up and fell again going to third. Everybody in the park was going crazy. Muscle should have had an inside the park home run but instead had to settle for a triple."

DICK BAILEY

Batboy for Kingsport in 1947

Florida football coach Steve Spurrier and I were both inducted into the Upper East Tennessee Sports Hall of Fame.

(Photo courtesy Sholes family)

"Muscle was a big, strong hitter who was feared by many pitchers. He reminded me a little of Ted Kluszewski who I pitched against when I was with Pittsburgh and he was with Cincinnati. I know I would start Muscle off inside with a fastball and hope he would pull it foul to get ahead in the count. Then I would go strictly to my curve. He was left-handed and I threw left-handed and I had pretty good success against him. But, if you made a mistake against Muscle, he'd take you out of the park and I saw him do it to a lot of pitchers."

PAUL LAPALME

LaPalme went 20-2 for the Bristol Twins of the Appalachian League in 1946 with a 3.16 ERA. Pitched in major leagues with Pittsburgh Pirates (1951-54), St. Louis Cardinals (1955), Cincinnati Reds (1956), Chicago White Sox (1956-57).

314

"I never saw Muscle play, but I heard a lot about him when I pitched for Burlington in the Carolina League in 1952 after I left Bristol. They were still talking about the 55 home runs he hit three years before. I finally met Muscle in 1993 when Bill Kirkland had a Carolina League reunion in Durham. It was a thrill to sit and talk with Muscle and what a likeable guy he was too. We'd get to talking and he'd say he was sorry he never got to hit against me. I told Muscle that I thought I could get him out a few times but I also told him that he would probably hit a few into the lights against me."

RON NECCIAI

The only pitcher in professional baseball to ever strike out 27 batters in one game. He did it on May 13, 1952 pitching for the Bristol Twins of the Appalachian League against the Welch Miners. Pitched in major leagues with Pittsburgh Pirates (1952).

*

"When he played at Johnson City in 1939, I was with Newport and then we later played together at Kingsport. He had a great eye for the ball and would wait until the very last second to swing. He had such a smooth swing. I use the expression that he looked good even when he struck out. I always tried to pitch him outside and low with a breaking ball and inside with the fastball. I didn't try to strike him out; I just tried to give him a pitch that he couldn't get much power on. I have the highest regards for Muscle Shoals of all those who I played with or against."

J. CRAFT (LEFTY) AKARD

Winner of 18 straight games for Kingsport Cherokees in 1945

*

"He could hit the ball as hard as anyone. He pulled everything down the line at first. I usually hit in front of Muscle and the first baseman would never hold me on if I happened to reach first base. With Muscle up at bat I could usually get a big lead because the first baseman would be playing so far back of the bag. Not many first basemen wanted to be close with 'Muscle' swinging."

CHUB ARNOLD

Saltville Alkalies of the Burley Belt League

Former Baltimore Oriole third baseman Brooks Robinson and I pose for the camera.
(Photo courtesy Sholes family)

"Muscle Shoals was one of the best hitters I ever faced and I faced the Aarons and the Mathewses. He was the most natural hitter I ever threw against. He had one of the more unorthodox stances; he was looking straight at you. And he has one of the quickest bats I ever saw. I was pitching for Johnson City, this was in 1955, and I was winning the game by one run with two out in the ninth inning. Muscle came to bat and I threw him my best fastball and he hit it out of the park but the umpire called it foul and I ended up walking him. He was so strong that he'd rip grounders that would handcuff second basemen. He had such

316

good bat speed and control that you couldn't get anything by him. If anything, I tried to pitch around him."

HOWARD NUNN

Pitcher for Johnson City Cardinals in Appalachian League in 1954 and 1955 and still holds Appalachian League record for strikeouts in a season with 249. Pitched in major leagues with St. Louis Cardinals (1959), Cincinnati Reds (1961-62).

*

"The reason that I signed with Kingsport out of Dobyns-Bennett High School was because of Muscle Shoals. As a kid I used to go watch him play and I always wanted to be on the same team with Muscle. I remember when I used to throw batting practice Muscle one time ripped one up the middle at me. After that I would never throw it across the plate to him and Muscle would get mad and slam that bat on the plate telling me to get it across. But I kept it in on his hands because I didn't want to get hit. He was the best player I ever saw. I remember one time we were playing at Middlesboro, Kentucky and Muscle was sick as a dog. But, he dragged himself up to the plate and hit two home runs and a double."

BUCKY COLLETTE

Pitcher for Kingsport Cherokees in 1953-54

*

"We started inviting Muscle to old-timers games with the Durham Bulls in the early 1980s. I had grown up in Greensboro and, although he was before my baseball consciousness, I heard stories of his home runs and knew he was the all time Carolina League home run king. I wanted to meet him so we invited Muscle to the old-timers games. I think this was the first recognition he had received from the Carolina League in many years and he was pleased to be invited. He was so gracious and good with the fans and he was a delight to have. Many of his old teammates and opponents were there and there were always great stories and good fellowship."

MILES WOLFF

Commissioner of Northern League

*

"I pitched against Muscle in 1951 when he was with Kingsport and I was with Johnson City. I didn't have anything but a fastball and I would just come after Muscle. The first couple of times you'd get Muscle, but when I started losing something off the fastball late in the game he would hit some ropes. I remember Muscle hit a home run one time, and it wasn't off me, that went over the bank in right field and on the other side of the fence into the football stadium. They later found the ball on the other side of the field on the track. Muscle wasn't too fast and I recall the first baseman and the second baseman playing back on the grass and the pitcher covering first base on a ground ball."

GARY BLAYLOCK

Posted a 23-6 record in 1951 with Johnson City with a league-leading 248 strikeouts which was the Appalachian League record until Howard Nunn broke the mark with 249 in 1955. Pitched in the major leagues for St. Louis Cardinals (1959), New York Yankees (1959).

*

"Nobody could hit them further than Muscle. I only got to see and play with him in the twilight of his career. He hit two home runs off Gary Blaylock of Johnson City that they're still waiting for them to come down. Once I was lucky to hit a home run in Welch, West Virginia, which I thought was a pretty good poke. But I tell you, Leo followed me at bat and hit one that made mine look like a bunt. I do believe they opened a new mine shaft where he drilled the ball into the side of the mountain. His legend will always exist.

WILLIS OAKES

Teammate of Shoals with the semipro Saltville (Va.) Alkalies

*

"Muscle was one tough out. When I threw to Muscle with men on, if he hit something it wasn't going to be a strike. You couldn't change up on Muscle. You'd fool him and he'd still hit it over the fence because of those quick wrists. I went 20-4 for Salem that year of 1955 but I also led the league in home runs given up with 25. I know Muscle must have hit five or six off me. I would pitch him outside and he would hit the ball to left field. I don't recall him hitting any home runs off me to left, but he hit his share the other way. Our center field fence in Salem was about 400 or 410 and he hit a home run over the center field fence that I swear was still going up as it cleared it."

PAUL JOHNSTON

Led the Appalachian League with 20 wins in 1955, his eighth and final season in professional baseball.

*

"Muscle was in his final season in 1955, but you couldn't tell he had slowed down any. I always tried to throw him fastballs in tight. But he would just lean back and with those quick wrists he'd smack the ball. You were a pretty good pitcher until you faced Muscle. I almost played with Muscle in 1955 at Kingsport but a friend of mine was managing Johnson City and I would go over and throw batting practice. One night Jack Crosswhite brought Salem into town and told me he'd give me $350 a month to pitch for Salem and I went."

CARMON DUGGER

Went 12-4 with Salem in 1955

319

Judging by the look on former Atlanta Braves pitcher Phil Niekro's face, I must be boring him with my stories.

(Photo courtesy Sholes family)

"I had the pleasure of being in the company of Muscle a few times. The first was my first year with the league in 1984 when he was gracious enough to appear at our all-star game. The other was 10 years later as we marked our 50th season. Muscle was a delightful person who really enjoyed talking about his playing days. He was mighty proud of that home run record and well he should be. I sincerely doubt it will ever be challenged. But he was in no way the least bit boastful about that or anything else."

JOHN HOPKINS

President of the Carolina League

*

Epilogue

Two individuals who knew Muscle Shoals as well as anyone were former teammate Cart Howerton and sports writer Bill Lane. Here are their memories of Muscle Shoals.

Bill Lane

Bill Lane is sports editor of the Kingsport Times-News and a longtime fan and friend to Muscle Shoals.

*

As a 13-year-old boy just getting interested in baseball, I first saw Muscle Shoals play for the Class D Kingsport Cherokees in the summer of 1954 at J. Fred Johnson Stadium. My neighbor kept telling me he wanted to take me to see a REAL ballplayer in action.

Just as we walked through the gate entrance, a bat sounded. The ball sailed over the flagpole in center field. I asked my neighbor if that was Shoals who'd just hit the ball. He said it was.

Constable John D. Parker ran part of his re-election campaign right there in the grandstand. He passed an army helmet through the crowd after Shoals' round-tripper. "Put some money in the hat," said Parker to the spectators, "and help this ol' boy out. And don't forget to vote for me on Election Day." The helmet came back filled with money. Before the game ended, Shoals hit another tape-measure homer. The helmet went around again and was stuffed with more money. One homer typically fetched $50, a second $25.

I didn't get personally acquainted with Shoals for several years after that, but he told me a fan always brought the gratuity money to him on the field and he'd put it in a coffee can on top of the dugout. "One summer," Shoals told

321

me, "I made my living out of that JFG jar and put my monthly paycheck in the bank."

I was the Times-News beat writer for the Appalachian League for about 15 years, covering rookie teams stocked by the New York Mets, Atlanta Braves and Kansas City Royals. I realize Shoals was much older than these rookie players when I saw him, but I've never seen anybody on a minor league team hit the ball with such authority then he did. Among the many sluggers I've seen come through were Joe Zdeb, Darryl Strawberry, Dale Murphy, Gregg Jefferies and Shawn Abner.

When Shoals was 52 years old, the Kingsport Royals invited him to participate in a home run derby against six of their best power hitters. Only one or two of the young Royals even managed to hit a ball out of the park that day. Shoals drove five pitches over the fences in right and center field. Several times he pulled inside pitches for 400-foot-plus fouls over the fences, striking the side of a medical building located across Memorial Boulevard.

Lightning wrist action was his thing. Shoals essentially could swing at a pitch, change his mind and yank the bat back fast enough to fool the umpire, getting a ball called.

During warm-ups before a game in Johnson City, Shoals and a couple of teammates were engaged in a game of pepper. Shoals, admittedly showing off his ability to control a bat, pivoted as he took half-swings, and poked several balls into the bleachers. Suddenly, he felt a pair of hands gripping his throat from behind. It was Branch Rickey. "As long as you're wearing one of my uniforms," said Rickey, who charged from the stands to reprimand Shoals, "don't you ever let me see you do that again." Shoals said he learned a lesson that day.

Bill Dale, manager of the Bennett & Edwards semipro team of Kingsport, lured Shoals out of retirement at the age of 45 to play first base and pinch-hit. Shoals lived 55 miles away and worked a fulltime job, so there was really no time to prepare for the season. In his first game, Shoals went

4-for-5, including a double, against defending state champion Greeneville (Tenn.) Magnavox club.

After he settled in Glade Spring, Virginia, I communicated with Shoals by mail and telephone for about 20 years. Each time he came back to Kingsport to watch a game, the fans would pour into the stadium hoping to see him and maybe get to talk with the legend.

George Fanning, who operated the Bluefield Orioles for many years, said of Shoals: "When Muscle Shoals hit 'em, you couldn't find 'em."

One night an old-timer told Shoals he had seen the game in which he hit a ball clear over that Tennessee Eastman smokestack (situated approximately a half-mile in the distance).

"Yeah," a smiling Shoals replied, going along with his admirer's recollection, "I remember that one well."

Every year that goes by, Shoals' feats seem to get larger. But there's no question, Muscle Shoals was a special player who never got to prove himself in the major leagues. Given the opportunity today's players have, the sky would have been the limit when determining his worth. It's a bit of a stretch, but he might have been co-owner of the ballclub.

Cart Howerton

*

Cart Howerton was 19 years old in 1949 when he joined the Reidsville Luckies as an outfielder. Howerton hit .254 with three home runs and 27 RBIs in 46 games in which he batted 193 times. Howerton, after his playing days were over, served in the Boston Red Sox organization as a coach at the major league level to managing in the minor leagues and then to scouting before operating the Winston-Salem franchise in the Carolina League.

I really don't know why Muscle never made it to the big leagues. He certainly had the talent. People seem to think it was his drinking which kept him out, but if that was the case there's a lot of guys who would never had made it up. His drinking was not as bad as some people would have you believe. He had some scrapes along the way, but he didn't bother anybody. Muscle was a guy who liked to carouse and have fun, but he was harmless. If he did drink as much as they say he did, he wouldn't have lasted long in baseball, and he certainly wouldn't have hit all those home runs.

Muscle would play the games and then the rascal would stay out all night but this was before he became a family man. I'll go over to Reidsville and they still talk about Muscle. One fellow over there told me not long ago, "Yeah, he'd sit on the porch swing and drink a case of beer and then get up to go to the ballpark and hit home runs that night."

Muscle was older than me by about 10 years when I played with Reidsville. But when I came, he sort of adopted me. A good friend of his who had played in the Carolina League and then in the major leagues was Bill Nagel. Leo would call me "Little Nagel" because I always had a chew of tobacco, a big honker and wore the bill of my cap down just like Nagel. Muscle would say, "Howie, you look like Nagel spit you right out of his mouth."

The whole time I played with Muscle I can remember only one time he came to the ballpark in no condition to play. We were taking infield and George Souter was down at third base. Zip Payne, our manager, hit a grounder to Souter and Souter fires it over and Muscle, who was a good fielder and fancy, put up his mitt and the ball goes right by his ear.

Payne hits another and Souter rifles the ball over and Muscle let the ball go by his ear again. Zip, who was visibly upset, walked two thirds of the way down to first base and shouted at Muscle to get off the field and to go back to the clubhouse. Muscle left and went to the clubhouse, which was behind the left field fence at Kiker Stadium. It was nestled back in among some trees. The door was locked, one of those heavy wooden doors. Well, Muscle laid into it and put that door right down on the floor, took it right off the hinges. He was strong as a bull.

Anyway, Muscle got dressed and left the park. The next day Zip cornered Muscle and put the law down to him. When we came to the ballpark Muscle was working like crazy putting that door back up.

He would always come to the park in a cab. I never saw Muscle much away from the park, although there were a few times my wife and I went out with Muscle and Helen. We'd go out and eat chicken livers at a place up toward the Rockingham line. The restaurant was behind a drive-in theatre. It had a private dining room and dance hall and the owner would put us away from the crowd.

As for his drinking, he may have drank a lot at night but a lot of that talk about him was overdone. He was just a guy who enjoyed living. But, if you get a reputation in baseball, it follows you for life. Every time I used to see Muscle at an old-timer's game, I would tell him honestly that one of my greatest experiences was playing on the same team with him. He would blush and say, "Oh, that can't be." But it is true.

He was a legend and one of the most colorful players ever. A lot of the old time scouts who have signed some great players over the years say he was one of the greatest minor league players they had ever seen and that he could have been a star in the big leagues. His arms were so big that he cut the sleeves short so that it wouldn't bind his arms when he swung the bat.

He was so powerful with those huge arms and strong wrists. We were awed by his strength. He had a little hitch in his swing, but when he'd check his swing his bat would be going like he was getting ready to pound a pitch and then, all of a sudden, the bat would stop and just shake. We all swore that we saw sawdust coming out of his bat handle when he gripped it.

I know one time in Burlington the bleacherites behind first base were on Muscle, riding him about cheap home runs. The right field line at Burlington was about 395 feet. I was on first base and Muscle was at bat. He swung and I can still hear that ball whistling through the trees beyond right field. I crossed home plate and turned to greet Muscle. As we were heading back to the dugout, he stopped, tipped his cap to the Burlington fans and shouted, "How'd you like to hang a week's work of wash out on that one."

But, like I said, Muscle would arrive at the park in a cab and he would leave in a cab and we never saw much of him before or after a game. The cab was always full of kids and it didn't matter whether the kids were black or white. Muscle didn't see color in a person, he just saw kids. He was a regular hero to those kids.

The Luckies gave us fan appreciation night with the players all getting some nice gifts. But, when they got ready to give Muscle his stuff, they drove in one of these flatbed trucks loaded down with furniture and all kinds of gifts. The people just loved Muscle, not only in Reidsville, but all over the Carolina League. No matter where Reidsville played, the fans came out to see Muscle Shoals hit a home run. The night he broke the league home run record in Winston-Salem, he got on the bus after the game and told the skipper to get this thing loaded up and out of town, because he was buying the beer.

But I won't forget those home runs he used to hit at Kiker. Kiker was maybe 325 down the right field line, but behind the fence was a steep, clay bank that must have went 60 feet up in the air and had trees on top. Muscle would stick the ball on that bank many times. When Muscle came to bat, kids would flock to that bank and when the ball landed, they'd hold it up to show the crowd how far it went.

He was a great player. A truly great player and, more than anything, a great friend who helped me so much when I was starting out.

Letters to Muscle

Dear Muscle,

I've studied several of the big home run seasons that have taken place in the minor leagues in the past and many of them can be explained partly by the size of the ballparks involved. Three of the 50-plus seasons were in Nashville, Tennessee. All of them involved left-handed hitters who benefited by the 256-foot right field fence at Sulphur Dell Field.

Two other places, Baltimore and Minneapolis, were noteworthy as small parks. Many of the bigger home run seasons took place in the Southwest. Joe Bauman (72 in 1954), Bob Crues (69 in 1948) and Frosty Kennedy (60 in 1956) all did their hitting in the dry, light air of the Texas and New Mexico deserts.

So far as I'm concerned, your 55 homers in 1949 was a greater accomplishment than some of those who actually ended up with higher totals in other places. About half of your home runs were on the road and the Carolina League had pretty decent pitching during that season.

To give you an idea of what a hitter's league the West Texas-New Mexico League was in 1948, by comparison to the Carolina League in 1949, consider the following: The pitcher that led the WTNM in earned run average in 1948 posted a 3.85 ERA. Eleven of the league's pitchers who worked in 150 innings or more had earned run averages of 6.00 or higher.

One Albuquerque left-hander had a 16-9 mark despite an earned run average of 6.18. Lamesa had a pitcher who spent 238 innings on the mound even though he gave up 7.64 earned runs per game. I'm not belittling Bob Crues 69 home runs during that same season, but it seems to me that if you'd been hitting in the same league, you might have gotten somewhere around 70-80 home runs.

While I was in Reidsville, I stopped at a barbershop for a haircut. The barber, who had been around town for a long time, talked about your seasons in that town. He said that he worked at Short Sugar's Barbecue in 1949 and that you often came in for lunch. Like a lot of persons who saw you play, he had tales of home runs that just might still be traveling through space. Your playing hasn't been forgotten in Reidsville, that's for sure.

Your friend,
Bob Gaunt

July 6, 1984
Dear Mr. Shoals,

To begin, I'd like you to know that I've written but few fan letters in my 48 years, the last one to a lovely young woman who used to give the weather forecasts some years ago for a local TV station. But for a long time I have wanted to let you know how much I enjoyed watching you hit baseballs out of sight during your 1949 season in the Carolina League.

In those days, when I was a teenager playing the local sandlots and you were making records hitting the long ball, a couple of friends and I attended just about every local game between Raleigh and Reidsville. Several times we left the stands before the end of the game to get your autograph, but none of us was ever able to summon the courage and ask for it. Finally, near the end of the season, my father got your signature for me. I still have that tattered old scorecard.

Since the Durham club came back into the league a few years ago, several of us have been going over to watch them play. Frequently we sit with Eddie Neville along the third base line and listen to his tales about the old days of the Carolina League. He has several good stories about Muscle Shoals and we never tire of listening to them, especially one about a tremendous drive you hit off him that carried over the smokestack on the building in right-center.

While listening to the recent all-star game in Salem, I heard the announcers talking about your probably never-to-be-broken home run record and the fact that you were attending the game. Later I obtained your address from Miles Wolff of the Durham Bulls and finally decided to drop you a line.

Obviously no player in this league ever hit 'em higher, farther or with more consistency than you did and I thank you for all the thrills and many happy memories.

With all the very best wishes, I am

Sincerely,
William M. Palmer, Curator
North Carolina State Museum of Natural History

YEAR	CLUB	LEAGUE	POS	G	AB	R	H	D	T	HR	RBI	BA
1937	Monessen	Penn State	1B	100	347	83	127	22*	8	18	74	.366
1938	New Iberia	Evangeline	1B	10	39	9	9	1	1	0	2.	.231
	Albuquerque	Ariz.-Texas	1B-P	86	342	71	112	21	7	10	90	.327
1939	Johnson City	Appalachian	1B-P	106	373	87	136	22	14	16*	91	.365*
1940	Tyler	East Texas	1B-OF	109	414	87	120	25	2	11	66	.290
	El Dorado	Cotton States	1B-P	20	75	13	26	9	1	3	21	.347
1941	El Dorado	Cotton States	1B-P	79	283	54	90	12	4	15	62	.318
	Marshall	Cotton States	1B	51	167	32	46	5	3	11	26	.275
1942-45	(MILITARY SERVICE)											
1946	Kingsport	Appalachian	1B-P	122	444	102	148	26	10	21*	106	.333
1947	Kingsport	Appalachian	1B	109	393	118	152	25	4	32*	124	.387*
1948	Charlotte	Tri-State	1B	116	411	76	118	22	6	21	82	.287
	Chattanooga	Southern	1B	22	72	10	16	2	1	3	15	.222
1949	Reidsville	Carolina	1B	144	501	131*	180	18	1	55*	137*	.359
1950	Columbia	South Atlantic	1B	89	318	57	83	21	3	7	42	.261
	Reidsville	Carolina	1B	44	116	18	26	4	0	5	16	.224
1951	Kingsport	Appalachian	1B	118	415	113	159	23	5	30*	129*	.383*
1952	Rock Hill	Tri-State	1B	113	369	85	118	20	2	17	84	.320
1953	Kingsport	Mountain States	1B	113	396	103	169	27	7	30	142	.427*
1954	Kingsport	Mountain States	1B	81	248	68	87	15	1	18*	59	.351
	Knoxville	Tri-State	1B	42	158	28	47	9	0	6	27	.297
1955	Kingsport	Appalachian	1B	126	431	113	156	24	2	33*	134*	.362
Totals				1800	6312	1460	2125	353	82	362	1529	.337

CAREER STATISTICS OF LEO "MUSCLE" SHOALS

Bibliography

Bristol Public Library

Lee Landers, President of Appalachian League

Monessen Public Library

Monessen Chamber of Commerce

El Dorado Chamber of Commerce

Barton Library in El Dorado

Tyler Public Library

Jeromy Rose, Richwood, W. Va. Chamber of Commerce

Olaf Lipscomb

Dale Taylor, Shawnee State University

Portsmouth Public Library

Ann Lorentz, Parkersburg Public Library

Henry Jenkins, retired from Johnson City Press-Chronicle

Bill Lane, Kingsport Times-News

Society of American Baseball Research

Albuquerque Public Library

Furman Bisher, Atlanta Journal-Constitution

The Sporting News Baseball Guides

David Weeks, Dacus Library Winthrop University

Bob Gorman, Winthrop University

Vanessa Curry

John Hopkins, President of Carolina League

Asheville-Buncombe Library

Charlie Harville

Association of Professional Baseball Players of America.

Bill Kirkland

USA Today Baseball Weekly

Reidsville Public Library

Reidsville Chamber of Commerce

New Mexico State Library

Tucson Pima Library

Central North Carolina Regional Library

Z.Smith Reynolds Library at Wake Forest University
National Baseball Hall of Fame
Jim Sumner, North Carolina Museum of History
Sherrod Library at East Tennessee State University
Kingsport Public Library
Minor League Baseball Stars, Society of American Baseball Research, 1984
Abayoni Manrique, Auburn Avenue Research Library on African-American Culture and History
Lisa Roth, Thronateeska Heritage Center, Albany, Ga.
Portsmouth (Ohio) Public Library
Ohio Historical Society
William J. Weiss, Baseball Statistics
Ray Nemec, SABR
Johnson City Cardinals
St. Louis Public Library
The Sporting News
Robert Van Atta, Greensburg, Pa. Tribune-Review
May Memorial Library
Spartanburg County Public Library
Arkansas Historical Commission

Books

Alexander, Charles C. *Rogers Hornsby*. New York: Henry Holt and Company, 1995

Green, Ernest J. The Diamonds of Dixie. Lanham, Maryland: Madison Books, 1995

Blake, Mike. The Minor Leagues. New York: Wynwood Press, 1991

The National Association of Professional Baseball Leagues. The Story of Minor League Baseball: 1901-1952. Columbus, Ohio: The Stoneman Press, 1952.

Wingler, Karl. The Appalachian League Black Book, 1950.

Russell, Fred. Bury Me In An Old Press Box. New York: A.S. Barnes and Company, 1957.

Obojski, Robert. Bush League. New York: Macmillan Company, 1975.

Perry, Thomas K. Textile League Baseball. Jefferson, North Carolina: McFarland & Company, Inc., 1993.

Adelson, Bruce. Brushing Back Jim Crow. Charlottesville: University of Virginia Press, 1999.

Sullivan, Neil J. The Minors. New York: St. Martin's Press, 1990.

Sumner, Jim L. Separating The Men From The Boys. Winston-Salem, N.C.: John F. Blair, Publisher, 1994

Gonzalez Echevarria, Roberto. The Pride of Havana. New York: Oxford Press, 1999.

The Encyclopedia of Minor League Baseball, Edited by Lloyd Johnson and Miles Wolff, 1993, Durham, N.C.: Baseball America

Friend, J.P., Cotton States League Golden Anniversary 1902-1951.

Holaday, J.Chris, Professional Baseball in North Carolina, Jefferson, North Carolina: McFarland & Co., 1998.

Newspapers

Monessen Valley Independent, 1937
St. Louis Post-Dispatch, 1938
Martinsville Bulletin, 1949
Albany (Ga.) Herald, 1939
Reidsville Review, 1949, 1950
Portsmouth (Ohio) Times 1937, 1938
New Iberia Weekly Iberian 1938
New Orleans Times-Picayune 1938, 1948
Albuquerque Journal 1938
Elizabethton Star 1939, 1946, 1951
Kingsport Times-News 1939, 1946, 1947, 1951, 1953, 1954

Johnson City Press-Chronicle 1939, 1946, 1947, 1951, 1955
Greeneville Sun 1939
El Dorado Daily News 1940-1941
Bristol Herald Courier 1946, 1947, 1951, 1955
Roanoke Times 1946, 1947, 1955
Roanoke World News 1955
Nashville Banner 1948
Atlanta Constitution 1948
Chattanooga Times 1948
Asheville Citizen 1948, 1952
Asheville Times 1954
Knoxville News-Sentinel 1948, 1952, 1954
Knoxville Journal 1953
Charlotte Observer 1948, 1952
Charlotte News 1948
Burlington Times-News 1949
Greensboro Daily News 1949
Winston-Salem Journal 1949
Winston-Salem Journal-Sentinel 1949
Durham Sun and Morning Herald 1949
Raleigh News & Observer 1949
The State (Columbia, S.C.) 1950
Rock Hill Evening Sun 1952
Morristown Daily Gazette and Mail 1953, 1954
Spartanburg Herald 1954
Smyth County News & Messenger 1996

Magazines

Thornley, Stew. "Unser Choe" Hauser: Double 60. The Baseball Research Journal (1991), pp. 20-22.

Vaughn, Gerald F. George Hausmann Recalls The Mexican League of 1946-47. The Baseball Research Journal (1990), pp. 59-63.

Moyer, Alan. 72 Homers. The Diamond (December 1993), pp. 34-36, 55.

Corbett, Warren. There Used To Be A Ballpark: Sulphur Dell Nashville. The Diamond (March-April 1994), pp. 43-46.

Hernandez, Roberto. Salvent Takes Aim at Batting Honors. The Sporting News (August 3, 1960).

Hernandez, Roberto. Peso Finish Marks Best Year Since '55. The Sporting News (September 28, 1960).

Spare A Ball?. Newsweek (June 8, 1953)

Dixie Baseball Loop May Fold Over Negro Player. Jet Magazine (August 12, 1954).

Negro Player Moved, Dixie Loop Resumes Play. Jet Magazine (August 19, 1954).

Former Players Interviewed

Tal Abernathy, J. Craft Akard, Charlie Allen, Chub Arnold, Gary Blaylock, Joe Bowman, Earle Brucker, Jr., Bucky Collette, Jim Constable, Boyce Cox, Crash Davis, Alton Denson, Bob Downing, Willie Duke, Carmon Dugger, Mike Forline, Dean Frye, Walter T. Frye, Mike Garbark, Tom Giordano, John Goryl, Bill Halstead, Hugh Hamil, Cart Howerton, Charlie Hummell, Raymond Johnston, Paul Johnston, Ivan Kuester, James Lamb, Paul LaPalme, George Lebedz, Carl Linhart, Bobby Malkmus, Charlie Metro, Joe McClain, Bill Monbouquette, Hugh Mulcahy, Paul Musselman, George Myatt, Carlton Nebel, Ron Necciai, Howard Nunn, Willis Oakes, Lee Peterson, Rance Pless, Pedro Ramos, Glenn Rawlinson, Wilmer Shantz, Dick Sipek, George Staller, Emo Showfety.

I had a great life in baseball. I wish I could do it all over again.

(Photo courtesy Sholes family)